TO Darren

All my love
forever

Ally
xxx

The Complete Book of Gardening

The Complete Book of Gardening

by Brian Leverett

Illustrations
by Ursula Sieger

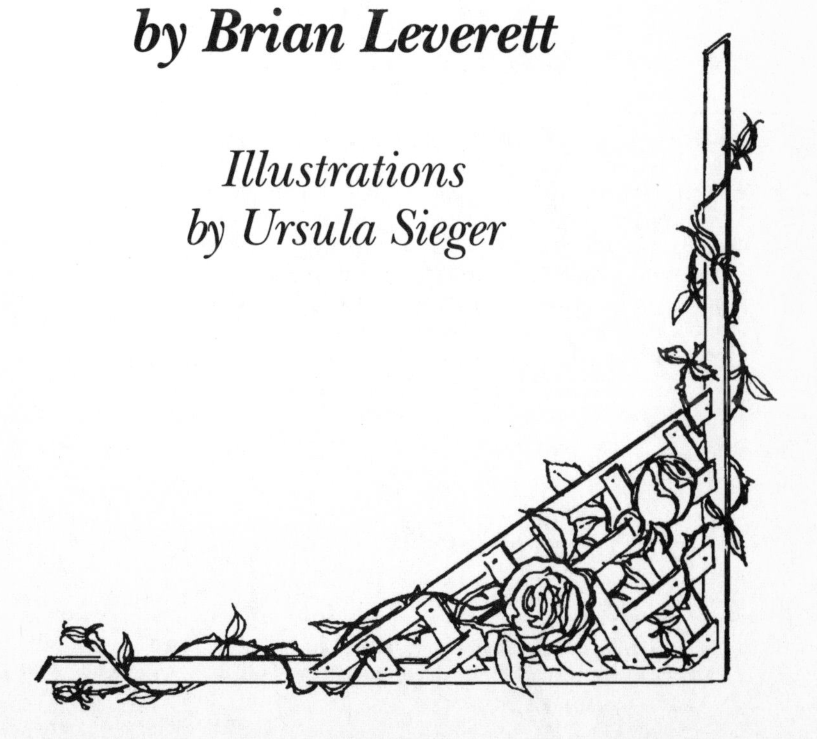

foulsham
Bennetts Close, Cippenham, Berks, SL1 5AP

ISBN 0-572-01986-6

Photoset by Encounter Photosetting, Fleet, Hampshire GU13 9SJ
Printed in Great Britain by St Edmundsbury Press Ltd., Bury St. Edmunds, Suffolk

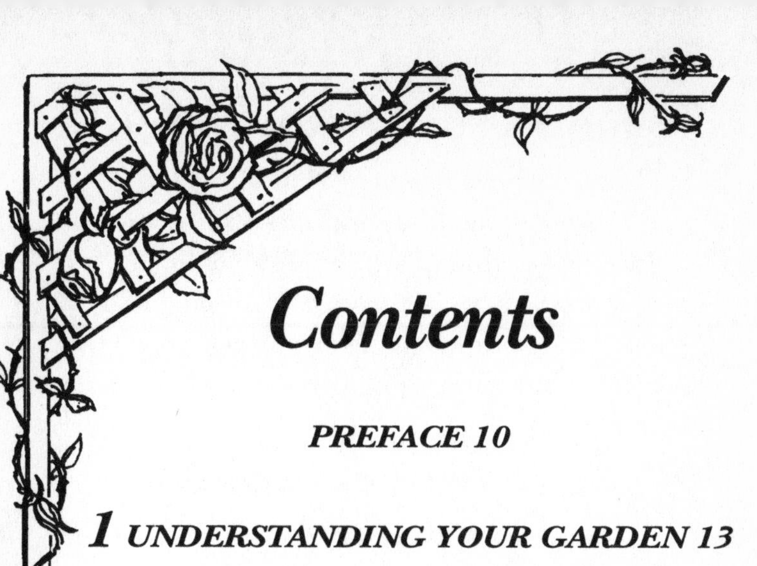

Contents

14 ROCK GARDENS 191

15 WINTER GARDENS 199

16 CUT FLOWERS 203

17 THE VEGETABLE GARDEN 213

18 THE HERB GARDEN 237

Preface

Every year gardening becomes more and more popular with increasing numbers of people participating in what must be the country's number one hobby.

Gardening has also been elevated to that late twentieth-century phenomenon – the status symbol. The first thing that the visitor to your house will see is your garden. That important first impression will have been formed. Every person walking past your house will see the garden. In a year hundreds more eyes descend on your garden than they do on the inside of your house.

Fortunately, gardening need not be difficult. Without any experience you can buy a plant, place it in the ground and usually it will grow. Increasingly plants are being sold with simplified instructions, and by following these you should enjoy some success. But gardening is not like a DIY activity where it is possible to perform a set task through a few step-by-step instructions and then walk away. Plants are living organisms that need constant attention. They require their own special environments, and without you providing for their needs they will die. Yet equipped with some knowledge of horticulture you can ensure that your plants prosper and that your displays outshine many others in the area. Furthermore, you can save yourself hundreds of pounds by propagating your own bedding plants and providing the family with healthy, fresh-tasting vegetables.

Gardening requires more than a few simple lessons. Just like in any other worthwhile activity, you continue learning throughout life providing that you have a firm foundation in the basic principles.

In this book I describe the basic operations and explain why we do them, so that you can adapt them to your own unique situation and be confident of success from day one. In addition to general principles, I have given brief details of all of our most popular plants together with some rarer species that in my opinion deserve to be better known.

I have included much information that is by no means essential for the beginner but which will almost certainly prove useful as your confidence grows and you become progressively more and more ambitious. So while this book has been written with the beginner very much in mind, it is hoped it will be of value to the more experienced gardener as well as the novice.

I had the benefit of receiving my early training in gardening from my father, and was handed down the lessons that generations had learnt through trial and error – with more than a little folklore thrown in. Today, science can explain much that our ancestors had to learn through observation, and the explanations are usually quite simple. I have included discussions of scientific principles wherever I feel they will be of practical help or add to your enjoyment of the hobby.

You may receive differing advice on how and even when to perform certain operations, but there is no single correct way of accomplishing a task in the garden. The methods explained in the text are those I have found work well and which I am confident will be equally successful for you. Where you know of a different method, try it out and decide for yourself which you think is the best. There are no hard and fast rules.

What we should never lose sight of is that gardening is a relaxation, a hobby which brings many people nearer to nature. It gives them an acute awareness of the seasons of the year, which they might not otherwise experience, and a realisation that to achieve anything it is necessary to work with nature not against it. I hope that gardening will give you the immense satisfaction over very many years that it has given me. My first piece of advice to any new gardener is just go out and enjoy your garden. See it as a pleasure, a challenge to achieve the best possible results, but never a task to be endured.

Brian Leverett
Poole

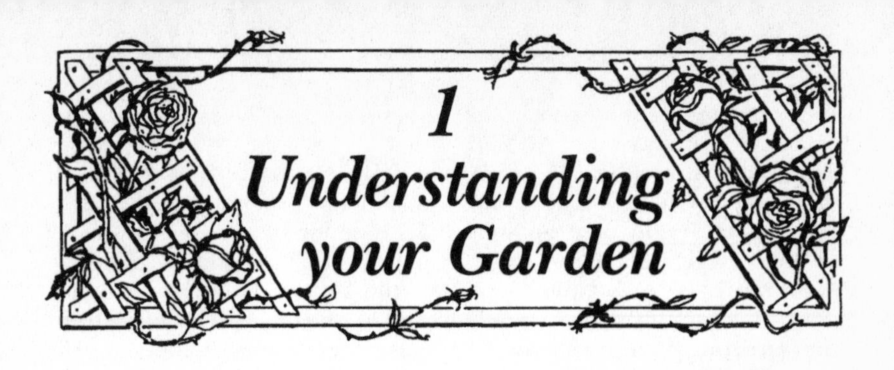

Walk down any street and you will see gardens that are masterpieces, where everything seems to prosper, yet in the same road there are gardens where the plants seem to die almost the same day they are planted

Often the owner of the unsuccessful plot is just as enthusiastic, cares as much about the plants, may even spend larger sums of money on his garden and work harder – only to find that much of his efforts are wasted. The harder he seems to work the less success he enjoys, whereas his neighbour, the owner of the magnificent plot, seems to spend less time labouring and more enjoying the fine results.

The difference between the winning and losing garden is seldom more than the knowledge and experience of the owner. While there is no short cut to experience, it is possible with just a basic understanding of plant requirements and a source of ready reference explaining the needs of particular types to go out and create the necessary environments for them.

The needs of plants

The plants familiar to us in gardens were originally collected, in their wild forms, from every part of the world, and from widely varying habitats. For instance, desert cacti only survive in the most arid conditions, while water lilies must have their roots and parts of their stems permanently covered in water. And bromeliads originate from high up in the hot humid rain forests of South America, whereas many alpines come from the dry windswept mountains of Europe. As these examples require completely different conditions to thrive, if we plant them close together in a similar environment it should be no surprise when some of them die.

While no one, of course, would attempt to grow pond dwellers without water, the requirements of other plants are every bit as exacting if less obvious. Unless you are able to cater for them adequately they will just as surely die!

The successful garden is not one but several environments, each tailored to the requirements of individual species and their varieties.

Many modern plants are the result of careful selective breeding to produce larger plants, brighter or more pleasing colours, better form, more compact growth or greater resistance to disease. Although the plants may seem far removed from their wild ancestors in appearance, their basic requirements, laid down through evolution over millions of years, will remain the same. However hard man tries, it is impossible to influence greatly the environmental demands of any particular species.

For any plant to prosper it will require grower-friendly conditions.

Soil

Soil provides an anchorage for the roots and a medium for retaining moisture and plant nutrients.

It will also contain chemicals which dependent upon their nature and concentration will make the soil acid, neutral or alkaline(chalky). They will have a profound effect upon the soil's ability to sustain certain plants.

A few plants will grow in any type of soil, virtually oblivious of its acidity or alkalinity, whereas others, such as camellias, rhododendrons and many heathers will only grow in acid soils. Chalk effectively locks out chemical elements that these plants require, thus starving them. But other plants *need* chalky conditions. Many vegetables benefit from a little lime in the soil.

The level of the soil's acidity or alkalinity is expressed as its pH, which stands for 'potential of Hydrogen'. The pH scale represents the concentration of hydrogen ions present. The scale runs from pH 0, which is the strongest acid, to pH 14, which is the strongest alkali. It is a logarithmic scale, which means that a change of one unit multiplies the acidity or alkalinity by ten. For example, a soil of pH 5.5 is ten times as acid as a soil of pH 6.5 while a soil of pH 4.5 would be one hundred times as acid as one of pH value 6.5. Most garden soils range between a pH value of 5.0 and 8.0.

pH as applied to soils

5.0	Very strongly acid
5.5	Strongly acid
6.0	Acidic
6.5	Only just acidic
7.0	Neutral
7.5	Only just alkaline
8.0	Alkaline
8.5	Strongly alkaline
9.0	Very strongly alkaline

You can buy kits to measure the pH of the soil, but for the reading to have any true meaning you must take the greatest care to ensure that the sample is representative and not just taken from one small area in the garden.

It is easy to adjust the pH of the soil upwards by the addition of lime. Most vegetable plots benefit from a light spreading of the powder once every three years. As well as raising the soil pH, the strongly alkaline powder releases the final traces of the nitrogen-rich ammonia from any mulch in its last stages of decay.

It is far more difficult to lower the pH of your soil. Very localised effects can be achieved by digging out areas of alkaline soil and replacing with peat or compost, but it is far better to concentrate on growing those plants which prefer chalk or can at least tolerate it.

Temperature range

Plants only grow over a very limited temperature range. Some, such as grass, can survive throughout most of the range, while some others will only grow well provided the temperature is within a few degrees of the ideal.

Temperature together with moisture are the two factors which trigger the germination of seeds after the dormant period. The usual reason why seeds will not germinate is because it is too cold, but seeds will also not shoot if the temperature is too high. This is a protective mechanism to ensure that they do not emerge into a world that is going to dry them out. It accounts for the difficulty experienced when trying to germinate lettuce seed during midsummer.

Frost is the biggest killer of plants, and for the tender or half-hardy subjects the timing of the last of the winter frosts and the onset of the following autumn frost dictate the length of time that they can survive out of doors. In Britain it is usually said that tender subjects such as tomatoes and bedding plants should not be planted until the first week of June. You are unlikely to get a frost anywhere after this date but it has been known – with nature there are no guarantees. Yet in many instances this could be unnecessarily late. Most plants benefit from being transported to their permanent positions as soon as possible, and a week or a fortnight gained at this stage is invaluable, always provided that they are not cut down by frosts. In any particular location there is a date after which frosts are highly unlikely and this is the time which should govern your decision as to when it is safe to plant out. It will depend very much upon the local conditions or *microclimate.*

Microclimate

The microclimate may be defined as the conditions that prevail in your garden as opposed to those quoted for the country as a whole or even your region or town in particular, which is only a statement of average conditions. You are no more likely to find standard conditions in your garden than you are to have the average 1.8 children!

It is the climate in your garden which is the only one of any importance.

Even within your garden there will be hot spots and cold areas. Once you know where they are situated you will be a long way towards establishing how best to utilise the available space.

The temperature in any position will depend upon when and for how long the garden receives direct sunlight. A site that is fully exposed will enjoy day-long radiation. Eastern aspects will receive early morning sunlight, gradually decreasing throughout the day, whereas western aspects will tend to receive little warmth during the early morning but the full intensity of the sun's rays late in the day. Northern aspects receive the least direct sunlight, but there are still many plants that will prosper in such locations.

South-facing walls have very

special microclimates. If you have a wall lying anywhere between south-east and south-west, plan very carefully what to plant against it as it will be one of your most valuable assets! Here you may grow peaches, nectarines, grapes and other fruits which are normally thought to be unsuccessful in this country. While the plants are receiving the sun's warmth during the day, the bricks of the wall absorb its energy, and, acting as a natural storage heater, will give out warmth during the night. Thus conditions are created that are several degrees warmer than in any other part of the garden.

Frost pockets

Cold air will settle in the lowest possible position and where such air becomes trapped, as in a natural depression like a valley or behind a wall in a sloping garden, it will become significantly colder than the surrounding areas. At times when the ambient temperature is almost down to freezing point, where the air is trapped it will become cold enough for frost to form even though the rest of the garden or area is clear. Such positions are termed *frost pockets.*

Become aware of any frost pockets on your land by walking the plot and checking on cold mornings. The months of May and October are crucial as this is when there is danger of localised but not widespread frost. Care should be taken not to plant any frost-tender subjects in such positions.

Most frost damage occurs as a

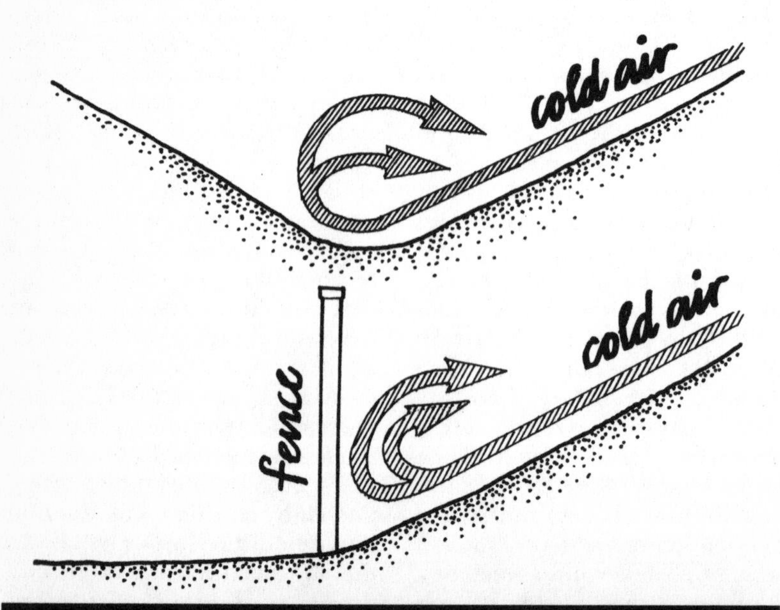

A frost pocket is a position prone to frost in late spring and autumn. It occurs where cold air settles at the bottom of a slope or is trapped behind a wall on a sloping site, becoming colder than the surrounding areas.

result of the sun's action producing a rapid thaw. The frost causes small crystals of ice form within the plant cells. When the sun's warmth falls on to the plant the crystals rapidly expand and burst the cell walls before melting.

It is sometimes possible to save plants that have become frosted by pouring very cold water over them while they are still frozen. This will initiate thawing but will cause it to be brought about slowly, allowing the cell to accommodate the changes.

Careful siting of important plants, so that they do not receive direct early morning sun, can save problems in the garden.

The flowers of camellias will turn brown if they are frosted, which is a problem as the blooming period is from February through until April – the time when frosts are most prevalent. A camellia should be sited in an open position where is does not receive the direct rays of the sun until midday, by which time the air will have slowly warmed up and the blooms will be safe except in the severest weather.

Wind

Wind can damage plants simply by its sheer power, breaking stems and branches. In addition, large volumes of cold air striking a plant can cause browning of the leaves. This is wind burn, the result of the rapid evaporation of large quantities of moisture from the surface of the leaves.

Some plants have evolved to cope with windswept environments, so wind causes them no problem. For example, ground-hugging plants, such as the alpines, experience few difficulties.

Consider two large structures close together with a gap in between them, such as a pair of detached houses. In a storm, the wind will be channelled through the gap with the result that the air travels with far greater force, creating a draught. As with frost pockets, areas so created should be planted with only the hardiest of specimens.

Wind can be controlled in several ways. Solid structures, such as walls, can create downdraughts in front and behind them which can cause other problems. More effective are screens and hedges, which will break the force of the wind and then allow it to pass with its destructive power greatly reduced. Windbreaks constructed from espalier fruit trees or trellis work covered in flowers are productive and decorative as well as functional.

Light

Plants cannot grow without light, which is needed to perform photosynthesis – the process that produces the glucose from which virtually all of the substance of the plant is built up. Some plants will not prosper without full light. In shady conditions such species grow long and thin trying to reach up to the life-giving sunlight. Seedlings germinated indoors where light levels are low, though with other growth promotors such as warmth and moisture present in abundance, will grow long and thin and be incapable of supporting themselves.

A plant produces light-sensitive hormones in its shoots. If it receives sunlight from one side only, e.g. a pot plant on a windowsill, the hormones move down the shoots and become more concentrated on the darker side where they cause greater cell elongation. This results in the plant bending towards the sunlight.

Plants grown in such conditions should be turned daily to ensure that all parts will, over a period of time, receive the same light intensity.

There are plant species that have evolved to exploit almost every environment on this planet. Some species require much less sunlight than others, having become adapted to using the light available very efficiently. But, as an outcome, if they receive too much bright sunlight they will not prosper. Such types must always be grown in a shady location.

Many of the spring-flowering plants grow under deciduous trees. They produce their leaves and blossoms in the period before the trees are covered in leaves, for the canopies create too much shade for them. So it is safe to plant most spring bulbs under trees which lose their leaves but they must not be placed under evergreens.

The intensity of light and the amount of daylight hours will influence the rate at which plants grow. As the days lengthen, plants grow more rapidly. The extra light, combined with the higher temperatures in the June-July period, make this the time best suited to plant growth. The growth rate for many plants is probably fastest just after the longest day, as by this stage the soil will have warmed up appreciably. In September, in spite of the soil being still fairly warm, the diminishing daylight hours make this time far less suitable for the taking of many types of cuttings.

Water requirements

The water requirements of various plant species can differ a great deal too. More plants are lost through too much or too little water than any other factor.

Constant attention must be paid to the amount of water in the soil. Not many plants can survive alternating drying out and soaking with water. With most plants the first sign of insufficient water is a wilting of the leaves. Wilting leaves is actually a protection mechanism as it reduces the water losses by transportation. If a plant is allowed to continue without water, its flowers will drop off, buds will fail to open and the leaves will turn yellow. Recovery is often possible but only at the expense of several weeks' growing time – the plant could fail to reach prime condition before the end of the season.

Except in drought conditions, rainfall will provide sufficient water to at least keep outdoor plants alive. But containers seldom receive all of the precipitation which falls upon them, because the leaves of the plants act as an umbrella, deflecting most of the precipitation away from the soil. Even early in the season before the canopy of leaves has fully developed over the container it may still get insufficient natural moisture. Containers should be watered regularly from the time that they are first planted (see pp. 131-133).

The humidity – the amount of water vapour in the air – is important to the health of every plant. Although seldom a problem out of doors, inside central heating systems produce very dry air that kills plants. Sometimes pot plants tend to lose their leaves even though there is an adequate temperature and the plants are watered regularly. This is probably the result of insufficient water vapour in the air. In such instances the humidity may be increased by standing the pots over a saucer filled with gravel which is kept constantly wet. Spraying the plant daily with a water mister will also help to alleviate the problem.

Where plants have a dormant season, withhold water in order that they may rest. If they are not allowed to follow their natural cycle and are kept growing through the winter months they tend to be less vigorous the following year, often failing to produce buds until late into the season.

Wherever water exists in the soil it will tend to evaporate from the surface, removing some of the available energy and lowering the temperature. This is another reason for greatly reducing the water given to tender plants that are being wintered inside.

The quantity of water that any plant requires is related to the amount of growth that it is making and the ambient temperature. Consequently far more water is required during the summer than the winter months.

Water straight from the tap is often at a far lower temperature than that in either the greenhouse or the lounge. If it is given straight to the plant it will be a shock to its system. Always leave some water standing near the plant so that it reaches the same temperature.

Tap water is ideal for most plants. The principal exceptions are the ericaceous subjects, particularly pot-grown azaleas, which will be killed by the chalk contained in hard water. If you live in a hard-water district, avoid the problem by catching and storing a quantity of rainwater.

Conserving water

With the ever-increasing need to conserve water it is important to ensure that the greatest amount possible of that put on the soil is taken up by the plants and not wasted.

Watering should always be performed when the air temperature is at its lowest, either late at night or early in the morning. This allows the maximum amount of water to soak into the ground without being evaporated away, which is what will happen if it is applied during the period when the sun is at its brightest.

Always saturate the soil – never give a light sprinkling. Small quantities of water are almost always wasted with virtually none of it reaching the roots. In addition, it will tend to consolidate the surface particles together causing a crust to form on the top of the soil. Many plants are watered too frequently. Once a week is usually sufficient for most outdoor plants providing that they have a thorough soaking. Only tomatoes and greenhouse plants will require a daily watering. With tomatoes water can be used more effectively if a small flower pot is sunk level with and next to the roots. This can be filled daily and will disperse the water in the vicinity of where it is most likely to be taken up by the plant.

Water can be retained around the roots of plants, especially trees and shrubs, by *mulching*. Cover the root area with a layer of organic material, such as leaf mould, compost, peat or wood bark, about 5 cm (2 in) thick, when the soil is saturated. An annual mulching at the end of February will simultaneously help to retain the winter moisture well into the dry season and suppress weed growth. Being weed-free itself, the only weeds likely to grow are from the soil beneath, but the young seedlings will not be strong enough to penetrate the thick organic layer and will perish. The mulch will gradually be drawn into the soil whose texture it will improve. The process is repeated the following year.

Nutritional requirements

By the process of photosynthesis, plants make the carbohydrates they need to build up their tissues from the moisture and carbon dioxide of the air. Oxygen is produced as a by-product, and some of it may be used directly in the plant's respiration while the rest is released back into the atmosphere.

In addition to carbon, hydrogen and oxygen, plants need three main elements: nitrogen, phosphorus and potassium.

Nitrogen

This promotes growth, for it is a major constituent of protoplasm which makes up the bulk of the plant. By feeding extra nitrogen it is possible to increase leaf area, generating volumes of lush dark green material. While this may seem the solution to producing bigger plants you must restrict the amount of nitrogen – give too much and you will get a lot of soft growth that is vulnerable to attack by fungi and viruses. No fast-acting sources of nitrogen should be given to plants during autumn or winter as the weak growth produced will be incapable of withstanding the rigours of the season.

Phosphorus

The element phosphorus is required by plants in the form of phosphates. Phosphates produce strong roots and if there is a deficiency in the soil you will never grow sturdy plants. Phosphates are a constituent part of enzymes, which are essential for all of the plant's biological functions, particularly the reproductive process. Without enough of this element, plants will fail to produce and ripen fruit.

Potassium

Usually referred to by its older name of potash, like nitrogen it is required for foliage, which it strengthens – making it more capable of resisting weather and both fungal and viral attacks. It also promotes the development of flowers and fruit.

The above mineral elements must be in a water-soluble form before they can be absorbed by the roots of the plant. Very soluble forms of these elements make quick-acting fertilisers whereas those which only dissolve very slowly are correspondingly slow-acting fertilisers. All the necessary elements are present to some extent in animal manure and in compost, which is broken down plant matter. Since both composts and animal manures originate from materials that were once living they are classified as 'organic', but it is often desirable to boost the supply of nutrients by the addition of factory-produced compounds, often termed 'inorganic'.

Since the plant roots are only capable of taking up water-soluble forms of the elements (ions) and since these will be the same whether they come from an organic or inorganic source, there would seem to be little to choose between the two classes of material. However, many of the fertilisers which are man-made are much faster acting and so can give a much needed boost when necessary. Balanced against this is the fact that these fertilisers do not provide any material which will contribute to the texture of the soil.

There are two basic types of quick-acting fertiliser. First, there are those which are high in nitrogen. These are more important in the early stages of a plant's growth and are given early in the season. Secondly, there are those which are low in nitrogen and suitable for use before the autumn and winter. This principle is very important in the formulation of lawn fertilisers.

On a fertiliser bag you may see its content of nitrogen, phosphate and potassium expressed as a ratio. The figures are percentages of the active nutrients, so if the contents are described as 6:6:6 it means that the fertiliser contains 6% each of the three main nutrients.

Some fertilisers such as Growmore, although man-made, tend to dissolve slowly over a long period and they are scattered at the rate of 50 g/sq. m. (2 oz/sq. yard) during the spring.

Foliar feeds are fertilisers which, in order to speed up their action, are sprayed onto the plant. Some is absorbed by the leaves but none is wasted, as that which falls to the ground will be taken up by the roots. The use of such treatments is best restricted to the May to August period although foliar feeds may be used on annuals almost until the time that they are removed from the ground.

Trace elements

In addition to the three main elements, plants need some components termed trace elements in very minute amounts. These are so widespread throughout nature and are required in such small quantities that there is seldom a deficiency problem, yet as a safeguard many of the proprietory fertilisers contain some trace elements. The one trace element most often required is magnesium. This element lies at the centre of the chlorophyll molecule and is used in the photosynthesis process. Tomatoes are often short of it – seen by a yellowing of the leaves. Should you detect this problem, water the plants with a solution containing a teaspoonful of Epsom salts per 10 litres (2 gallons) of water.

Some plants have special nutritional requirements if they are to produce what is desired of them. For example, we want our roses to continually produce firm growth and flowers, and our tomatoes should have good growth, plenty of flowers and fruit which will ripen. Special proprietary fertilisers have been developed to cater for these particular needs. If you are trying to grow the highest quality produce, such fertilisers hold distinct advantages. But if you do not wish to go to the extra expense of individual fertilisers, perfectly good results can be obtained by using all-purpose feeds.

Among the organic fertilisers, dried blood is a quick-acting source of nitrogen. Many of the others are slow release, such as bone meal, which being high in phosphate is excellent for placing in the hole before a tree or shrub is planted. 'Blood, fish and bone' is a faster-acting, all-purpose fertiliser, but it is not totally organic in that it contains added potassium sulphate to increase the potash level.

Manures and composts

Fertilisers are like pep pills. Though they give the plants a boost, their effects are only transitory. They are not a substitute for manures or composts, which improve the texture of the soil.

The aim should always be to improve the quality of the soil, a process that should continue throughout the time you occupy the plot.

Animal manures

There are several different types of animal manures, some of which may have incorporated with them large quantities of straw. Although the composition of manures will differ according to the diet of the animal from which they originated, they are all rich sources of soil-improving humus together with varying and usually very worthwhile amounts of nutrients. Fresh manure needs stacking before it is used. It contains strong chemicals that will burn plants. Furthermore, during the aging process the manure is broken down by bacteria which themselves require nitrogen and would take this nutrient from the soil if the manure were to be dug straight into it. The result would be an initial drop in fertility. So either buy year-old manure or stack fresh manure for at least nine months before digging it into the ground.

Composts

Composts are top-rate soil conditioners and improvers. For many gardeners compost is the only practical way to provide the soil with bulk organic material. Used in conjunction with fertilisers it is just as effective as manures, which are practically impossible to obtain in sufficient quantities in urban locations.

Any plant matter may be composted but woody material needs to be broken up by a shredder, the purchase of which can only be justified if you intend processing large quantities of the material. Several different types of proprietary compost maker are available. Basically, they are all containers with aeration holes in the side. Although they successfully produce limited quantities of compost, they are only suitable for the small garden. It is a simple matter to make your own compost bin, one which will produce large amounts of soil-enriching material, and you will soon realise that this is the powerhouse of your garden. *Most successful town gardens have a large compost-making facility.*

It is best to make twin containers so that you have one from which the compost may be taken and a second container which is being filled. Size will depend upon the amount of material you have for composting, but if each bin is 100 cm square and 150 cm high (3 x 3 x 4½ ft) then this will be sufficient for the average garden. Make the containers out of second-hand timber, constructing a frame from four pieces of wood 5 x 5 cm (2 x 2 in). Nail timber 1.5 cm (½ in) thick around three sides leaving the front open. You will need to be able to remove the front boards. Achieve this by placing a piece of timber behind each front support and a similar sized piece just in front to create runners. The timber can then be slid down the runners. If space permits, it is more convenient to make a double unit. Place a layer of plant material 15–20 cm (6–8 in) deep in the bottom of the container. Then sprinkle with a layer of compost activator, which feeds the bacteria that bring about the decomposition. Continue with alternating layers of plant material and activator until you reach the top of the container. Avoid thick layers of grass mowings or other fine materials – these soon become compressed and form a solid mass, which stops the composting process. Try to mix your mowings with other materials. Garden rubbish, excluding woody material, is the main source of plant material for composting and should not be wasted. Roots and weed seeds may be included in the compost heap as they will be broken down and completely destroyed by the heat of decomposition. Diseased

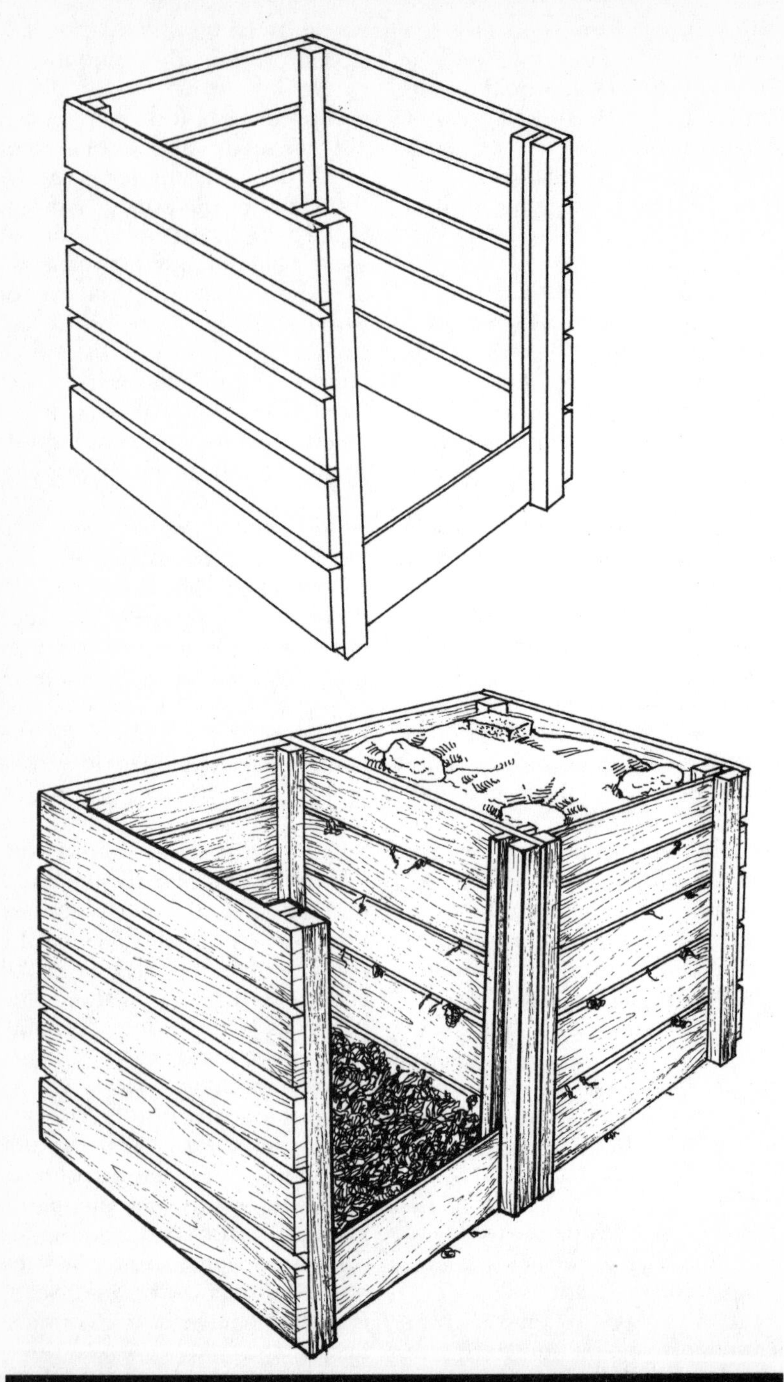

Home-made slatted wooden compost bin, single and double

material should always be burnt. While the composting process will destroy most of the germs, it is the spread of viruses and spores to the atmosphere before they are rendered harmless which causes the problems. Avoid including materials that have been sprayed with weedkiller. Animal remains and scraps of food can be composted but they should not be added to the heap as they will attract rats and other vermin.

A month after you have filled the container turn it over and return it to the bin. This has a twofold benefit. It will ensure that all of the material spends some time at the centre of the heap which is at a higher temperature than that on the outside, and it will incorporate the large quantities of air essential for the breakdown process. Rainfall should provide the small amount of water that is needed. During a drought small quantities can be given but it is usually not necessary. Only if the heap is fully exposed will it receive too much water. Should this happen, it will become a slimy mass excluding the air and stopping the decomposition process. To avoid this, cover the top with plastic weighed down with bricks during wet spells.

The compost should be ready for use in six to nine months, by which time it will be a dark brown-to-black material, clean to handle and odourless.

Liquid manure

Many of the nutrients present in well rotted manure will be in the form of soluble salts, which are easily utilised by the plants, and the material may be used to brew a very effective liquid manure. At one time this was the only available liquid feed, and very effective it was too!

To make liquid manure, place three generous spadefuls of well rotted manure in the centre of a large piece of cloth. Gather up the corners and tie at the centre of a large stick such as a broom handle. Then suspend the 'bag' in a container holding 100 or more litres (20 gallons) of water. Allow the manure to remain immersed for ten days before removing it from the liquid. The barrel may be filled with water a second time and the nutrients extracted again, but after that the manure should be assigned to the compost heap. Ideally, have two barrels, one from which the concentrated liquid manure can be drawn and a second one where the extraction process is occurring.

Liquid manure prepared in this way is too concentrated for feeding directly to plants and must be diluted with three times its own volume of water. Feed tomatoes, other vegetables and bedding displays every week throughout the months of June, July and August.

Worm-worked compost

Nature wastes nothing. In the garden, dead and decaying materials are recycled naturally, either by bacteria – a principle we utilise in the compost heap – or by being consumed by lowly creatures, notably earthworms. Virtually any organic material will pass through a worm's digestive system and emerge as a black powdery substance that is both odourless and inoffensive. Notice the worm casts on your lawn; they may well be a blot on your carefully manicured sward but they are not unpleasant to handle. Kitchen scraps, peelings and scrapings from plates, materials that cannot be placed on compost heaps, can be converted into top quality compost by creating your own worm factory. Obtain a large plastic or metal dustbin and make several holes in the lid to allow air to enter. Starting 5 cm (2 in) from the base, create a series of drainage holes extending to 15 cm (6 in) up the side of the container. Place it in a tray to collect the liquid (diluted threefold, this makes an excellent feed). Fill to the top drainage holes with gravel and cover with a board also drilled with holes. Then place a layer of compost 10 cm (4 in) thick on top of the piece of board.

Next, add the workers – the earthworms. To create good compost use brandlings. This species is easily recognised by its yellow and dark brown bands, and is found in any compost. You can buy these worms by post from specialist suppliers, or you may be able to obtain them locally from an anglers' shop. You will require about a hundred worms to begin your wormery.

Start by adding the household scraps. The worms will consume virtually all human food, both animal and vegetable, but bones are not acceptable. Although the worms appear to reject very little, they probably will not appreciate the remains of last night's curry.

Decaying food tends to be acidic and the worms are very sensitive to a sour environment. To keep the mixture sweet, at every 25 cm (10 in) from the bottom up add a covering of broken egg shells or cracked cockle shells. Continue filling in this way until you are within 15 cm (6 in) of the top.

The worms will require both moisture and an adequate temperature. Whether it will be necessary to provide additional moisture will depend upon the nature of the waste material provided. Often it is not necessary, but if the compost does become dry give a light watering from a can. As with all biological processes the operation is very temperature dependent. Below 5°C (41°F) the worms become inactive. During the summer months the problem is keeping the system cool. Place the bin out of doors in a shady location. Bring it into a shed or garage as winter approaches.

On average it takes 4–6 months to convert the waste into nutrient-rich compost, which should then be completely removed from the container. During the compost-making process the worms will have continually reproduced and there will be a large number of worms distributed throughout the medium. Use some of the compost to start a second drum of worm manure.

The compost is too strong to use direct and should be mixed with the same amount of both peat and grit to make a top quality potting compost.

A competitor-free environment

Most ground will support growth, as can be seen from any piece of waste land. As soon as the surface is exposed, almost overnight it becomes covered in weeds. So you may ask 'why bother to feed and carefully cultivate soil?' But stop and look carefully at the weeds growing on the uncultivated ground and compare them with any specimens that have escaped the gardener's attention on a well maintained plot. Those growing by the wayside or on undeveloped land are individually poor specimens whereas those left to grow in a garden are positive monsters by comparison. Seeds falling on waste land may germinate, but, while they will have the potential to produce plants of the same quality as those growing on well maintained soil, the environment in which they grow will restrict them to being poor, stunted specimens. Weeds are the survivors, the product of natural selection, unlike many of our garden plants which have been developed to satisfy man's idea of the perfect plant. These will only survive providing we ensure that they are not subjected to the competition of the survival of the fittest, which they would most certainly lose. The gardener must see that his plants do not have to compete for space, nutrients and water by not planting them too close to each other and by seeing that the self-sown competitors – weeds – are not allowed to grow and choke them out. Garden plants must also be protected from pests as they may have had some of their natural immunity and inbuilt defences bred out of them.

Controlling weeds

Annual weeds emerge as small seedlings and are easily removed by hand or hoeing. It is important to destroy them while they are still small. Among them there will almost certainly be seedlings of some perennial weeds, and if these are allowed to remain they may well prove difficult to remove at a later stage.

Perennial weeds are of two main types. Those with crowns, such as dandelions and plantains, do not present too much of a problem. They can easily be dug out (make sure you remove the centre and the root). Alternatively, they may be treated with a weedkiller. The other type of perennial weed often has some form of creeping underground stems, which facilitate vegetative reproduction, leading to the emergence of fresh plants some distance from the parent. Such weeds may be almost impossible to remove once they get between the roots of perennial plants or shrubs without digging up the cultivated specimens first, or using chemical weedkillers. These must be handled with the greatest care so that they do not come into contact with the cultivated plants (see p. 269).

All ground should be thoroughly dug or forked over before planting and all traces of weeds removed. *Do not simply turn weeds over with the soil believing that they will rot. Many perennial weeds will survive the treatment and if they are broken up in the digging process this will serve to facilitate their propagation.*

However carefully you turn over the soil, some pieces of root capable of generating new plants will survive. These pieces will give rise initially to plants with a far weaker anchorage than undisturbed weeds. Providing that you regularly examine the ground you should be able to easily pull them out as they appear.

Where virgin land is being cultivated for the first time or you are taking over a neglected plot, it is advisable not to make any permanent plantings during the first year. Give priority to the removal of perennial weeds. This is achieved by digging the ground with a spade in either the autumn or spring and digging over again, or otherwise simply removing the weeds which emerge during the summer.

New vegetable plots are best cleaned up by planting a crop of potatoes. The shoots are strong enough to compete with the weeds. The hoeing and harvesting of the crop will provide opportunities to remove any remaining weeds.

Garden hygiene

Hygiene is just as important in the garden as any other activity in life. By good management it is possible to reduce the chances of attack by pests and diseases or to limit their numbers to manageable levels. Keeping areas weed free and not overcrowding the plants will reduce the available cover, allowing predators every

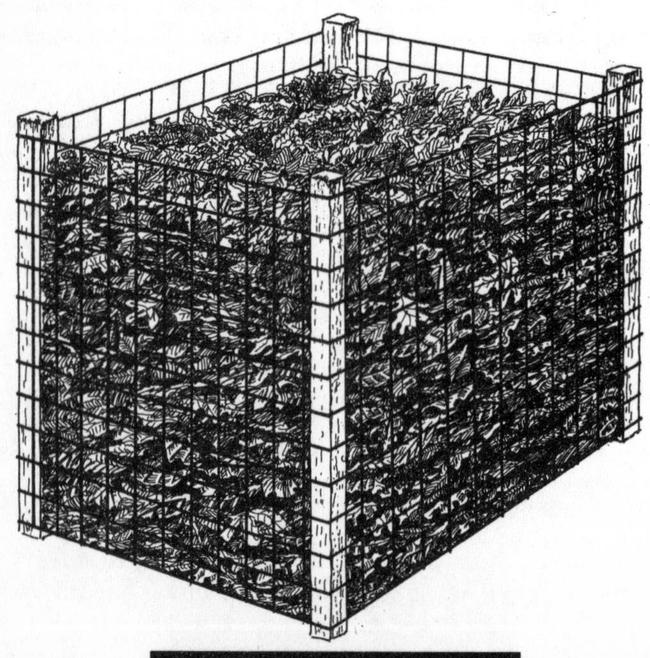

Wire bin for leaf mould

opportunity to destroy pests. All rubbish should be removed as this offers hiding places for both the pests themselves and their eggs. Turn over a large stone and it will reveal hordes of snails and slugs. Rotting pieces of wood similarly provide homes for woodlice and earwigs.

Autumn leaves can provide hiding places for a wide range of pests. Where large quantities of deciduous leaves fall they should be gathered up and placed in a storage area made by placing four posts in a square arrangement in the ground and wrapping wire netting around it to form an enclosure 1 metre square by 1 metre high (1 sq. yd x 3 ft high). The leaves will break down to form an excellent mulch.

Gather up fallen fruit. Any left on the ground will provide an environment for a whole range of pests and diseases.

Tools

Some tools are necessary, some desirable and others luxuries. Listed below are the most important items that you will need to acquire at the outset.

Spade

Essential for digging ground, removing old plants, shrubs and trees. A spade is required when soil has to be turned over completely or trenches dug.

Fork

A fork is needed for turning over pre-dug soil, to extract the roots of perennial weeds and for spreading manure. It is also required to aerate lawns.

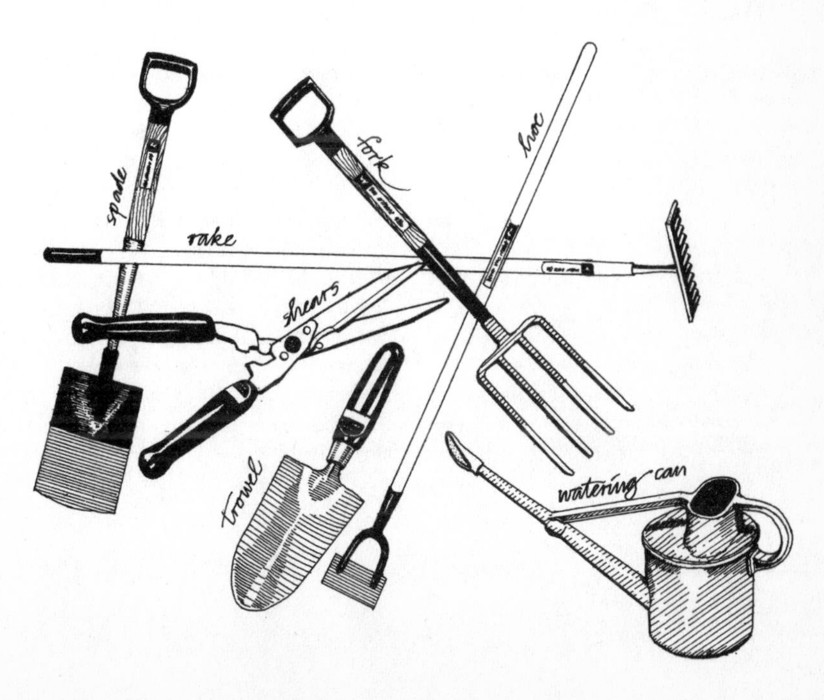

Rake
Necessary to level soil, the back of a rake is the most practical tool for forming seed drills. A rake is also used to scarify the surface of a lawn and remove debris.

Hand trowel
This is required for setting out seedlings and other small plants.

Hand fork
Required for weeding and simultaneously aerating small areas of beds where hoes are impractical. Consider buying one with a long handle to avoid back strain.

Hoe
Used for chopping off seedlings as they emerge and for simultaneously aerating the soil.

Watering can
For providing water when transplanting seedlings, for attending to hanging baskets and growing bags, for limited watering of beds and applying liquid feeds.

Secateurs
Essential for pruning shrubs and trees.

Pruning saw
Used in conjunction with secateurs where there is a large number of trees or shrubs including ones with branches too thick for secateurs.

Shears
Required for hedge trimming, tidying plants and for cutting the edges of lawns. This can all be done with the same tool, but a pair of long-handle shears for trimming lawns will save a great deal of backache.

Lawn edging tool
This half-moon spade-like tool is essential for cutting and keeping sharp the edges of lawns. If a spade is used in its place you will always be able to see a separation mark between each individual cut.

Bulb planter
This will produce a flat-bottomed hole of the required depth, vastly superior to using a trowel.

Care of your tools
Correctly looked after, your tools will last you a lifetime. Their worst enemy is corrosion. Always clean your tools thoroughly, wipe them over with an oily rag and hang them up in their allotted space in the shed. Never leave tools out of doors. Secateurs, shears and all metal parts of other tools should be covered with a thin film of oil before putting away for the winter.

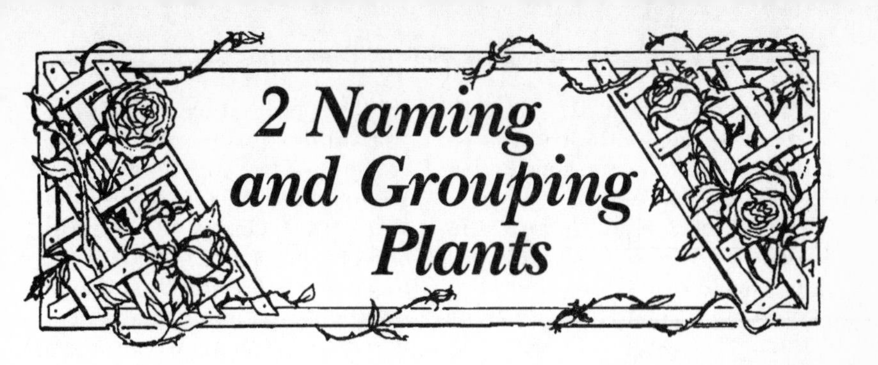

2 Naming and Grouping Plants

The naming of plants causes great confusion among many gardeners. Basically there are two distinct options – to use the common or vernacular names, or to use the scientific names.

Virtually all our popular plants, especially those that have been grown for generations, have names with which we are all familiar. Everyone knows what you mean by a foxglove – the name is understood throughout Britain. But many plants are known by different 'common' names. For example, what to many is the rowan tree is called the mountain ash by others. And if you live in England, a bluebell is a bulbous woodland plant, but the bluebells of Scotland are the harebells of England.

Clearly the use of common names is unreliable. But in the scientific method of naming every distinctive type of plant has a name by which it is known throughout the world.

Every plant is assigned to a major *family* group, e.g. the Scrophulariaceae. All members of a plant family have certain features in common, suggesting a true relationship. Within the family are usually several subdivisions into groups called *genera* (a single group is called a *genus*). A genus consists of closely related *species.*

Species are the basic units in plant classification. The individuals of a species are mutually fertile; they cannot interbreed with other species unless they are closely related in the same genus.

Within the Scrophulariaceae family is, among others, the genus *Digitalis.* One of the species belonging to this genus is *Digitalis purpurea* – the common foxglove. This name relates to the naturally occurring wild form. Cultivated hybrids, such as 'Shirley Hybrids', are correctly referred to as *Digitalis purpurea* 'Shirley Hybrids', although you are quite likely to see these described as Foxglove Shirley Hybrids in seed catalogues.

The characteristics of plants are passed on by their genes. New varieties sometimes arise in plants by gene mutation, known as 'sporting'. For example, among a population of plants that is normally blue-flowered a white individual may appear. If the seed from this white plant breeds true then we have a new variety. More often, however, it won't come true from seed, but it might be possible to propagate it vegetatively (see Chapter 4). A variety produced in a garden and maintained by a horticultural technique such as this is termed a *cultivar* – culti(vated) var(iety). The offspring of individuals of different varieties or species are termed *hybrids.*

Some seed packets bear the words 'F1 hybrid'. Such seeds are the product of crossing two perfectly true-to-type parent strains with desirable characteristics and are the 'first filial' generation – hence the symbol. Seedsmen are developing and producing the crosses yielding superior offspring. They are often more vigorous than either parent (hybrid vigour), disease resistant, and uniform in habit and growth. The disadvantage is that they are expensive. Production cost is high because it involves hand-pollination and isolation of the plants for breeding. Their special characteristics will only remain for one generation. Any seed produced by the hybrids will not breed true and are likely to be disappointing.

Convention in writing scientific plant names

Each species has a two-part Latin name, conventionally printed in italics. The first part is the generic name, which always has the initial letter capitalised. The second part, which pin-points the species, is not capitalised.

The Latin name of the common snowdrop is *Galanthus nivalis.* A doubled-flowered version, that originally occurred as a sport, is named thus: *Galanthus nivalis* 'Flore-pleno'. Actually, there is no need to repeat the generic name once given; just the capital letter with a full stop will suffice: *G. nivalis.*

Hybrids produced by the crossing of two different species are indicated by a multiplication sign. An example is a cross between two species of foxglove: *Digitalis grandiflora* x *D. purpurea.* Another example is *Forsythia* x *intermedia* which is a cross between *F. suspensa* and *F. viridissima,* and is a naturally occurring cross between two species of forsythia. There are man-bred versions of forsythia too, for example *F.* x *intermedia* 'Spectabilis'. The point to remember is that the part of the name indicating a cultivar is conventionally printed in roman rather than italic type, with an initial capital letter.

The naming adopted in this book

In seed catalogues and gardening books Latin names are often used, sometimes side by side with the common names. But no one, unless they are a terrible show-off, would refer to *Lathyrus odoratus* when they mean sweet peas. There can be little justification in using the scientific names of common annual plants, except when the genus name is the only one in common usage (e.g. cotoneaster), when it is unavoidable of course.

In this book, where common names are generally agreed upon and widely used these are given in preference to the Latin names. Conversely, a Latin name will be used in any instance where this is the more widely used, with the popular name, if there is one, alongside it in brackets.

Latin names aren't as difficult

to remember as you might think. You'll find certain words appearing again and again in different plant names, and these often tell you something about the plant, such as its appearance or habit . Thus, for example, the epithets *pumila* or *nana* will tell you that the plant is dwarf in habit, while *giganteum* tells you it's the opposite. And *rotundifolia* indicates round leaves, *fragrans* scented, and so on.

A knowledge of scientific naming will help you choose the right plants for your garden. Remember, only a very slight difference in name may mean a vastly different plant.

Classification according to life form

As well as being classified according to their genetic relationships, plants may also be grouped according to their life form. One widely used system groups plants according to the position relative to soil level of the buds that survive during the dormancy period to sprout anew in the following season.

Accordingly, the biennials and perennials are divided into four groups. One of these contains the trees and shrubs, whose survival buds are well above ground level. In the next group are found plants whose survival buds are close to ground level. This includes bushy plants whose aerial parts die away to leave buds at a stem base, creeping plants and very compact cushion plants. A third group consists of plants whose buds are at ground level, all aerial parts dying away, and includes rosette plants such as dandelion, daisy and some saxifrages. In the fourth group the survival buds are below ground (or water, in the case of water plants). It includes all the bulbous and rhizomatous plants (these are discussed in Chapters 4 and 6).

A fifth group is made up of the annual plants. These have no survival buds, depending on their seeds instead.

Annuals

Plants that complete their life cycle from germination to seed production in one year. They are divided into two classes: the hardy annuals, which can withstand frost, and the half-hardy annuals, which can be grown out of doors but are not frost-hardy. Annuals must be sown afresh each year.

Biennials

Plants that require two years to complete their life cycle. The seed germinates in the first year, the plant stores up food, overwinters and the following year produces flowers and seeds. It then dies.

Perennials

All plants except annuals and biennials are, strictly speaking, perennials – they continue their growth from year to year. But what most gardeners mean by perennials are the *herbaceous* perennials, the non-woody plants. The parts above the soil die back at the end of the season, to be replaced by new shoots in the following year from underground structures that live through the winter. Not all herbaceous perennials are deciduous, however. Some, such as bergenia and dianthus, have evergreen foliage.

One could say that climate determines what is perennial. Some garden plants that would be normally perennial in warmer climates die in the winter in this country. These must either be brought indoors to overwinter or else be treated as half-hardy annuals.

Trees and shrubs

These have permanent woody stems above ground that form the starting point for each new season's growth. This characteristic enables some of them to reach a very large size. Some retain their leaves throughout the year (evergreens), the others lose their leaves in winter, i.e. they are deciduous.

Botanically there is very little difference between trees and shrubs. We tend to call 'trees' those with a single stem or leader – the trunk – from which all other stems emanate. Shrubs have several woody stems originating at ground level. (See Chapters 10 and 11.)

Plants such as lavender and the heathers are sometimes called 'sub-shrubs' because they are halfway between shrubs and herbaceous perennials. Although they are relatively low-growing and the tops are herbaceous, their stems become quite woody. Such plants require regular pruning to generate fresh growth.

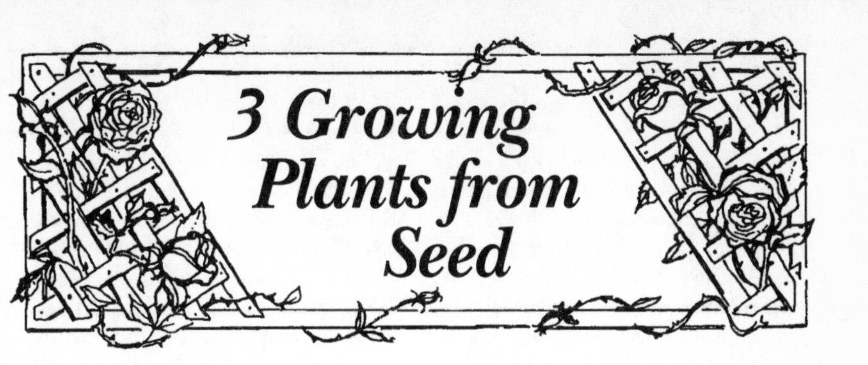

3 Growing Plants from Seed

The most economical method of obtaining garden plants is from seed. Normally expensive high quality bedding plants, vegetables and many decorative pot plants can be easily raised in this way, often for just a few pence each.

A seed contains an embryonic plant in a state of dormancy. It simply requires the right conditions to initiate germination. Sufficient food is stored in the seed to nourish the developing seedling until it is capable of supporting itself.

Nature designed certain seeds to remain viable for years while awaiting the right conditions for germination to occur. Yet there are others, such as the delphiniums, that decline very rapidly and need to be sown during the first spring after harvesting.

The majority of seeds of cultivated plants will germinate readily once they receive water, sufficient air and a suitable temperature. The moisture must first penetrate the seed's protective outer coating. If the seed has a particularly tough, thick covering (e.g. sweet peas), germination will be speeded up if you nick the seed coat with a sharp knife. Take care that you only cut the skin and do not damage the seed beneath.

Some seeds benefit from soaking in water for a few hours before they are sown. Generally they should not be soaked for longer than four hours, which is sufficient for moisture to penetrate most seed coats. Soaking for days will cause them to rot. Once your seeds have been soaked, the germination process has probably been set in motion. Plant them immediately and take care not to not allow them to dry out.

Each kind of seed germinates best at a certain temperature. At temperatures much higher than this optimum, germination will fail to occur. At lower temperatures than the optimum, germination will take place more slowly or, if really low, not at all. Cold, damp soil can cause seed to rot, so do not sow seed outside until the ground is warm enough to allow germination to take place reasonably quickly. Seed packets usually indicate the ideal temperatures and the time of year for sowing.

As well as hard seed coats, there are other explanations why seeds can remain dormant in spite of favourable germination conditions. They may need special treatment. Some kinds only germinate in darkness and others only in light (many others have no any preferences in this respect). The seed of some plants actually needs to be kept for a period of several weeks at a temperature near freezing to break dormancy (stratification), when good germination should follow. In most cases, seed germinates better when it is fresh, but in some instances (e.g. lettuce), the freshly harvested seed is often slow to germinate. Although apparently mature, it will continue to ripen during a period of storage.

Sowing times

Several factors affect the times one should sow, such as the length of the period between sowing and harvesting (or blossoming, in the case of flowering plants), the prevailing weather conditions (for seed sown out of doors), and the time needed for the particular type of seed to germinate.

Even under ideal conditions, different kinds of seed vary widely in the time they take to germinate. With some, such as cabbage, germination will take just two or three days, while others, such as parsley, will take several weeks to sprout.

The seed companies usually provide details of the germination time and sowing period, together with easy to follow instructions. However, like all gardening instructions, these can only deal with average conditions. To establish the best time to sow, you need to know your local climate and be prepared to adjust your sowing date according to the current situation. *It is the moisture and temperature levels, not the date on the calendar, to which the seeds respond.*

Seed can be sown earlier following a mild, dry winter, when the ground will be warmer than in an average year. Whenever soil is wet or frozen seed should never be sown, irrespective of the date.

It is often suggested that parsnips and other crops requiring a long growing season should be sown in February. But germination at this time of the year is very erratic and you will lose nothing by delaying sowing for a month.

Nevertheless, do not delay outdoor sowings unnecessarily because, other factors being equal, early sowings mean bigger and better crops. If in doubt about when to sow, choose the mid-point of the times recommended on the packet. It is at the extremities that problems occur. Too early, the seeds may rot; too late and the plants may not have sufficient time to reach maturity, or, like late-sown peas, they may be vulnerable to the mildews and pests prevalent in late summer.

The timing of indoor sowings is less variable as we are able to control the conditions. The only consideration in this instance is when it is safe to plant out, which does not vary a lot from year to year.

A common mistake is to presume that because seeds are on sale at a particular time of the year it is safe to sow them then. This may not be so. Seed companies despatch their seed packets in batches to the retailers

SOWING OUTDOORS

Rake the soil over to produce a fine tilth

Mark the position of the drill with a taut line

Draw out a V-shaped drill using a hoe with the blade resting on the line

Sow seed thinly

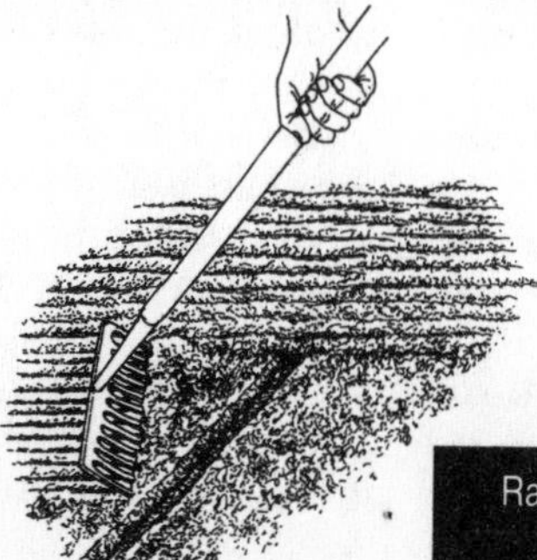

Rake soil over the seeds from both sides of the drill

who will display them as soon as they arrive. It is a good idea to buy early and store your seed. Unfortunately, some shops keep seed packets in their displays long after the sowing date is past.

Many seeds are marketed in foil packets, affording them protection from humidity. Providing these packets remain unopened, the seeds in them will usually remain viable for several seasons. Once the seal on the packet has been broken the seeds are no longer protected, so it is advisable to sow them during the current year. When seeds are not stored in a protective packet they should be bought fresh each season.

To store seed, keep it somewhere cool and dry so as not to trigger germination.

Sowing seed out of doors

The majority of hardy vegetables and annuals may be sown straight into the ground either in their permanent position or in a bed for transplanting when large enough. Direct sowing, apart from the work that it saves, has the advantage that it yields completely hardy plants with no tendency to become straggly.

Step-by-step guide to sowing directly into the ground

1. Select a site that is sheltered but not in the shade.

2. Dig over the soil (preferably this will have been completed during the previous autumn as the winter's frost helps to break up the soil). Remove all roots of perennial weeds and any stones.

Rake the soil over to produce a fine tilth, adding some fertiliser such as Growmore.

3. Stretch a taut line across the ground to mark the position of the drill. Fix the line to a stake. Draw out a drill to the depth required, using a hoe with its blade resting on the line. Where there is limited space and you intend to transplant the seedlings later on, drills may be created in a number of concentric circles using a piece of pointed wood.

4. Sow the seeds thinly. Where they are too close together it will be necessary to thin the seedlings later on. Not only is this wasteful, you will need to be very careful that you do not disturb the seedlings that you wish to remain.

5. Cover the seeds by raking soil over them. Generally the depth of soil should not be more than twice the length or diameter of the seeds.

6. Mark the position of the ends of the row with a label and write on it the type and variety of seeds that you have sown.

7. Scatter slug pellets around. Tender freshly germinated seedlings are the favourite breakfast of slugs and snails.

8. When large enough to handle the seedlings should be transplanted or thinned out

Do not attempt to complete the thinning out in one session. You can never be sure how many plants may be lost through pests or other causes. If you thin out too much and too early you will have no reserves. With the increasing popularity of mini-vegetables, which may be cooked whole, more mature thinnings may be used in this way.

A slightly different technique is used for members of the pea and bean family. The ground should be prepared by the general method of seed sowing (see p. 38) or by trenching (see p. 215). Make a flat drill 20 cm (8 in) wide by 5 cm (2 in) deep using the wide edge of the hoe blade. Sow the seed in three rows, the first at a distance 5 cm (2 in) in from the edge of the drill, the second a further 5 cm in from the first with the first seed in a position equivalent to the mid-point between the first and second seeds of the first row. The third row, 5 cm from the second, is commenced with the first seed in line with that of the first row. Three rows staggered in this way allows you to sow the greatest number of seeds in the smallest possible area at the same time, providing ready access to all of the plants when they are fully grown. Other types of seed including root vegetables, which are always sown straight into their final position, may be spaced out in this way. Where space is limited seeds may also be sown in blocks. A block about 1 metre square is divided into a series of short rows about 20 cm (8 in) apart and the seed is sown at the recommended distance into these rows.

The majority of seeds are small. Some, such as begonias, are so tiny they appear as dust and there does not appear to be a right side up. Simply scatter them on the surface of the compost.

SOWING PEAS AND BEANS

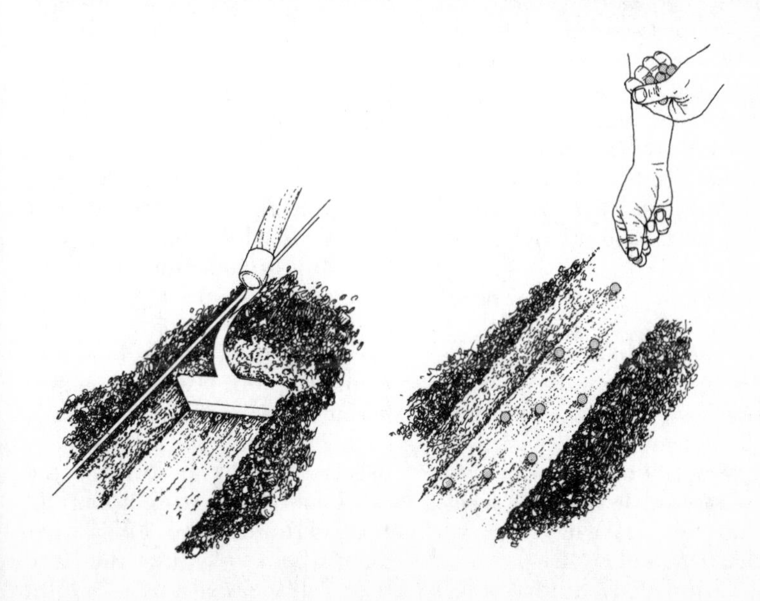

With bean seeds it is not difficult to plant them the way that they will grow. The majority of bean seeds are kidney shaped. At the top of the bean there is a flat black piece, and it is from here that first the root and then the shoot will appear. When bean seeds are sown at random they will rotate themselves, under the influence of gravity so that they are aligned in the right direction. Make it easier for them by sowing the beans with the thinner of the two ends pushed gently into the soil.

Members of the marrow family, including melons, cucumbers, gourds and pumpkins, should be sown with the pointed end downwards.

Raising bedding plants from seed

Bedding plants are usually hardy or half-hardy annuals. Annuals complete their life cycle within a year. Hardy annuals can be sown outdoors where they are to flower, but if you want plants to be ready as early as possible you must start them off inside in artificial heat. Half-hardy plants must be raised indoors or under glass and are planted outside when spring frosts are over.

Step-by-step guide to sowing seeds indoors

1. Provide a margarine tub or similar container with holes in the base for drainage. Fill it to within a centimetre of the top with seed compost. Water the compost until it is evenly moist, but do not soak it. Make the surface firm and level.

2 Sow the seeds thinly on the surface. Then cover lightly with the same compost to the depth recommended on the packet (remember, fine, dust-like seeds should be left uncovered).

3. Insert the tub into a polythene bag and provide gentle heat by placing it on a south-facing window-sill or by a radiator. Germination is greatly assisted by using a bottom-heated propagator, if available. Do not insert the tub in a polythene bag when using a propagator.

4. After the seedlings have emerged and established themselves they should be removed from the heat source or taken out of the plastic bag and placed in a sunny position. Higher temperatures are usually required for seeds to germinate than to grow. If seedlings are allowed to remain at the elevated temperature, especially in dull light, they will become spindly. From now on try to maintain a temperature of 9–15°C (50–60°F). Water them using a fine spray, just sufficient to keep the compost moist.

5. Once the seedlings are about 5 cm (2 in) tall and large enough to handle they should be transplanted into a seed box or tray. If making your own seed box, drill the necessary holes for drainage. A standard seed try is large enough to allow for the development of 48 seedlings – in eight rows of six – of most bedding plants. There is only sufficient room for 24 salvia or begonia seedlings, which are grown in six rows of four and allowed to develop into larger plants before setting out into beds. Fill the seed tray with John

Innes No. 2 or a general potting compost. Ensure that the surface is damp, but not soaking.

When transplanting, handle the seedlings with very great care. The slightest damage at this stage can result in the plant being killed as it will have very little defence against fungal attack. A batch of plants may be dug out with the tip of a penknife, individually separated and replanted in the seed box. Handle them by the leaves only.

6. Allow the plants to grow to two thirds of the required size. They should then be hardened off by taking the box out of doors during the daytime and bringing it inside at night. This is necessary to reduce the rate of growth, allowing the development of firm cells and tissue.

7. Continue to bring the seedlings indoors each night as long as there is any danger of frost. As soon as this has passed, plant them out in the beds.

If you do not own a propagator or some other means of providing artificial heat, it is possible to sow hardy annuals during September using the method described above but relying solely on ambient temperature. Transfer the seedlings to seed boxes and stand on the greenhouse or conservatory shelf throughout the winter. Harden off a fortnight before planting out. Seedlings raised in this way are among the earliest and hardiest.

Special technique for very fine seeds

Very fine seeds do not contain sufficient nutrients to carry the stem through the soil. Never

RAISING BEDDING PLANTS INDOORS

cover such seeds. To ensure a good spread, mix the seeds with a quantity of fine dry sand. Do this by placing the sand in the seed packet and giving it a shake to obtain an even distribution. To ensure that you control the sowing of the seed and that they do not all aggregate together, take a piece of paper and fold it to form a groove. Place the seed and sand mix in the groove and gently tap the piece of paper just above the surface of the sowing pan.

Special technique for growing geraniums from seed

Geranium plants yield only a small number of seeds and since the very best F1 hybrids require controlled pollination, seeds can cost 50p or more each! With such seeds it is even more important that they virtually all germinate and develop into top quality plants.

Seeds sown in mid-January will produce flowers during May. Modern geraniums flower perpetually throughout the summer and you will not gain maximum blooms from the plants if you delay until later in the season.

1. Fill a 10 cm (4 in) flower pot to within a centimetre of the top with sowing compost. Stand the pot in 2–3 cm (1 in) of water until the compost is damp. Sow the small number of seeds in the packet as far apart as possible. Cover with one millimetre of compost. Insert the pot in a polythene bag, closing the top with a rubber band.

2. Place the pot in a temperature of 21–24°C (70–75°F). The seeds may start germinating within three days but it can take longer even under ideal conditions. It is unlikely that all of the seeds will germinate at once. Leave the pot undisturbed for three weeks after sowing – no more are likely to emerge after this time.

3. When all the seeds that are going to have germinated, remove the polythene bag and maintain the temperature at 21°C (70°F). The plants will grow towards the light, so turn the pot through 180 degrees every day.

4. Four to five weeks after sowing, transplant the seedlings into individual pots and maintain at 15–18°C (60–65°F).

Where it is impossible to meet the above fairly exacting requirements, the seeds may be sown in September in the same way, allowing them to stand in the greenhouse at ambient temperature. By mid-November they will be about 10 cm (4 in) tall. Grow them on throughout the winter at about 4–7°C (40–45°F). This value is not critical, but the plants must never be exposed to frost or to lounge temperatures.

During March, the by now large seedlings must be brought into a warmer environment, 15–18°C. Seedlings raised in this way are just as advanced as those that are January-sown but, like bedding plants sown in the autumn, you have all the work of over-wintering them. In future years you will find it more convenient and cheaper to overwinter rooted cuttings of your favourite geraniums (see pp. 48–50).

Raising herbaceous perennials from seed

So far we have looked at annuals and plants that flower during their first season. Many of the handy herbaceous perennials are easily raised from seed too. They are sown one year and the foliage will die back and produce a flowering plant the following season.

The most convenient way to raise perennials is to prepare a nursery bed which is not in a prominent position but which will receive maximum sunlight. The best place for this is often furthest from the house and screened from the rest of the garden.

1. Prepare a seed bed as described in the step-by-step guide to sowing directly into the ground (p. 38).
2. When the seedlings are about 4 cm (nearly 2 inches) high, transplant them from the seed drills into rows or square formations, allowing adequate room for the plants to grow and develop.
3. Give the plants a weekly liquid feed until the second week in August. During October, but before the first frosts, transplant the small perennials to their permanent positions.
4. Most herbaceous perennials die down during the winter, so clearly mark the position with a plant label.
5. As the shoots emerge the following spring give a dressing with fertiliser and slug pellets.

Raising trees and shrubs from seed

Everything about the life cycle of trees and shrubs takes longer to complete than for other members of the plant kingdom. While there are exceptions, many trees take several months, a year or even more, to germinate. The process can be speeded up by pre-chilling some tree seeds prior to sowing.

1. Place the seeds on the surface of a tub filled with moist compost and seal inside a polythene bag.
2. Allow to stand in the greenhouse or on a window-sill at 15–21°C (60–70°F) for four days.
3. Place the seeds in the chiller compartment of the refrigerator. The time period for this stage will vary according to the type. Where periods are quoted on the seed packet, they should be allowed to remain for that time, but where no time is suggested or the seeds are gathered from the wild allow them to remain for 21 days.
4. Inspect the seeds every other day. As soon as they show any signs of germination they should be taken out and placed on the surface of a flower pot filled with moist sand and placed in a greenhouse or on a window-sill.
5. Where no signs of germination are observed in the refrigerator, the seeds should be removed after the prescribed period and treated as in 4 above.
6. Allow the seeds to stand until they have germinated. This may take several months.
7. Keep the soil moist but not soaking. Do not keep the seed pan in the polythene bag. While this would retain the moisture, the humidity and lack of air circulation can result in fungal disease which will rot the seeds.

An alternative but longer method for germinating tree seeds is to plant a single seed in a flower pot and leave in a cold frame or a sheltered area where it will receive maximum sunlight. It will be necessary to keep the soil moist for months or even years. This is usually a far longer method for raising trees, but if you have the patience you can almost guarantee success.

Aids to germination

Realising that the most difficult part of raising plants from seed is the germination stage, seed companies now sell by mail order pre-germinated seedlings growing in small plugs of compost.

Every year an increasing selection of the more difficult or spectacular subjects are available in this form. This is an easy way of raising bedding plants just as long as you can provide the correct conditions for them to grow on and develop.

Propagators

There are two types. The simplest are those that do not provide any additional heating and consist of a seed tray or base and a clear plastic cover. Placed on a window-sill they will trap heat by the greenhouse effect. But they hold little advantage except for appearance over the polythene bag method. Propagators with a base containing a heating mantle are a great aid to seed-raising and will allow you to germinate all seeds early in the season. They are also extremely useful for rooting cuttings.

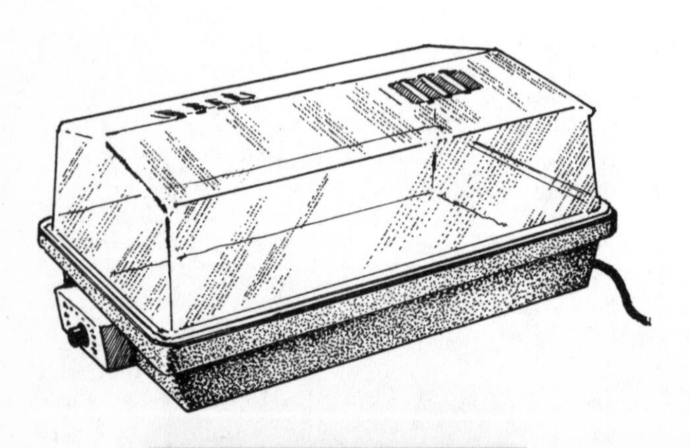

A bottom-heated propagator

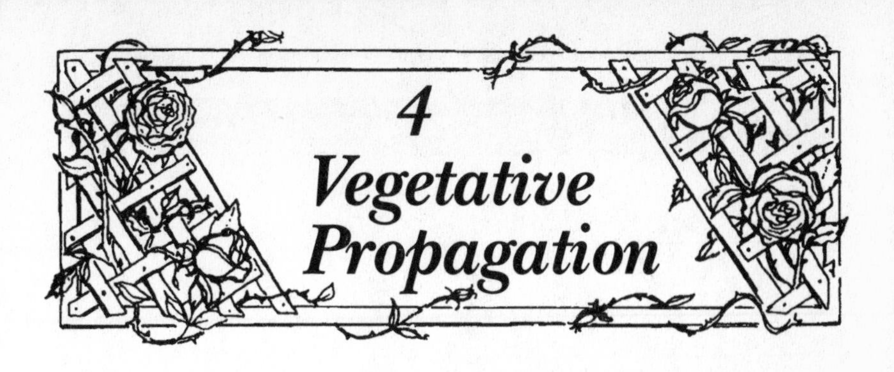

4 Vegetative Propagation

Certain plants as they grow older lose their vitality, their zest for life, and they need to be replaced with something more youthful. As an alternative to propagation by seed, plants may be increased by vegetative means. Most vegetative methods of increase involve taking tissue that is in its first year and rooting it. The young plants will be clones, identical to their sole parent in every respect. Vegetative propagation is the only way of increasing the stock of many of the new and spectacular varieties that have been developed in recent years.

There are three basic methods of vegetative propagation: simple division of a crown where the roots are already present; the separation of structures such as bulbs or bulblets, which have an inbuilt root-producing mechanism; and the inducing of plant material, mainly shoots, to generate the life-supporting roots.

Simple root division

As the crown of a herbaceous perennial increases in size the centre will get woody and the whole plant loses vigour. Lifting and dividing it every four or five years will rejuvenate the plant and increase your stocks. In the early spring, cut back all the dead material and lift the whole of the crown. Place two forks back to back in the centre of the crown and pull it apart, dividing the root into equal parts. Further divisions to form extra, smaller plants may then be performed. Providing that the pieces have their own roots and three or four buds it is often possible to obtain several young plants from one parent. With those plants which increase the size of the crown by growing out from the centre it is the pieces nearest to the circumference which have the greatest vigour and which give the best results.

Before replanting any herbaceous perennials use the opportunity to scatter slow-acting fertiliser into the hole. Delphiniums and other plants that have a relatively small crown should be carefully lifted during March or early April. At this stage the buds will be developing and clearly visible. With a sharp knife cut through the central tough tissue to form two halves, each with their own buds. Unless a plant has a very large crown, restrict the propagation to simple division by two.

Paeonies are a special case. They resent being moved and will often not flower the next season or even the one after that

PLANT DIVISION

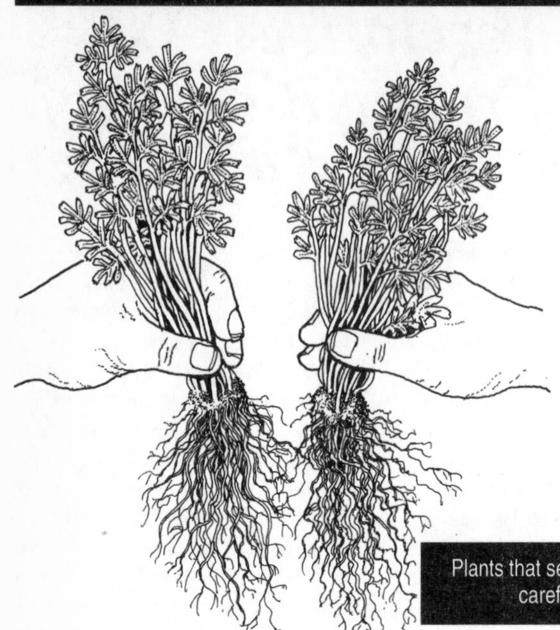

Plants that separate easily should be carefully pulled apart

Perennials that have grown too big should be lifted and divided

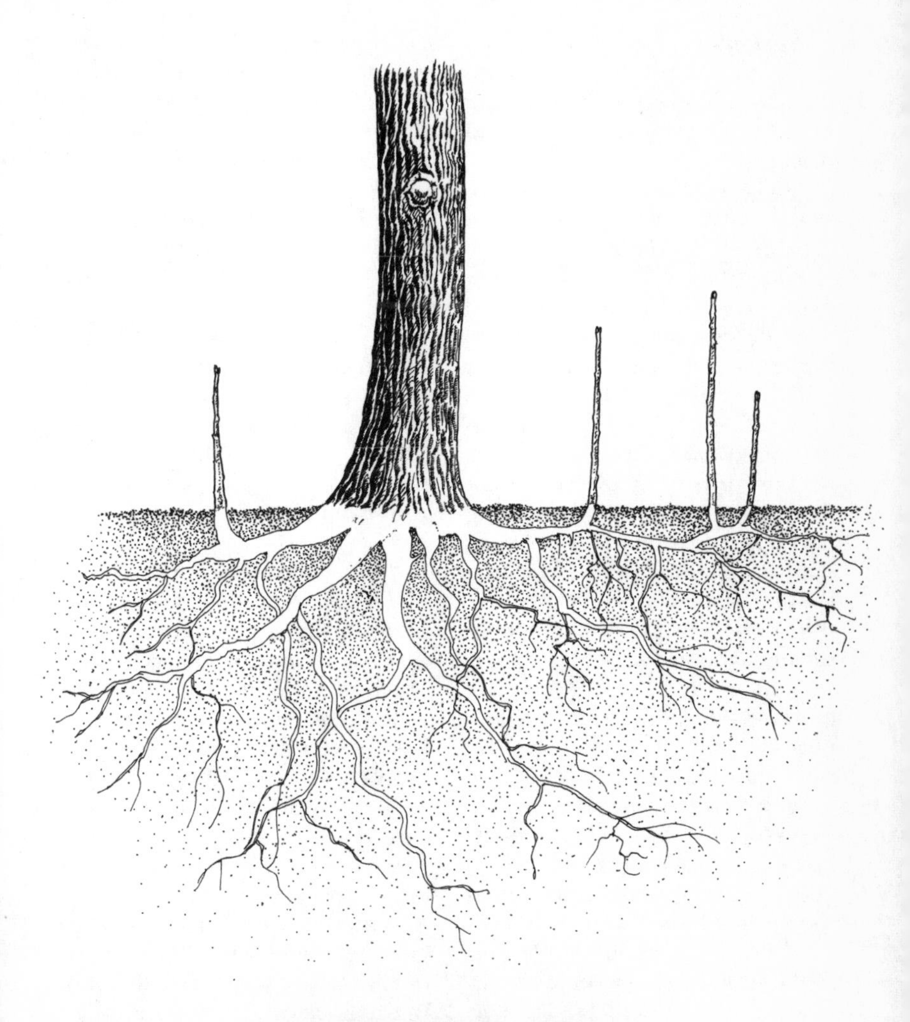

Suckers, formed by many trees and shrubs, are a ready means of vegetative increase, but do not propagate from grafted rootstocks following division or transplanting. Reduce the delay in producing the next crop of flowers by lifting the plant in September, dividing it into two or more by means of a sharp knife and immediately replanting it into its new position.

Suckers

Shrubby kinds of perennials can be increased by removing suckers from the plant and replanting.

Suckers occur on certain woody plants whose roots are capable of producing buds at various points away from the main crown. The buds develop into shoots that form new plants. Suckering can be so prolific in some cases that if left unchecked they will spread throughout the garden. Remove suckers with a portion of root by severing from the parent with, depending upon the size, either a sharp spade or trowel. This operation should be performed as soon as the new season buds emerge through the surface of the soil.

Some trees, particularly members of the genus *Prunus*, produce several suckers around their base. Usually these do not develop until quite late in the tree's life, by which time its history is unknown. Since so many fruiting and ornamental trees are grafted onto different rootstocks, severing and replanting saplings obtained in this way could lead to an unexpected type of tree. Such suckers should be dug out as soon as they are noticed and discarded. The appearance of a large number of suckers is a sign that root-pruning is required (see p. 72).

Cuttings

The aim of taking cuttings is to induce a severed piece of plant tissue to form roots. Where plant tissue is broken it is usually possible to encourage newly emerging cells to develop into root-forming material, but as with all other operations success depends upon getting the conditions correct. Tissue from some plants, mainly those with succulent growth such as busy Lizzies, root so easily that all you have to do is to break off a piece, place it in damp compost and wait for it to grow. Others, especially woody ones from trees and shrubs, are extremely difficult and you must take the greatest care, yet there are very few plants that are impossible to root from cuttings.

Softwood cuttings

These are cuttings taken from plants such as geraniums, which do not form any woody cells, and immature shoots of shrubs such as fuchsias taken when the plant has just started into growth. Select a shoot 7–10 cm (3–4 in) in length. It is important that you make a clean cut with a sharp knife – a jagged surface is a larger surface for fungal disease to enter. Once the shoot has been removed, trim the stem just below the leaf joint (usually there is the greatest concentration of growth-stimulating hormone at this point).

Remove the lowest leaf, or leaves if they grow in pairs, and dip the cutting into a combined

TECHNIQUE FOR GERANIUM AND OTHER SOFTWOOD CUTTINGS

Select a healthy side shoot about 7.5 cm (3 in) long and cut it from the plant with a sharp knife. Cut the stem again just above a node (where a leaf joins the stem). Remove the leaf from the node and any flower bud on the shoot

Dip the end of the shoot into a rooting powder

Fill a flower pot with a cuttings compost. Insert four or five cuttings around the edge of the pot at a depth of 2–3 cm (1 in). Firm them in well

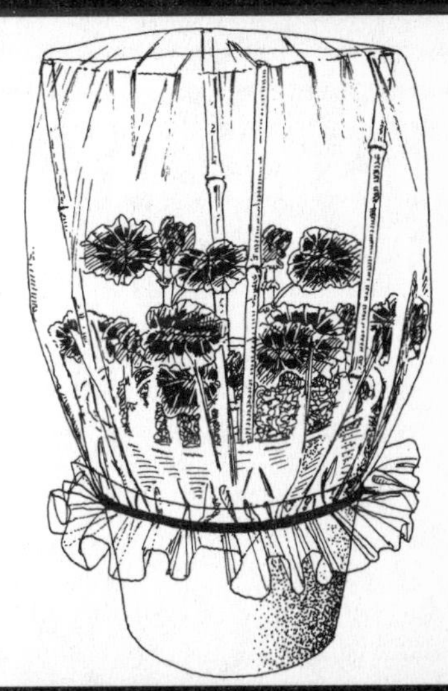

Place a polythene bag over the flower pot and leave in a warm position for a month to six weeks

When the cuttings have rooted, transfer them to individual pots

rooting hormone and fungicide, which will simultaneously encourage root formation and afford protection from the many germs that prosper in the conditions that favour root development. Place about six cuttings around the edge of a 12 cm (5 in) flower pot filled with either a loam or peat-based compost. Cover the cuttings and pot with a clear plastic bag, securing it in position by means of a rubber band. The pot should then be placed in a warm position shaded from the direct rays of the sun.

How quickly the cuttings will root will depend upon the time of the year, the temperature and the number of daylight hours. Softwood cuttings root best between June and August but they are usually successful from late spring through until early autumn. After a fortnight, establish whether there is any fresh growth and take away any cuttings that have obviously died. Unless you are sure that the cuttings are growing, replace the plastic bag.

Check their progress every week, removing the bag only when you are sure that the cuttings are now fully self-supporting. Do not worry if you allow the bag to remain longer than that – it is unlikely to do any real harm.

When the pot becomes overcrowded the cuttings should be removed and planted individually in pots.

To root clematis cuttings, adopt the same method but use internodal cuttings, i.e. taken midway between two leaf joints.

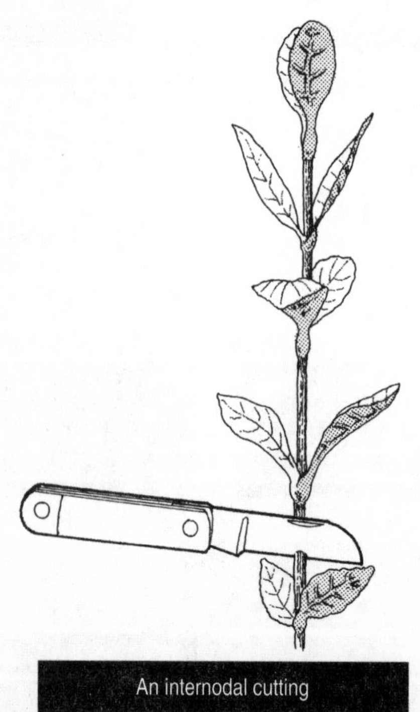

An internodal cutting

Semi-hardwood cuttings

These are cuttings taken from shrubs of the current season's growth when the shoot is just beginning to turn woody. The period for taking them is usually about July but may be up to the end of September. Semi-hardwood cuttings root easier if they have a heel attached. This is the sliver of bark and underlying wood from where the shoot is attached to the main stem. Like the nodal position on the softwood cutting, this is where their growth stimulants concentrate and it is where potential root-forming cells are most likely to be situated. Select a semi-softwood shoot of about 10 cm (4 in) in length and carefully pull it downwards so that it is torn away from the stem. Trim any jagged edges, dip it into the combined rooting compound and fungicide and proceed as described for softwood cuttings.

Hardwood cuttings

This is a method of propagating deciduous trees and shrubs and conifers. Larger cuttings about 25–30 cm (10–12 in) are taken during September with a heel or cut with secateurs. Prepare a nursery bed by selecting a well drained site and working some sharp sand into the loam so that it will not become waterlogged during the winter. Bury the cuttings one third of their length in the soil.

During the spring the cuttings will be seen to produce new growth, but this does not mean that they have rooted. The sap contained within the stems will

HARDWOOD CUTTINGS

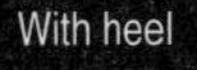

With heel

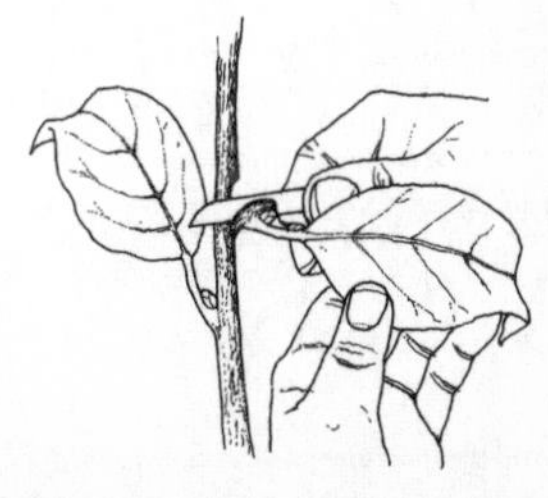

With bud

be sufficient in many cases to generate some leaves. From now on it is important that you keep the cuttings regularly watered throughout the summer months when the increasing temperature will stimulate root formation.

With all methods or propagation there are always some losses and these tend to be greater with hardwood cuttings. But some of the cuttings will still be growing by the end of the summer, which is a sure sign that they now have independent roots and will be ready for transplanting into their permanent position during the following autumn or spring.

If in spite of all your efforts the cuttings do not root, try a variation of the semi-softwood method again in September. Prepare the cuttings in the same way, dipping them into rooting compound and fungicide before planting them individually in flower pots. Then cover them with a very large, clear plastic bag and leave them in the greenhouse until April when the bag may be taken off. The pots should be kept watered throughout the summer.

Root cuttings

The roots of most hardy herbaceous perennials are capable of producing independent shoots and the plants may be propagated by means of root cuttings. In late February or early March lift part of the crown of a herbaceous hardy perennial to expose the roots. Sever two or three of the fleshiest roots at the base of the crown. Roots that are more than 5 mm (¼ in) in diameter should be cut into pieces 5 cm (2 in) long. The thickest end of the piece of root, i.e. that nearest the crown, should be given a square cut and the thinner end a slanting cut. Do not use rooting powder. Insert the thick cuttings vertically into a flower pot filled with soil or compost, with the slanting cut end towards the bottom of the container. Thin roots (those with a diameter of less than 5 mm) are cut into strips 7–10 cm (3–4 in) in length and are laid across the surface of the compost and then covered with 1 cm of compost. Root cuttings should be kept in the greenhouse until the young plants have become established.

New plants from rhizomes

Some types of irises have thick, fleshy rootlike structures near the soil surface. Technically, they are not roots but swollen stems and are termed rhizomes. They grow horizontally, producing roots from their lower surface. Undisturbed, the rhizomes will gradually crowd themselves – there will be too much root competing for the available nutrients and the plants will lose their vigour. Regenerate and propagate them simultaneously by digging up the rhizome clump after the plant has finished flowering. Examine the clump and you will find that the younger parts, which grew in the current season, are at the extremities. Select pieces of the new young growth with at least one new shoot or bud and some roots. Sever a piece 7 cm (3 in)

ROOT CUTTINGS

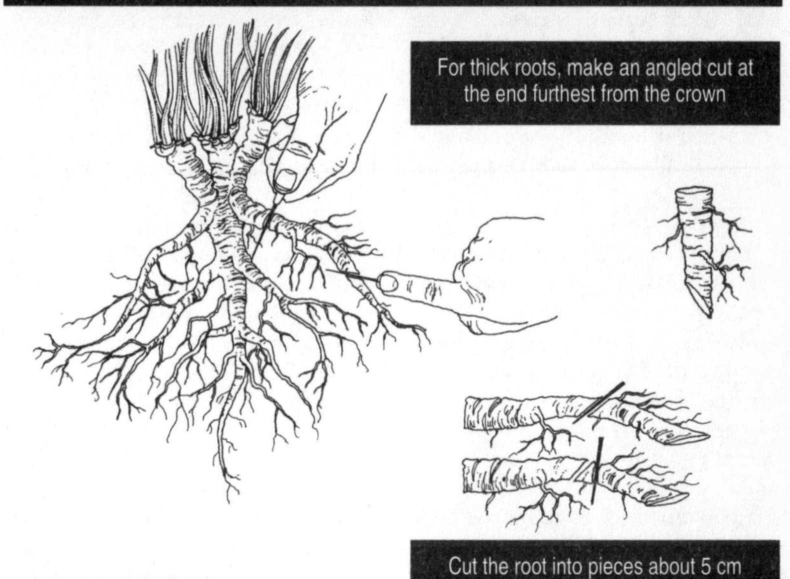

For thick roots, make an angled cut at the end furthest from the crown

Cut the root into pieces about 5 cm (2 in) long

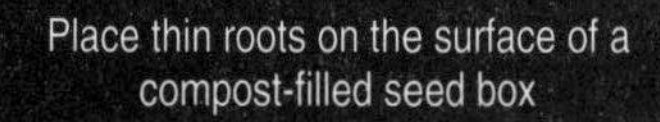

Place thin roots on the surface of a compost-filled seed box

Insert thick pieces vertically in a flower pot of compost

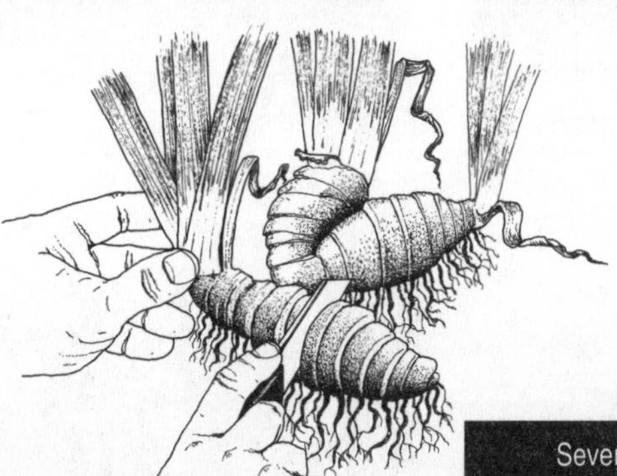

Sever rhizomes with a knife

long from the parent and place it horizontally at the same depth that it occupied before being removed. Cut back the leaves on the new iris plants by half – a large leaf area will lose water more rapidly than the reduced amount of roots can take up.

Leaf cuttings

Correctly treated the leaves of certain house plants will root and produce shoots. Two different techniques are employed. For large flat leaves such as *Begonia rex*, select a fully mature leaf showing no sign of damage. With a sharp knife make a series of cuts 2 cm (nearly an inch) apart halfway through each of the main leaf veins. Place the leaf on the surface of a flower pot containing moist compost and pin it to the soil by means of a bent paper clip. Then place the flower pot in a plastic bag just as you would for softwood cuttings and treat the leaf cuttings in the same way.

With long leaved plants such as streptocarpus or mother-in-law's tongue, the leaf should be cut into a series of strips 2–3 cm (1 in) wide. Push the leaf strips vertically into moist compost contained in a flower pot. Again place the pot in a polythene bag and treat the cuttings as described for softwood cuttings.

Leaf-stalk cuttings

African violets (*Saintpaulia ionantha*), some foliage begonias and many other plants will generate roots and shoots around the leaf stalks. During May or June insert the stalk of

AFRICAN VIOLET LEAF-STALK CUTTINGS

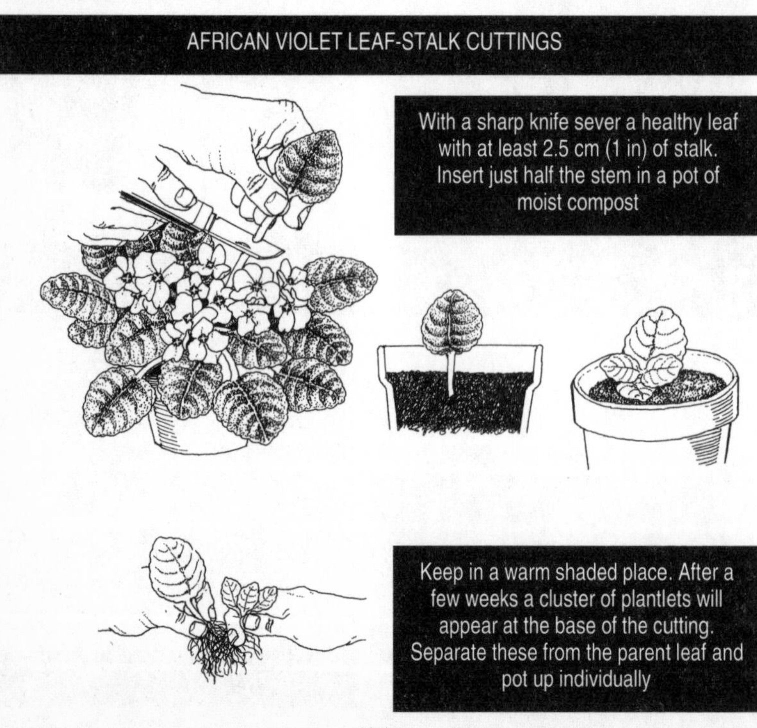

With a sharp knife sever a healthy leaf with at least 2.5 cm (1 in) of stalk. Insert just half the stem in a pot of moist compost

Keep in a warm shaded place. After a few weeks a cluster of plantlets will appear at the base of the cutting. Separate these from the parent leaf and pot up individually

STREPTOCARPUS LEAF CUTTINGS

Select a healthy and still vigorously growing leaf and with a sharp blade cut it into strips about 2.5 cm (1 in) wide

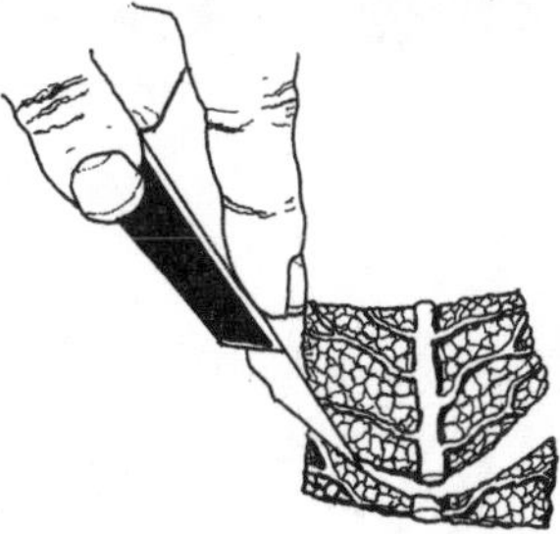

Trim the pieces to a gentle point. Insert several pieces in a pot of moist compost and cover with a polythene bag

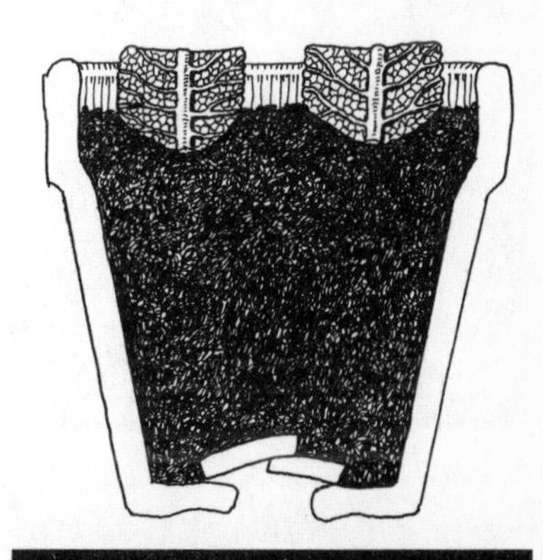

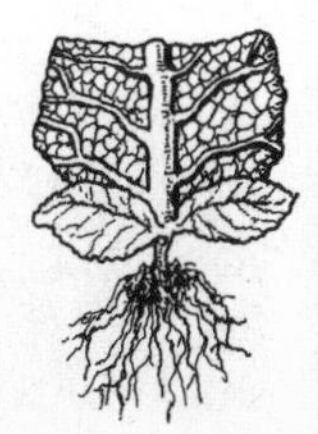

Keep the cuttings out of direct sunlight and in a warm, even temperature. Remove any that shrivel and die. After several weeks the rest will develop plantlets at the point where the midrib meets the compost

the leaf into moist, sandy compost and again proceed by the method given for softwood cuttings.

Propagation from leaf cuttings of all types is a slow process. Without heat, two to three months may go by before there is any sign of new plants developing – with this method you must be patient.

Root cuttings and leaves in water

African violets, balsam (*Impatiens balsamina*) and other succulent growths will root easily in water, but this is not an effective method of propagation. While root production occurs readily it is extremely difficult to pot the plants without damaging the roots.

Layering

Layering is a method of plant propagation intermediate between cuttings and division. It is used for woody shrubs such as camellias, which may be extremely difficult to root if you do not possess a propagator. Layering consists of creating an open wound that can produce

PROPAGATING A SHRUB BY LAYERING

Select a branch and bend it so that it touches the ground about 30 cm (1 ft) from its tip. Then make an oblique cut in the part of the branch lying over the ground. Keep the wound open with a sliver of wood

Place some sharp sand under the partially severed branch to encourage root formation. Firmly anchor the branch using a stake. Keep the soil moist until the branch has acquired roots (up to a year)

roots, yet the material from which the new plant is to be generated remains attached to the parent plant. There are two variations: soil and air layering.

Soil or normal layering consists of selecting a shoot during springtime that is capable of being pinned to the ground. Make an oblique cut a third of the way through the branch about 30 cm (1 ft) from the tip. Place a sliver of wood in the cut to keep it open while still leaving the maximum cut surface area exposed. To encourage root formation, place a quantity of sharp sand under the partially severed branch. With a piece of bent wire, pin down the cut surface so that it is resting in the sand. Place a stake in the ground and secure the branch to it. The soil under the wound must be kept moist throughout the summer. It may take up to a year for the partially severed branch to acquire roots and it should be allowed to remain attached to the parent plant for a further year.

Air layering is used for branches that are too high to be propagated by the normal layering method. Again, make an oblique cut a third of the way through a branch 30 cm (1 ft) from its growing tip and place a slither of wood in the gap to keep the wound open. Onto a piece of transparent plastic place a damp mixture of equal parts sand and peat. Create a sleeve by tying the ends of the plastic on either side of the wound. It may take several months to produce the roots, which will easily be seen through the plastic.

Increasing bulbs and corms

The cultivation of corms and bulbs is discussed in Chapter 8. Here we will look at how we may

Gladiolus corm with cormlets

propagate them. Although they produce seeds, many have some kinds of vegetative means of multiplication as well.

Many bulbs produce new bulbs, known as secondary bulbs or offsets, around the parent bulb. In the case of narcissi, an offset is at first enclosed in the same scaly covering or tunic as the parent. By the following year it will have separated to the extent that it is only attached to the base. At this stage it can be separated and grown on to become a flowering-sized bulb in a year or two.

Certain bulbs and corms generate numerous minute bulblets. These bulblets will take three or four seasons to reach flowering size and should be grown in a small nursery bed of rich soil. The ones that surround gladiolus corms are about the size of sweet pea seeds and are referred to as spawn.

Hyacinths are extremely reluctant to form new bulbs, but they may be stimulated to do so by notching the base of the bulb before planting. Make V-shaped grooves about 3 mm ($\frac{1}{8}$ in) deep (see diagram). The bulb should then be grown in a pot in the greenhouse without forcing throughout the winter. After the greenery has died down lift the bulb and you will discover that several small bulblets have formed. Remove these and grow in the greenhouse until they are large enough to be planted outside in beds.

Certain members of the lily family produce aerial bulbils in the leaf axils. These bulbils may be removed and grown in a pot in the greenhouse until they are large enough to raise a flowering

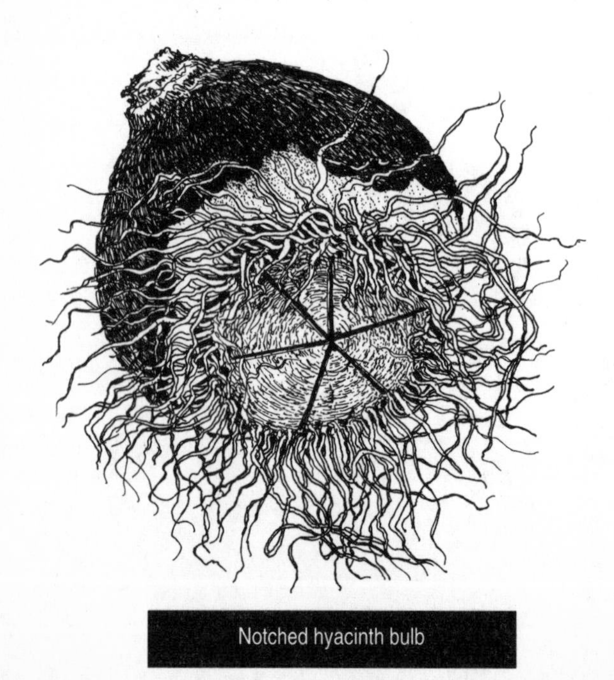

Notched hyacinth bulb

plant. The bulbs of lilies consist of several overlapping fleshy scales. Lily plants may be propagated by gently pulling all of the scales away from the bulb and inserting them base down in compost in a large flower pot. In a few weeks bulbils will form which will be ready after the end of the flowering season for potting individually.

Grafting

Grafting is a means of reproducing plants that are difficult or impossible to propagate by other methods. It differs from the other methods in that the plant you are seeking to reproduce does not generate its own roots but relies on another plant to do that part of the process for it. Basically, a piece of the stem of one plant, called the scion, is induced to unite with the rooted part of another, the stock. The technique is well within the capabililities of the amateur whose only problem is likely to be that of obtaining suitable rootstocks.

Rootstocks are available from specialist suppliers, but amateurs most commonly graft hybrid tea roses onto dog roses (*Rosa canina*) which are easily grown from seeds. Even if you do not graft yourself, a knowledge of the principles involved will help you to better understand the planting, maintainance and pruning of grafted stock.

There are two main reasons for grafting:

1 It is the most satisfactory method of propagating trees and shrubs other than species, which grow true to form from seed.

2 Grafting may be used to create tree or shrub specimens with the characteristics of both the stock and the scion.

Grafting allows for the creation of certain dwarf conifers from material that might not generate its own roots or, if it did, the trees would become too large. We can grow bizarre forms such as twisted hazels that will not come true from seed and are reluctant to root, by grafting them onto the root of the wild hazel.

Grafting is not only a technique restricted to hardwood subjects. It has been extended to tomatoes, where superior flavoured varieties are grafted onto vigorous growing rootstocks. Cacti are also frequently grafted.

As grafting is a tissue-fusing operation, to be successful it is necessary to use plants that are closely related. The ring of green living cells within the woody stem just below the bark is called the cambium layer. The cambium tissues of the two plants have to be bought into close contact and firmly kept together until the union is complete.

The grafting of trees and shrubs is best performed during the spring just as both the stock and scion are coming into growth. Scion material, which should be hard woody shoots that grew during the preceding season, is cut in winter and stood vertically in a nursery bed.

There are several different cuts used in grafting but they are all variations on a basic theme.

Splice grafting

This is the simplest and most widely used of all grafts. Cut back the stock to the point where the graft is intended, usually 15 cm (6 in) above ground level. Make the cut slope at an angle of 45 degrees. Take a scion of near identical diameter to the stock and make a sloping cut to match as closely as you can that of the stock. Remember, the better the pair match up the greater your chances of success. Place the scion on the stock – don't forget, it is particularly important that the cambium layer just below the bark is in close contact as it is through this that the life-giving sap travels. Bind the joint with rubber grafting strips, raffia or plastic adhesive tape.

Saddle graft

This is a more secure union and is usable for all hardwood grafts. Select a scion that has about the same thickness as the rootstock, which is cut off 15 cm (6 in) above the ground. On either side of the stock, at the top, create an inverted V-shaped form 2 cm ($^3/_4$ in) in length. Then take the scion and cut a corresponding V-shaped depression into it. The two Vs must fit into each other exactly. Bind the union securely.

Budding

As the name implies, this involves the insertion of a bud into the rootstock. Budding has now taken over as the main commercial method of

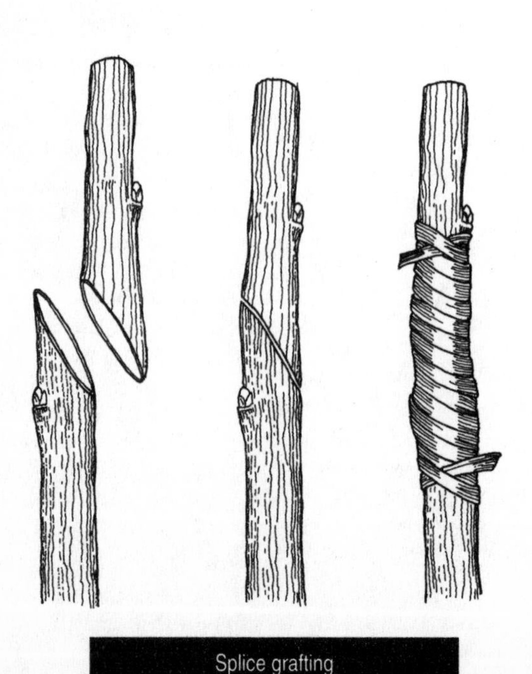

Splice grafting

propagating roses. During the summer, select a bud from halfway down the stem of a rose that has just finished flowering and with a very sharp knife make a cut 2 cm (¾ in) above the bud so that you have a sliver of bark and wood complete with a bud about 4 cm (1 in) long. Trim the edges and remove the sliver of hardwood. Make a short cut in the rootstock 10 cm (4 in) from the ground and parallel to it. Make a vertical cut to 2 cm (¾ in) above it and 2 cm below it. With the tip of the knife and your fingers, very carefully lift the bark of the rootstock and insert the bud in the space created. Bind the bud in position both above and below where it protrudes. Once the bud becomes established the stock is cut off just above it.

The majority of fruit and ornamental trees are grafted about 15 cm (6 in) above ground level. This allows sufficient clearance to ensure that the union is not below ground level, which could result in the scion forming roots that would take over and nullify the part played by the rootstock. The shape of bush roses is such that they start branching just a few centimetres above ground level, necessitating a graft or budding much closer to the soil. Rose rootstocks will develop buds that grow from the ground as suckers. Leaf stems of hybrid tea roses carry five leaves whereas those from the briar stock have seven leaves to a stem.

Saddle grafting

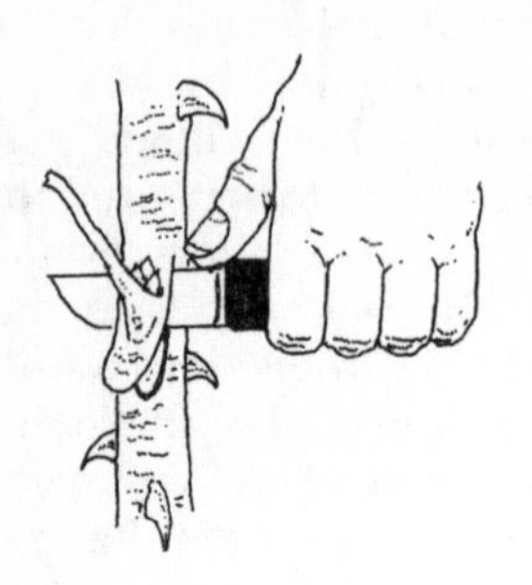

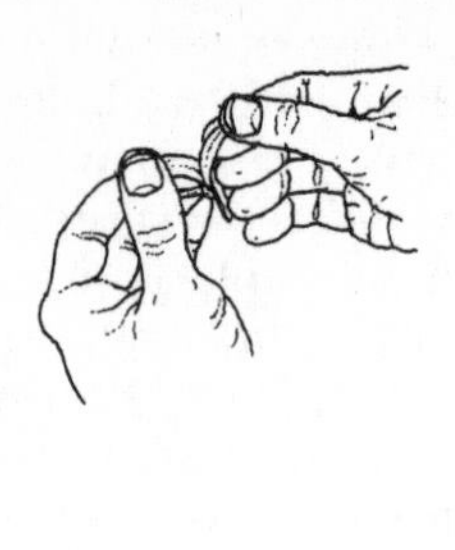

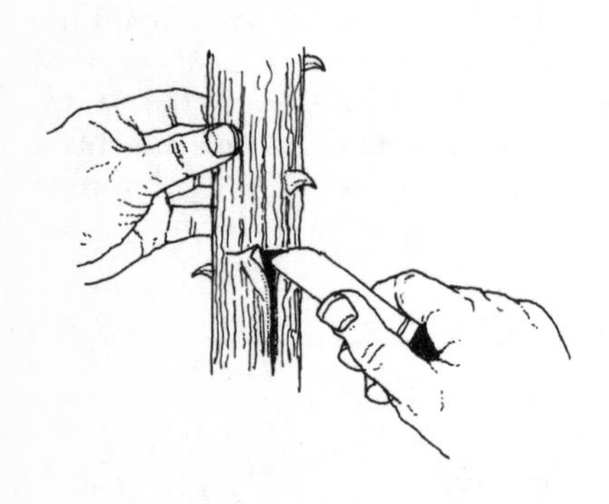

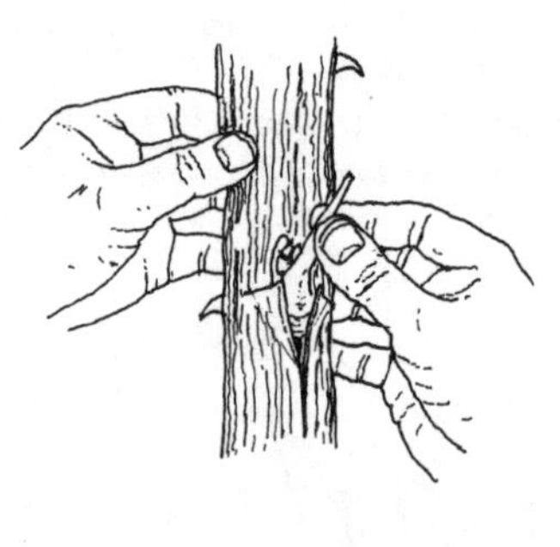

Budding roses

As soon as briar stems are detected they should be pulled away from the roots.

Standard roses are grafted just below the canopy. The strong single stem, provided by the stock, is a trained dog rose. Due to the different position of grafting, special pruning techniques must be employed.

Reversion

Often special named varieties of rhododendron seem to revert to the wild form. First the flowers on part of the bush change to purple and gradually the whole does so. What has happened is that the variety has been grafted onto the more vigorous growing common form and a bud from the rootstock, which will always have a tendency to produce shoots, will form a stem.

Due to its stronger growth it will prosper at the expense of the named variety. Left unchecked, it will drain the nutrients and become the dominant form until the original grafted variety is completely destroyed.

Similarly, a variegated plant can gradually revert to an all-green form if the green shoots are not cut out when they appear.

Wherever shoots of a wild or common form is seen coming from the ground close to any tree or shrub it is a sign that the rootstock is beginning to take over. Remove the stem with secateurs as near to the root as is practical. Once the tendency has been detected it is almost certain to reoccur and the plant must be inspected periodically.

5 Pruning

Pruning is the least understood of all aspects of gardening. Many gardeners feel they should prune trees every year, neither knowing the reason why nor how to do it properly. Trees and bushes grown naturally are things of beauty, but there is seldom sufficient room to grow trees completely naturally in gardens. We tend to cultivate our trees in confined spaces. To satisfy our landscaping aspirations we train trees to grow in unnatural shapes. With fruit trees, we try to obtain the maximum quantity of fruit from the smallest tree. For demands such as these we need to be able to control the rate and direction of growth.

There is a natural balance between the root system below the ground and all of the tree above. From the seed or cutting stage the amount of root determines the quantity of top growth. The root will push a certain quantity of water and nutrient-rich sap through the tree's circulatory system and the maximum growth that this quantity of liquid can sustain will occur. Reduce the top growth and there is an excess of the life-giving sap. Immediately the tree responds by creating more greenery. But pruning encourages growth in another way. Rising up from the roots are growth promotors, organic chemicals that stimulate the tips to grow. At the same time these tips send back growth inhibitors, which stop the ancillary buds on the branches below the tips from growing. Pruning stops the supply of growth inhibitors, with the result that secondary buds develop from the side branches. This is the reason why hedge clipping, which is the crudest form of pruning, results in the development of a dense barrier.

The exact method of pruning will depend upon the kind of tree or shrub, but certain principles are common to all pruning. Shape is always important and you should first form a picture of the mature tree in your mind. Inspect the tree for any signs of unhealthy growth. Damaged or diseased shoots must be cut back to healthy tissue. Any weak, spindly growths must be cut out at the origins. Often good strong branches develop, but instead of growing away from the centre of the tree they grow inwards towards the middle while other branches grow across their neighbours. These must be removed to stop the tree from becoming a tangled mass.

SOME PRUNING TOOLS

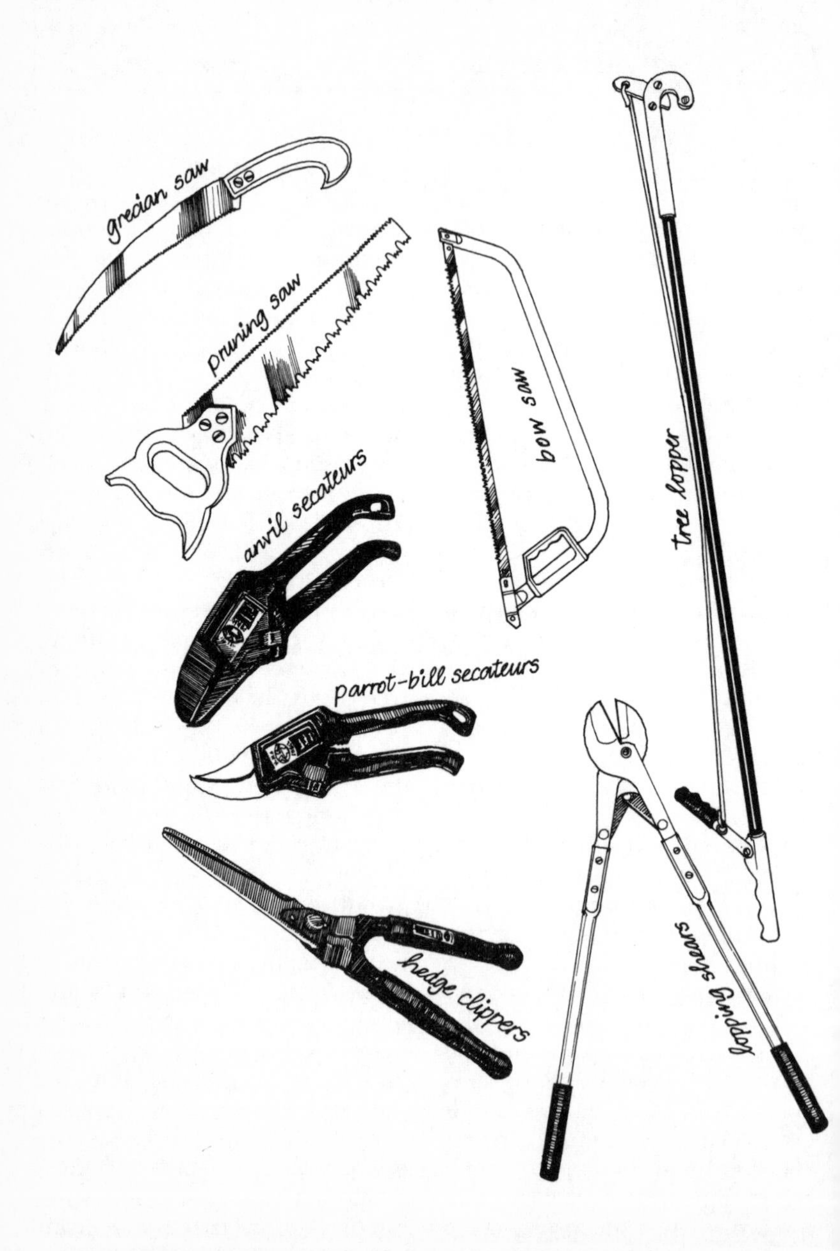

All secateur and saw cuts should be clean. Any jagged edges will increase the area through which disease organisms can enter. Cuts should be made just above a bud and sloping down and away from it at an angle of 45 degrees. Branches are sawn off with a pruning saw flush with the trunk. An initial cut is made about a third of the way through underneath the branch before sawing through from the top. This will ensure that the weight of the branch will not cause it to fall and tear a large quantity of bark from the trunk as would happen if the branch were cut through entirely from the top. Small cuts will heal themselves but large areas can become infected before they form protective callouses. Overcome the problem by painting with special pruning sealant.

Conduct the pruning during mild spells in February or March. The extent of cut-back will depend upon the vigour of the growth.

Roses

When pruning hybrid tea roses, first remove any weak growths or branches growing inwards towards the centre, cutting them out at their origins. Aim to leave no more than three or four strong leaders, which should be pruned back to an outward-facing bud about 15 cm (6 in) above the ground during the first year and to 23–30 cm (9–12 in) subsequent years.

A standard rose is just an HTR on a pole, so perform a similar

PRUNING CUTS

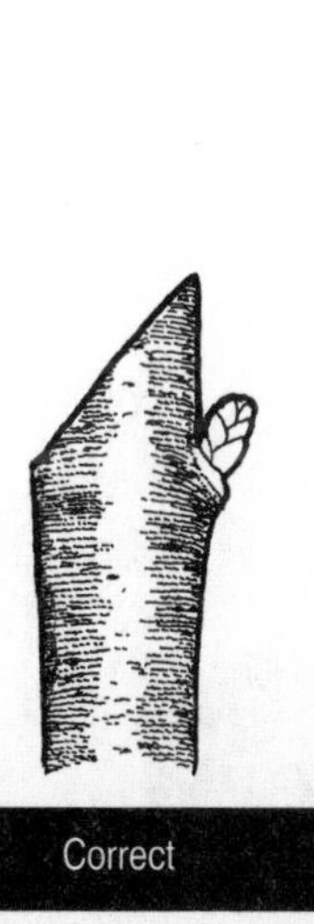

Correct

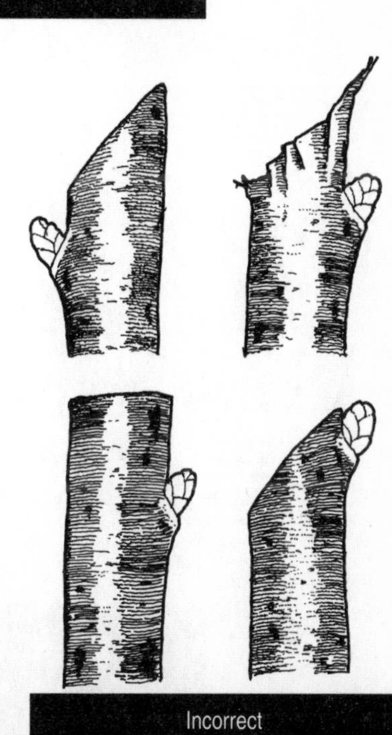

Incorrect

PRUNING ROSES

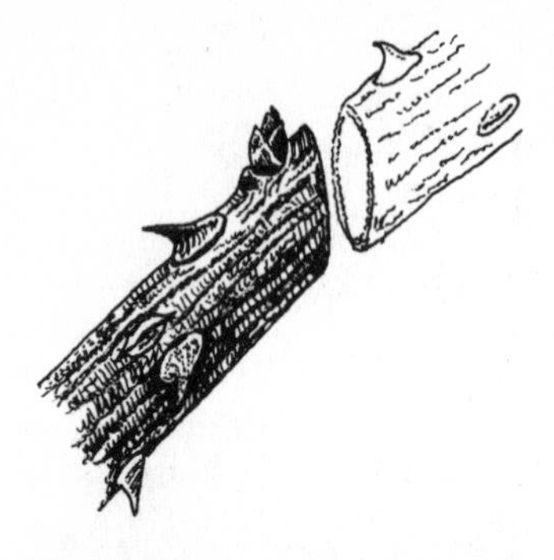

Always prune roses back near an outward facing bud

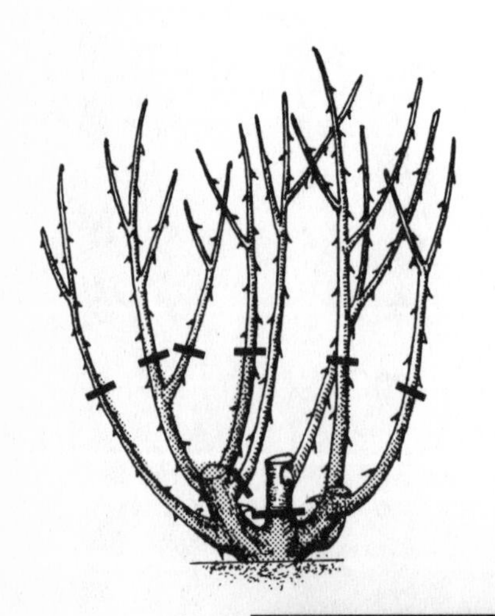

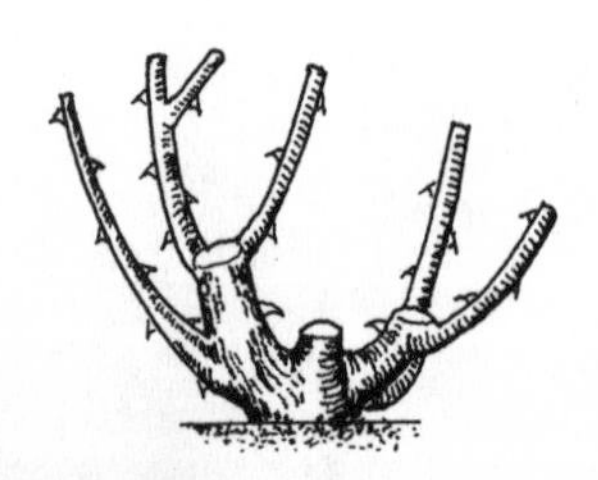

Established hybrid tea roses: remove weak growths and crossing stems at their origins; cut back shoots to about one third of the original height

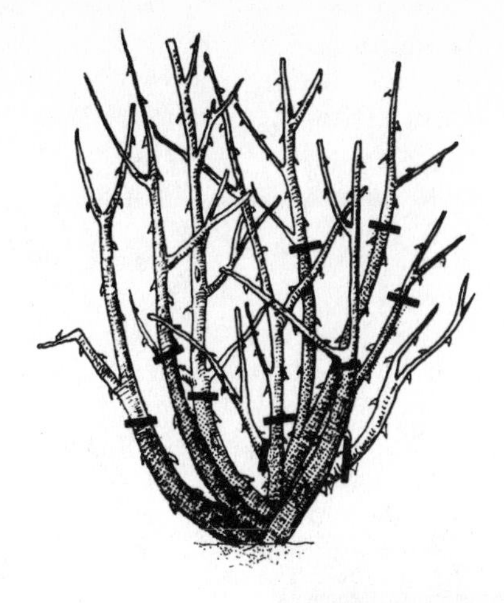

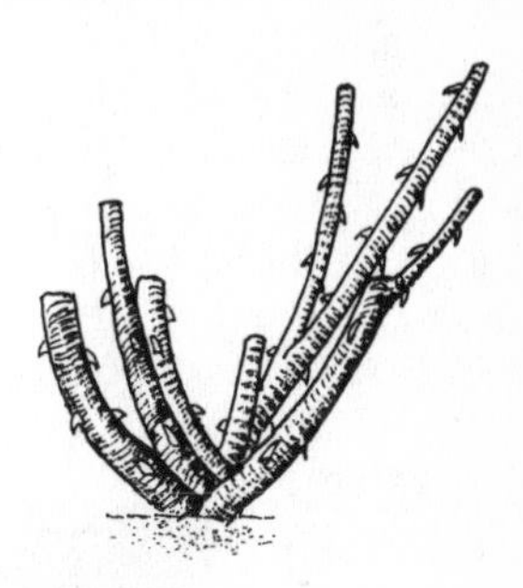

Established floribundas: remove weak and crossing stems; shorten the strongest stems to five or seven buds.

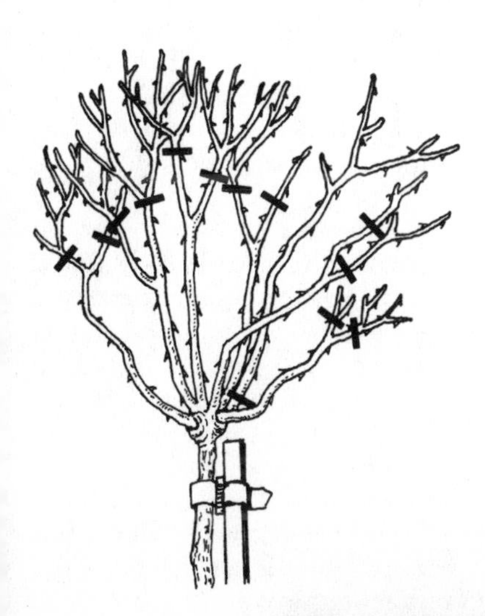

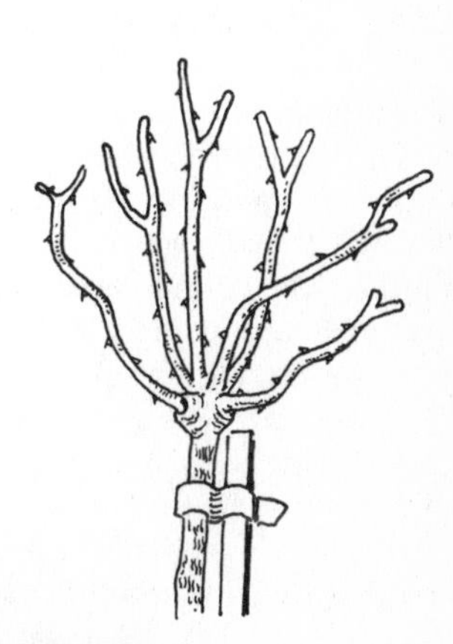

Standards: prune as for hybrid tea roses, but only back to about seven buds from the graft union

operation to the bush though less severely. Remember the graft is just below the canopy and this should be the position from which the imaginary measurements are taken.

Floribundas are generally more vigorous than HTRs and the pruning should be less severe, to 23 cm (9 in) in the winter that they are planted. In the following years cut out all weak and inward-growing growths at their origins. Leading growths should be reduced by about a half. Selection of the correct bud to cut to – one that is large and outward-growing – is more important than the length of the branch remaining.

Climbers should only be very lightly pruned by tipping new growths back to a bud and removing any weak growths. Try to picture climbers as floribundas or HTRs emerging from the thick, strong growing laterals, which are similar to the trunks of standards, and prune accordingly. Tie in those pieces needing support.

To control ramblers, cut them back to ground level when flowering is over. Miniatures should be pruned back to an outward-facing bud on the main growths in a manner similar to floribundas. Old Roses do not grow so vigorously and pruning should consist of removing weak growth and any branches that are growing towards the centre.

Deciduous trees

Trees can take several years to reach their true potential and as well as achieving a pleasing form in the mature tree you should be trying to create a thing of beauty throughout its development. During the early growth stages it is important that you maintain the size of the head in keeping with its height. Mentally divide the tree into thirds. Prune the lowest third of the tree back to the trunk completely – this fraction of the tree should be devoid of branches throughout its life. The next third will be an area of dense growth and should be pruned back to three or four buds to stimulate growth. Leave the uppermost third unpruned. As the tree approaches its natural or desired height, allow the branches to develop without interference apart from keeping the bottom third bare. When the tree has reached the height you want, cut the growing tip out. Deciduous trees are usually pruned between leaf fall and spring. The main exception is the genus *Prunus,* which should only be pruned during April when there is much less tendency for the tree to bleed.

Fruit trees

In addition to shaping them, fruit trees are pruned to increase the yield. Instructions on pruning specific fruit trees and bushes are described in Chapter 19.

Conifers and other evergreen trees

Many evergreens have low sweeping branches and from the moment they are planted these should be retained. Several fully grown evergreens have branches which actually touch the soil. The ever popular Lawson's cypress (*Chamaecyparis lawsoniana*) and related varieties are prone to branching of their leaders. As soon as this is noticed the weaker or more mis-shapen branch must be cut out where it divides. Where chamaecyparis and similar types are to be trained as a hedge they should be fully pruned at all stages to encourage branching. If at any stage they are pruned back to the trunk, they will remain brown because, unlike many trees and shrubs, they are incapable of regeneration. Evergreens should be pruned during the early spring.

Shrubs

There are two classes –

1 *Shrubs that produce flowers from buds that developed the previous season.* Some shrubs, such as camellias, begin to form buds on wood that starts growing as soon as the current season's flowers have died. The dead flowers should be removed and any light pruning that is necessary should be carried out immediately. Often these bushes require very little pruning and if in doubt they should be left undisturbed.

2 *Shrubs that flower on the current season's wood.* Some shrubs, such as buddleias, produce their blooms from buds that form during the same season that they flower. Left untrimmed these plants will become straggly with a reduction in both size and number of their flowers. Depending upon the size of the bush, you may reduce it by a third during the period November to March, though this is not a hard and fast rule. Dogwood and most other species grown for the colour of their bark in midwinter must be cut back to ground level during the spring. The colours are more pronounced in new wood and the almost whiplike character of the new stems is part of the charm of this group.

Evergreen shrubs and dwarf conifers

Both of these require the minimum amount of pruning. Inspect them annually during March and remove any diseased or damaged branches. Occasionally foliage shrubs develop yellow branches. These spoil the appearance and should be cut out at the origin. Far more of a problem is that associated with the many yellow or golden forms of evergreen shrubs. These plants result from mutations that genetically deprive the plant of the full capacity for making the colouring matter chlorophyll, which produces the plant's food. Frequently whole branches revert to the more stable green form – these will be much stronger growing and will ultimately take over the whole plant. As soon as one is seen it should be cut out at the origin.

Root pruning

When a tree is growing too strongly, and consequently producing few flowers or fruits, it is possible to reduce its vigour by root pruning. During wintertime, dig a trench two thirds of the distance from the trunk of the tree to the area where the bottom branches reach. When the root has been exposed with a spade or an axe sever every other root. (This

REMOVING A LARGE BRANCH

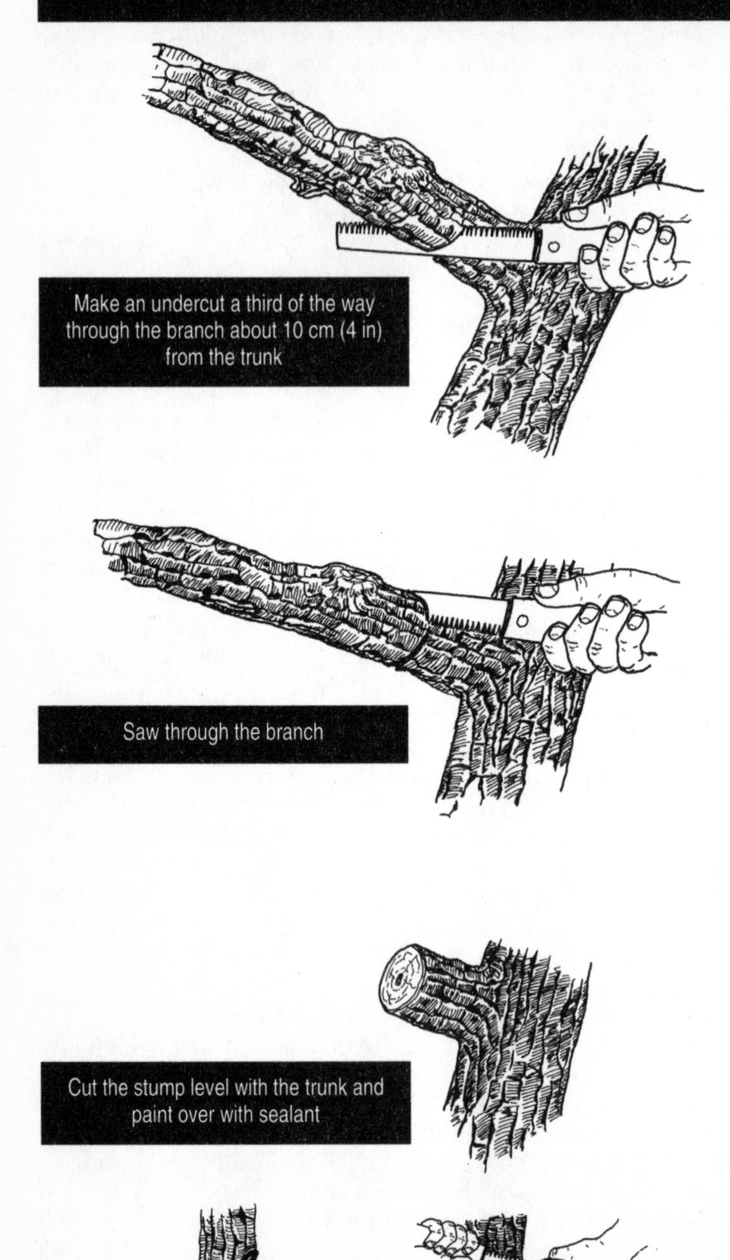

Make an undercut a third of the way through the branch about 10 cm (4 in) from the trunk

Saw through the branch

Cut the stump level with the trunk and paint over with sealant

decrease in rooting capacity will reduce the amount of nutrients that reach the top growth thereby reducing its vigour.)

Regenerating established trees

You may inherit an established tree which, as it gets older and reaches its maximum size, will tend to lose vigour or even become diseased. Or it may simply become too large for the site. No one likes removing trees, especially when it is possible to save them. In fact much can often be done to regenerate them.

Dead wood, perhaps the result of infection, and all other dead and decaying material should be cut back flush with a main growth and painted over with wound sealant. Cutting into live wood will stimulate growth, as in the case of coppicing and pollarding, neither of which are usually applicable to ornamental trees. Severing large limbs may be too drastic an action and can result in the destruction of the tree. Plan to remove the oversize branch over a number of years.

Old trees tend to develop holes in the trunk, which, untreated, become reservoirs for water and cause the tree to rot. If the holes are filled with inert material the tree will heal itself and may continue to grow for many years to come. First protect the tree from further damage by paring the edges of the trunk with a knife until you come to live material. Make sure that the whole of the surface around the opening of the hole is cut back to live material. Then prepare a very stiff concrete mix of two parts cement to five parts sand. Use an absolute minimum of water – the wetter the mixture the greater will be the contraction when it dries. Fill the hole level to where the bark meets the cambium layer. Do not cover the live tissue, which will form callouses that will more than cover the tiny area left by the contraction of the cement and form a watertight joint.

Removal of trees

By law you may not be allowed to remove certain trees from your own land. If the trees in your garden are the subject of a Tree Preservation Order you will need the permission of the local planning authority. Neither do their powers end there. You need the council's permission to crown thin (reduce the number of branches in the canopy), crown lift (remove the lower branches) or do any other work on the tree. And this is a law that you ignore at your peril, for felling a tree subject to a TPO without permission in England and Wales can incur an unlimited fine.

It is a wise precaution to check at an early stage whether your land is subject to a TPO. Once you have obtained the information that your land is free of restriction you may cease worrying as land may not be subjected to an order without the owner being notified. Fruit trees are not generally covered by TPOs but this only applies to those normally grown for their edible crops.

Where a very large tree needs to be removed, it is not a job for the amateur – it is dangerous and requires skill. However, old apple trees and others of similar size may be removed by a strong, fit person. To fell trees you will probably need to use a chain saw, which can be hired by the day. Should you decide to employ such a tool, make sure that you are fully conversant with its use as it is potentially very dangerous. Where it is only necessary to fell one tree or you have plenty of time, you can use a cross-cut saw.

Reduce the size of the tree by sawing the large branches from the canopy. Then saw through the trunk 1.5 m (5 ft) above ground level. The roots of a tree extend a very long distance and near the trunk they are so thick you will find it virtually impossible to cut through them. You may need to start digging the root out a distance of a metre or even more from the trunk. But do not dig further away than is needed, to avoid having to lift an unnecessarily large root ball.

As you dig, the spade will strike roots, and these must be cut through with an axe. When you have dug all around the trunk, move it by rocking backwards and forwards. Should you find that the root will not move, widen the trench and start excavating under the root, chopping additional roots as you find them. From time to time rock the trunk until you experience a definite movement – a sure sign that you are almost through the root system. Constraints on the trunk movements will indicate where the roots are attached and these may be cut accordingly.

As an alternative to removing a tree, consider using as a support for a climber such as clematis. If a stump is cut close to the ground, bore holes in it and plant with aubreta or trailing lobelia.

6 Bulbs and Corms

It is easy to be confused about the differences between bulbs and corms. Bulbs are underground buds consisting of an embryonic flower, surrounded by modified leaves. Contained within the bulb is the food store that will support the plant until its leaf system together with the roots can do it for themselves. Corms are somewhat different. They are basically swollen stem bases containing food stores, with one or more buds attached. Since both bulbs and corms are organs of vegetative reproduction containing food stores, it is convenient to consider the two together. (In popular usage, the word 'bulb' has come to include corms and in some instances even certain types of tuber.)

As bedding plants, bulbs may be left for several years in the same place where they will form

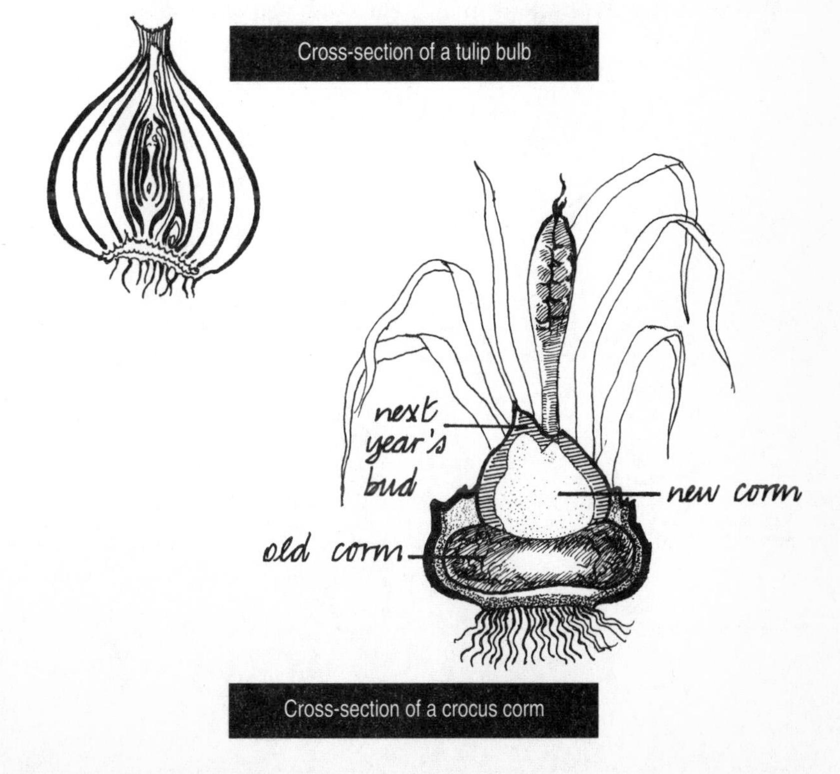

Cross-section of a tulip bulb

Cross-section of a crocus corm

large clumps (certain alliums for example). Or they may be removed after they have flowered (for instance, daffodils and narcissi), to be replanted again the following autumn.

Another way of using bulbs is to naturalise them, by planting them in a grassy area and leaving them undisturbed. It is only possible to naturalise bulbs in areas where the grass need not be cut until a least six weeks after the flowers have died. With many varieties of daffodil this may not be until mid-June, by which time the grass will be very high. Grass seldom grows well under trees, so make use of the fact by naturalising daffodils beneath deciduous trees where they can be left throughout the whole of their growing season.

More exposed positions may be planted with snowdrops and crocuses, especially the early flowering species. These can be naturalised in any area where cutting of the grass can be delayed until mid-spring, but even these are not for top quality lawns, which will need cutting throughout the winter when conditions permit, and weekly from mid-March onwards.

Bulbs can be purchased either by mail order or in a variety of shops, packeted or loose. The danger of buying bulbs loose is that they are often disturbed and you may not always get the variety you thought you had purchased. This is not a problem with packeted bulbs – they are protected and usually come complete with detailed growing instructions. The one big disadvantage of purchasing bulbs

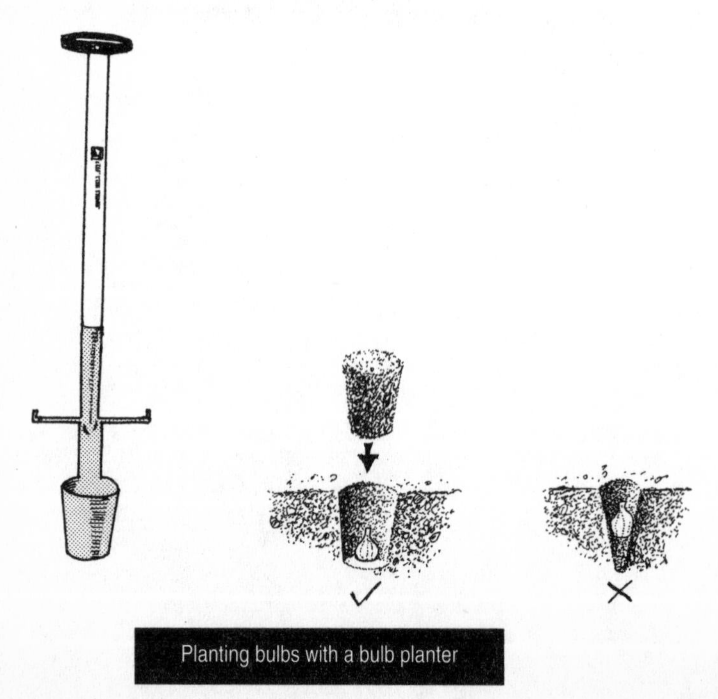

Planting bulbs with a bulb planter

this way is that the bag tends to warm up and the bulbs may start shooting if they are kept in it for too long a period.

Reject any bulbs, corms or tubers that have started into growth. Lack of light will have caused them to grow long and thin. Not only will they be very brittle but they will have depleted the reserves of food simply to produce a shoot that is never likely to yield more than a low quality bloom.

The majority of bulbs that we grow in the garden are spring-flowering, but for virtually every month of the year you will find some species that bloom then. Spring-flowering bulbs should be purchased and planted immediately they are available, which is usually from mid-August onwards. It is not natural for them to be out of the ground and for a limited number of species this is harmful – they should always be planted 'in the green' (see pp. 85 and 115).

Remember that while there is no activity above ground until the turn of the year, almost as soon as a bulb is planted it will start producing roots. For a good display, it is necessary to have a fully developed root system before the shoot begins to emerge.

Towards the end of the planting season, usually in November, bulbs are often sold off much cheaper than earlier in the season. Providing that they are firm, with a minimum of shoot development, and no sign of damage or disease, such bulbs can be good economical buys for naturalising or planting in pots. They may also be grown in beds but do not always give the best results in the first year.

Planting

To plant a bulb, first remove a core of soil with a bulb planter (or a trowel if you do not have one). If no detailed instructions on planting depth are provided, make the depth two and a half times the height of the bulb. When using a trowel, make sure the hole has a flat bottom and not a pointed base. Where a hole becomes narrower as it gets deeper the bulb will lodge some distance down the hole, leaving a hollow beneath it. This will act as a natural reservoir and the trapped water will rot the bulb.

Before planting bulbs for naturalising, allow them to gently fall to the ground from a height of a few inches, taking care not to damage them in the process, and plant each where it falls. This leads to a totally informal effect.

Because bulbs and corms contain the majority of the food necessary to produce a flower they will do well in virtually any position during their first season. Providing that the soil is not waterlogged they will grow in sunlight or in shade, on heavy or light ground and in acid or chalky soils.

Bulb renewal

You may if you wish consider bulbs expendable, grow them for one season and then discard them. This is unnecessary, expensive and wasteful. With care, you can build up a stock of bulbs for the following year. As they are self-propagating, you will find that in a few years single specimens will have become large clumps.

After flowering a bulb completely renews itself and begins producing offshoots or bulblets that will mature and flower the next year or even several years later. A corm, instead of renewing itself, actually shrivels completely spent, but at the same time a new corm is formed above it to ensure continuance of the plant. It also produces a number of cormlets around its base. Sufficient nutrients in the soil are necessary for bulb or corm renewal and offshoot development. The leaves also play an active part, producing nourishing material that the sap carries down to the bulbous part. If bulbs are moved without being allowed to complete their growing cycle, or a clump becomes so large that several bulbs are fighting for the available nutrients, the bulbs will not be able to renew themselves adequately, let alone be generating offspring. The bulbs simply regenerate a main bulb that does not contain an embryonic flower sufficiently well developed to bloom next year. When this happens the bulbs are said to have gone *blind.*

For a continuance of healthy bulbs that will produce good sized flowers, first ensure that the soil is in tip-top condition when they are planted. Work into the ground either well rotted manure or compost. Since bulb renewal does not accelerate until about the time of flowering, scatter some blood

A group of early spring bulbs: snowdrop *(Galanthus nivalis)*, *Crocus chrysanthus*, *Iris reticulata* and *Scilla siberica*

fish and bone or Growmore around the shoots or feed the plants with a high potash liquid fertiliser while the leaves are growing. In the case of daffodils this would be about mid-March.

Once a daffodil flower is dead it must be removed together with the swelling – the ovary – at its base. If left, the ovary will develop seeds. Seeds of hybrids, if they grow at all, will not be true to form and will take several years to generate flowering-sized bulbs. Anyway, seed production diverts large amounts of energy away from new bulb creation. However, when naturalising snowdrops (*Galanthus nivalis*), allow the drooping seed heads to remain because snowdrops spread rapidly by self-seeding as well as by bulb division.

Where snowdrop bulbs are allowed to develop into a large group, every four or five years it will be necessary to divide the group so that they do not starve each other out. When the flowers have faded lift them with a fork. Pull the clump apart with your hands and immediately replant them.

Unfortunately, when blooming is over the leaves of many bulbs, in particular daffodils and narcissi, tend to be very untidy, flopping all over the beds, at the critical time of the year the ground is needed for replanting with summer bedding. So you may be tempted to remove the plants before they have had the opportunity to die back. Research has shown that bulbs need a period of at least six weeks after flowering before the greenery may be removed, otherwise they

Daffodils naturalised beneath a tree

will go blind. It is better to allow them to remain for a longer period than the minimum.

Often the leaves of daffodils are cut back to about 15 cm (6 in) above ground and then tied together. Another practice is that of bending the leaves over and tying them back. Both procedures, while making the plants look quite tidy, drastically reduce their food-generating capacity.

Where bulbs that have not died down are in a prominent location and must be moved to be replaced with summer bedding, allow them to remain in their flowering position as long as possible. Remove them only immediately prior to replanting the site. When digging out the bulbs, take great care to cause the minimum amount of root disturbance. Handle the foliage carefully so that it does not become damaged. Transfer the bulbs to a ditch lined with a piece of netting or similar material. Fill it with soil leaving a small piece of the netting protruding. Allow the bulbs to complete their growing cycle. When all of the leaves have died back the bulbs may be harvested by loosening the soil and pulling out the netting, which should ensure that none of them remains in the ground.

Some popular bulbous plants

Alliums

These are ornamental members of the onion and garlic family, most of which are characterised by a globular head of many minute flowers grouped together. The smaller members may be grown in groups but the larger species, which can attain a height of about 90 cm (3 ft), are very impressive grown singly in a mixed or herbaceous bed. They occur in bright yellow as well as every shade of red from a pinkish lilac through to carmine. As with all members of the family, if they are damaged they emit a pungent odour.

Most of the genus flower during June and are among the last of the autumn planted bulbs to come into blossom. Once planted alliums are best left undisturbed. The natural species rather than cultivars are grown, and while an increasing number are becoming available in garden centres a wider range can be obtained from specialist bulb suppliers. The easiest and most popular species for the garden include:

A. caeruleum. Deep blue, growing to about 60 cm (2 ft). The globes are rather small for the size of the stem, so grow them together in groups for the best effect.

A. giganteum. Deep rose-red and the largest of all the alliums. The globes may be as much as 10 cm (4 in) in diameter. These are expensive bulbs, best grown singularly.

A. moly. Bright yellow, and one of the most popular of all alliums. Height 20–25 cm (8–10 in). Best grown in a group.

A. oreophilum (formerly known as *A. ostrowskianum*). Light red in colour, the flower has a somewhat open structure, appearing flatter and less globular in shape than the above species. Height 12–20 cm (5–8 in). Grow these in groups for the best effect.

A. siculum. Individual flowers have red centres with white edges. This is a tall growing species up to 120 cm (4 ft) with an almost flat head of individual flowers.

Bluebells

These familiar woodland plants are only suitable for naturalising in large areas under deciduous trees and shrubs. Placed in borders they will spread very rapidly and colonise the whole area in a short period of time. Once established they are extremely difficult to remove. Like snowdrops they are thin-skinned bulbs and are best planted in the green.

Varieties with white and pink bells are available as well as the usual blue form.

Colchicums

These are often incorrectly called 'autumn crocuses', as the flowers look very similar to the autumn and the more familiar spring-flowering crocuses, but they are not members of the same genus, or even family. The confusion arises because both colchicums and crocuses produce their flowers direct from the corm.

Most colchicums bloom during September and October. They occur in white, pink or lilac shades except for the spring-flowering *C. luteum,* which is yellow. The corms may be naturalised beneath trees, which is satisfactory as their leaves, which of course require the sunlight, do not appear until spring. An alpine setting suits them too. The leaves are broad and can be obtrusive, so bear this in mind when selecting a planting site.

Crocuses

Winter-flowering crocuses are grouped into two classes: the species, which are the first to bloom, with the flowers in many instances appearing before the leaves; and the slightly later, large-flowered varieties. The treatment is the same for both groups. They look good planted in alpine gardens, where their bright colours show well against the rocks. Crocuses may also be naturalised under deciduous trees, or planted in lawns that do not have to be cut at the beginning of the season.

Recommended species are *C. chrysanthus, C. sieberi* and *C. tommasinianus.* Try also *C. laevigatus,* the earliest of the winter-flowering species, blooming from mid-December onwards. It has the typical long, thin petals of the genus in a pale shade of lavender, which are followed by the leaves. This bulb is a must for planting under trees, as it is one of the few flowers that will be out during the shortest days of the year.

An autumn-flowering species is also to be recommended, *C. speciosus.* The flowers are lilac-blue and look very effective naturalised in grass.

The larger flowering varieties as well as being ideal for planting out of doors in all locations may be grown in bowls and forced for flowering early in the New Year.

Daffodils and narcissi

No spring garden is complete without a selection of daffodils and narcissi (they are all members of the same genus). The name daffodil is applied only to one group of narcissi, those in which the trumpet is at least as long as the surrounding petals (perianth) and there is only one flower to the stem. Because there are so many different varieties of narcissi they are split into 11 different classes or divisions. Most of these have cups either over a third but less than equal to the length of the perianth or less than a third its length. Some narcissi have one flower per stem, others may carry several.

There are varieties of daffodil and narcissus where the petals are swept back (reflexed), and there are others that are fully double. Some flowers are of only one colour, the selfs, while others, the bi-colours, have two shades. The colours are usually yellow, orange or white, but some modern hybrids have trumpets in pinkish shades as well. The range is too large to describe individual members and the best advice is to consult a specialist supplier's catalogue or the illustrations at your local garden centre before deciding which varieties to purchase.

Miniature daffodils and narcissi are to be found in a range of shapes and colours as well, and are treated in the same way as their larger counterparts. Generally, though, they are only suitable for growing in alpine gardens or among heather, the standard varieties being more suitable for general bedding purposes.

Narcissus 'Ice Follies'

Narcissi are excellent subject for forcing and specially heat treated bulbs may be purchased for the purpose.

Fritillaries

The members of the genus *Fritillaria* differ quite considerably from each other. The one feature that they have in common is their bell-shaped flowers.

F. meleagris (also known as the snake's head fritillary) is a native of the British Isles. The species has purple chequered markings on a white background. Several hybrid forms exist too, including white ones. They can be grown in borders or in pots, but they are best allowed to naturalise where they can seed freely.
F. imperialis (crown imperial). A tall, stately species in which the bells form a crown encircling the top of a 60 cm (2 ft) stem surmounted by a tuft of leaflike sepals. The round bulb has a hole in it, so it must be planted with the opening to the bulb in the vertical plane to avoid trapping water. Named varieties are available in shades of red, orange and yellow.
F. persica (Persian fritillary). This stately plant some 90 cm (3 ft) in height is definitely one for the back of the borders. The flowers are of a blackish-purple shade making them one of the darkest of all blooms. Though not easily obtainable these April–May flowering bulbs are among the easiest to grow.
F. michailovskyi. This species, which grows to about 15 cm (6 in), has from one to three blooms per stem. The bells, relatively large for their height, are deep purple with a light yellow edge.

Fritillaries should be protected by slug pellets, and the tall growing imperials and Persians benefit from a dressing of sulphate of potash as soon as the shoots emerge.

Hyacinths

Hyacinths possess one of the finest of all spring scents and their perfume is a delight wherever they are grown *en masse.* Failure with these can occur because of confusion between ordinary garden hyacinths and prepared bulbs for forcing.

Prepared bulbs are subjected to storage at a low temperature in order to create an artificial winter which when followed by a moderate rise in temperature will induce the bulbs to shoot early. These should never be grown in the garden. Nor is it advisable to plant out bulbs that had been grown in pots the previous year – what to them was maltreatment – until they have had an opportunity to build up their strength again in a nursery bed.

Once forced, hyacinths are probably best discarded. Saving them, unless you are very patient, is a false economy. For planting in the garden, buy hyacinth bulbs sold specially for the purpose. They are usually cheaper than bulbs for forcing. Once planted the bulbs may be left undisturbed for several years but they should be given a sprinkling of sulphate of potash each spring and autumn. During the spring, both before and after they have flowered, they should be protected by slug pellets.

Hyacinth varieties

Variety	Colour	Flowering period	
		Forced	Garden
Ann Mary	Rose pink	End Dec	Early
Blue Jacket	Bluebell blue	End Jan	Mid-season
Blue Magic	Purple		Mid-season
Carnegie	White	End Feb	Mid-season
China Pink	Pink		Early
City of Harlem	Primrose	Mid-Feb	Late
Delft Blue	Blue	Mid-Jan	Mid-season
Distinction	Burgundy	Mid-Jan	Mid-season
Gipsy Queen	Apricot	Feb	Mid-season
Jan Bos	Red	Mid-Jan	Early
Lady Derby	Shell pink	End Jan	Mid-season
L'Innocence	White	End Jan	Early
Ostera	Navy blue	Mid-Jan	Early
Pink Pearl	Pink	Mid-Jan	Mid-season

The exact time of flowering will depend upon location, microclimate and the time of planting

There are several named varieties of hyacinth yet there is rather less difference in the shape and size of the blooms than with the varieties of most other bulbs. Multistemmed forms do exist and there are slight differences in overall shape and closeness of packing of the individual flowers on the stem, but the main variation is the colour and the time of flowering.

Irises

The irises are a very large family of flowers. Some grow from bulbs, others from thick rhizomous roots. Here we are only considering those that form bulbs. One of the main bulb types is the English, which has large, elegant flowers of almost paperlike texture carried on a tall stem. Dutch irises are of a similar height with a slightly smaller flower. Spanish irises are similar but tend to flower later.

All the above varieties can be grown in borders and make ideal cut flowers. After flowering, the seed heads should be removed and the soil fed with an all-purpose fertiliser. Give a light sprinkling of sulphate of potash during October.

When the bulbs become crowded lift them as soon as the foliage has died back and replant singly.

Dwarf irises grow to little more than 10 cm (4 in), yet they possess an almost full-sized iris head. They may be grown individually in an alpine setting or in groups as part of a bedding scheme, but they are not suitable for naturalising. Dwarf irises are particularly effective when placed in between winter-flowering pansies.

The colours of *Iris reticulata* vary from deep blue through to light blue, while *I. dandfordiae* is a bright yellow.

Lilies
See p. 119.

Muscari (grape hyacinth species and varieties)
Grape hyacinths will grow in virtually any type of soil, but prefer full sun. They produce dense spikes of small tubular flowers. Except for a white form the commonly grown types are in various shades of blue. Once planted, they should be left undisturbed.

Nerine
See p. 121.

Scilla
A tiny plant with open almost star-shaped flowers. Scillas thrive in all soils and should be grown in an open, well drained position. They exist in various shades of blue and look good with miniature daffodils.

Snowdrop (Galanthus species and varieties)
Few flowers are more welcome in the garden than the snowdrop, which is one of the first to bloom (January and February). Individual bulbs or small groups may be grown in rock gardens, but they are at their best when naturalised. Under trees, in open position, on moist banks, under hedges – all are equally suitable locations for this cheerful flower that defies the worst of the winter weather.

Snowdrop bulbs are very thin skinned and they do not like being out of the ground for prolonged periods. It is far better to plant them while they are still 'in the green' than to put in bulbs in the autumn.

Planting 'in the green' is the transplanting of bulbs together with their foliage immediately after they have flowered. Providing snowdrops are planted to the same depth that they were growing previously and they are not allowed to remain out of the ground for too long, they will not suffer any setback and virtually all the bulbs will flower the following spring. When planting in the green do not divide the group into individual bulbs, but plant small groups of about half a dozen. The same technique should be used when dividing patches, which can be performed every four to five years. But periodic division is not essential – one of the charms of snowdrops is their sheer mass at a time when there is little else producing colour.

It is possible to obtain little clumps of snowdrops from florists – once the blooms are over they are particularly cheap. Your choice will almost invariably be restricted to the common snowdrop *Galanthus nivalis.* To obtain other forms consult one of the gardening periodicals during February, when specialist suppliers will be advertising.

Other varieties include:

G. nivalis 'Flore Pleno'. A double form of the common snowdrop.
G. nivalis 'Sam Arnott'. An extra large, sweetly scented single.
G. nivalis 'Viridapicis'. Both the inner and outer petals have a green tip.
G. elwesii. A different species with emerald green inner segments.

Snowflake, Leucojum aestivum

A plant that everyone knows but few can name. It consists of a stem about 45 cm (1½ ft) tall carrying several snowdrop-like flowers that are white with green tips. Flowering during April to May, these bulbs thrive in cool, damp locations. *L. aestivum* 'Gravetye Giant' is an improved version of the wild species.

Tulips

There are probably more cultivars of tulip on sale than any other type of spring bulb. Like narcissi, they are classified into divisions (15 in all). It is important that you choose the correct type for the specific purpose you have in mind. Tulips can be roughly classified according to their flowering season. Earlies bloom during March and April, mid-season varieties during April and May, and lates from May onwards. There are both single and double forms in bloom throughout the flowering period.

Tulips are particularly suitable for growing in containers out of doors. Drainage is always very important with any vessel used for growing plants, and particularly critical when cultivating winter bulbs in this way. Do not be tempted to prolong the flowering season by planting bulbs that flower over an extended period as at no time will the container be seen at its best.

A better approach is to use more than one container and only move each into the display area when it is in its prime.

Tall, late-season varieties are

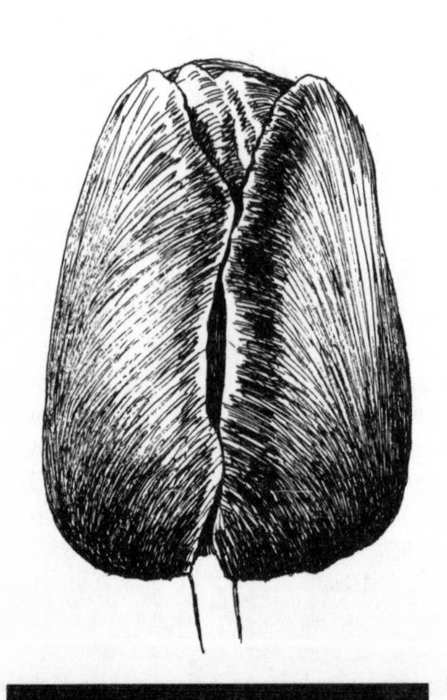

Black tulip

TULIP HYBRIDS COME IN MANY FORMS

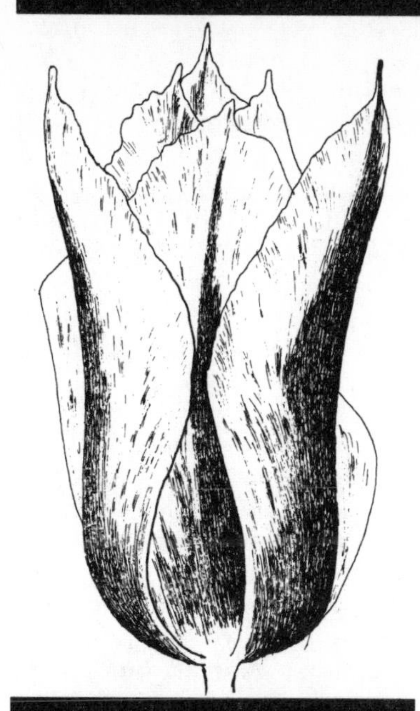

Lily-flowered

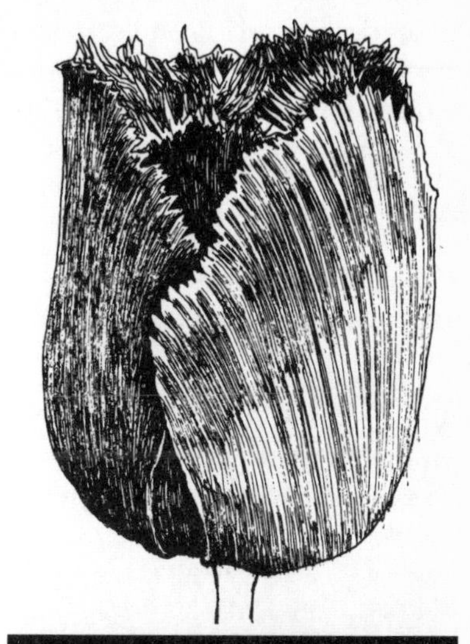

Fringed

Parrot

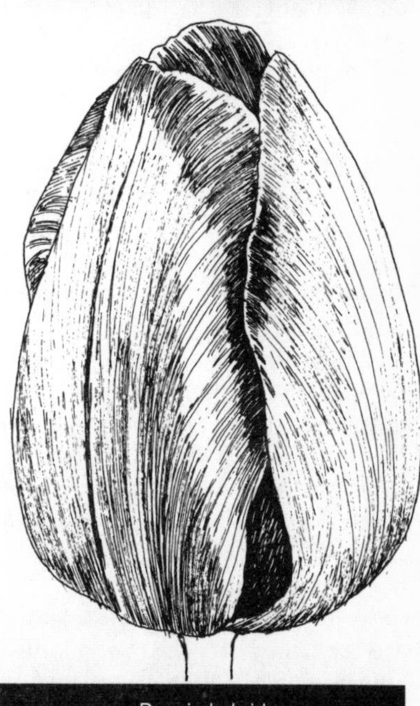

Darwin hybrid

particularly effective grown together with wallflowers. Low-growing types, such as hybrids derived from *T. kaufmanniana*, are best with polyanthus and pansies. Where tulips are grown as solitary flowering subjects in a display, seek out the more spectacular forms. As the name implies, paeony varieties have dense double flowers similar in shape although slightly smaller than the well-known perennials. They are among the most dramatic of spring flowers. Lily-flowered tulips have waisted flowers with pointed petals while parrot tulips have twisted and fringed flowers.

As well as numerous varieties of the flower, they can be obtained in white, yellows, oranges and pinks through to purples and reds that are so deep that they appear almost black, and there are pretty pastel shades. As well as striped varieties there are the verdiform tulips, which have green-backed petals. It is impossible to describe them all. You will find more than enough types in the garden centre to satisfy your needs. Check colour, form and flowering period before purchasing.

Unfortunately tulips are prone to a variety of virus diseases. The petals tend to harbour these infections, so as soon as the flower is over remove them. When the foliage starts to turn yellow lift them. Tulips may be prematurely lifted as described on p. 80. When tulips are removed from the ground you will find that there are a number of small bulbs attached to the larger one. These will not flower for three to four years. Should you wish to use them they may be grown and left undisturbed in a nursery site until such time as they are of size suitable for planting in a flowering location.

Unlike hyacinths, tulip bulbs are not specially prepared for forcing in pots, but earlies can be planted in bowls and brought indoors when they have shoots that are 5 cm (2 in) tall.

Pot culture of bulbs

Bulbs grown in flower pots provide colour in the home at a time when there is little else available. They are easily raised by anyone without extra lighting, heating or specialised equipment. Not all bulbs lend themselves to pot culture. The best are hyacinths, narcissi, crocuses and tulips.

For the earliest hyacinth blooms, buy bulbs specially prepared for forcing. To force bulbs, plant them in bowls with either bulb fibre, potting compost or loam. The exact composition is not that critical as the medium is mainly to provide anchorage rather than nutrition. Keep the bowls in a cool, dark place in the house or bury them up to their rims in a sheltered position out of doors.

Let them remain there until the last week of November, by which time shoots will have already emerged from the bulbs. If they have not developed to this stage, delay the operation until such time as the shoots have emerged clear of the neck of the bulb. Then, if they are outdoors, bring the hyacinths indoors and keep them in one of the cool rooms for at least three weeks. If they are already indoors, bring them into the light in a room at only a slightly higher temperature than that to which they had been acclimatised. When the plants are confronted with only slightly warmer conditions, the rise in temperature will be enough to confuse their biological clock mechanism already reset by the preparation treatment the bulb received before you bought it. Thinking it is spring, the plant will then proceed to flower weeks earlier than it would do if grown naturally.

Even at this stage it is far better to keep the bowls in a hall, kitchen or other area that is not maintained at the highest living temperature. The emergence of the flower, the time that it is in its prime and how soon it dies is reached sooner the higher the temperature. To extend the flowering period, maintain the plant at the lowest possible temperature always remembering that if the plant bulb were growing out of doors it might well be experiencing frosts.

A well grown pot of hyacinths

Bulbs for a succession of flowering over six months of the year

Month	Type of bulb	Colour	Use	Height		Planting distance			
						depth		apart	
				cm	in	cm	in	cm	in
Jan	*Crocus* spp.								
	chrysanthus	Y,P/M,W	N	5	2	5	2	5	2
	tommasinianus	P/M	N	5	2	5	2	5	2
	Snowdrops	W	N	7.5	3	5	2	6	2½
Feb	Crocuses (large)	P,Y,W	N	7.5	3	5	2	5	2
	Snowdrops	(as above)							
	Iris reticulata	P	Be	15	6	5	2	10	4
Mar	Daffodils and narcissi	Y,W,O	Be,C,N	30	12	15	6	15	6
	Fritillaria meleagris	P,W	N	20	8	5	2	10	4
	Early tulips	R,Y,W,P	Be,C			Various			
Apr	Daffodils and narcissi	(as above)							
	Muscaris	B,W	Be,N	12	5	7	3	10	4
	Scillas	B	Be	30	12	10	4	10	4
	Hyacinths	R,W,B,M	Be	22	9	10	4	10	4
	Mid-season tulips	R,W,Y	Be,C	30	12	10	4	15	6
	Crown imperials	Y,OR	Be	60	24	15	6	Use singly	
May	Late tulips	R,W,Y	N	30	12	10	4	15	6
	Bluebells	B, also W,P	N	20	8	10	4	7	3
	Leucojums	W	Be,N	30	12	7	3	10	4
Jun	Anemones	R,B	C	22	9	6	2½	7	3
	Alliums	W,R,B,Y	Be			Various			

(**Colours:** B, Blue; M, Mauve; O, Orange; P, Purple; W, White; Y, Yellow.
Uses: Be, Bedding; C, Cutting; N, Naturalising.)

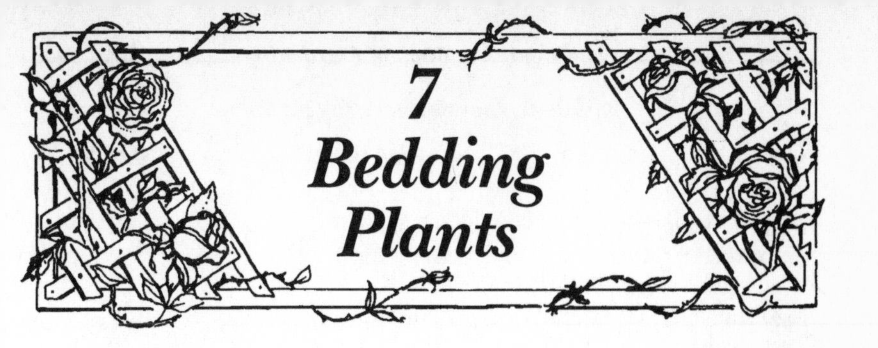

7 Bedding Plants

The summer bedding display is for many the most important feature in the whole garden. In front gardens its presence is like a jewel offsetting the dreariness of the road and the sameness of town or suburban dwellings. It is the item above all others upon which the world will tend to judge your gardening ability. Yet summer bedding is one of the easiest aspects of gardening, both to create and maintain. With a little skill and the necessary facilities you can raise your own plants from seeds, or alternatively you can purchase young plants ready for placing straight into the ground.

Apart from the obvious saving of costs, there are several advantages in raising your own plants. You may be sure of obtaining the variety of your choice, and by using good quality compost you will have vigorous plants growing in ideal conditions. And before planting out you will have properly hardened them off, to ensure that they are sturdy, to give the best results.

Raise your bedding plants by the general principles described on pp. 40–42. For sowing times check the table on page 92.

Every year bedding plants are on sale earlier and earlier. No sooner is Easter over than they start appearing in the shops. This is far too early to plant them out. Many of our bedding plants are only half-hardy. If you buy these and plant them before the last frosts are over, they will be killed and you will have wasted your money. In mild areas, the earliest date considered comparatively safe to plant out half-hardy subjects is the second week of May. In other regions, it may be necessary to wait until June.

Another factor you will need to take into account when planting out summer bedding is how much longer you need to keep the spring-flowering plants in position. It will not be safe to move narcissi until at least mid-May and tulips even later (see p. 80). Subjects such as wallflowers (cheiranthus) that are only allowed to remain in the ground for a single flowering season may be removed as soon as they have bloomed. Universal pansies will flower throughout the winter and, if left undisturbed, right into the summer, so they must be dug up while still flowering.

Bedding plants will produce wave after wave of flowers, but this makes very great demands upon the soil. Ensure that the texture is correct and that there is an adequate supply of

Guide to summer bedding plants

Name	Colour	Sowing time	Closest distance cm	in
Antirrihinum	W,Y,P	Feb–Mar	30	12
Ageratum	B	Mar–Apr	15	6
Aster	B,Pu,W,R,P	Feb–Apr	30	12
Begonia	R,P,O,Y,W	Feb–Mar	25	10
Busy Lizzie (impatiens)	R,P,O,W	Feb–Mar	25	10
Calendula	R,O,Y	Mar–Apr	30	12
Dahlia	W,R,P,Y	Mar	60	24
Lobelia	B,W	Feb–Mar	15	6
Marigold	R,Y,O	Mar–Apr	30	12
Pansy	B,Y,W,M	Jan–Mar	23	9
Pinks (dianthus)	R,W,P	Feb	30	12
Petunia	R,W,B	Feb-Mar	15	6
Salvia	R,W	Feb–Mar	45	18
Stocks	R,W,P,O	Feb–Mar	45	18
Tagetes	Y,O	Mar–Apr	25	10
Viola	B,Pu,W,R,Y	Feb–Mar	20	8
Zinnia	Y,R,O	Mar–Apr	30	12

(**Colours:** B, Blue; P, Pink; Pu, Purple; R, Red; W, White; Y, Yellow.)

nutrients – if you don't, the money and effort already expended will be wasted. Each year, prior to planting, work in well rotted manure and/or mushroom or garden compost and scatter Growmore or blood, fish and bone at the rate of 50 gm/sq m (2 oz/sq yd). This more than any other factor will bring success.

You will have grown or bought your plants in boxes and the number of plants you have will almost certainly not conveniently conform to the theoretical planting distances you may see quoted in books or catalogues, which are at best only a guide. Be prepared to adjust planting distances to make the best use of your seedlings in the space available.

When you remove the seedlings from the box, they will almost certainly come away as a solid group with the roots intertwined. Prise the plants apart, lay them on the surface of the bed and then move them about until you have obtained an even distribution. Dig a hole beside each of the plants. Fill each hole with water before placing the seedling in the hole.

In spite of the vast improvements in colour, form and the ability to produce flowers continually throughout the summer, the plants we grow in our gardens are governed by the same laws of nature as their wild counterparts. What drives them to produce flower after flower is the urge to reproduce.

The flowers are the first stage in this process, their role being to attract pollinating insects.

If you remove the flower as soon as it withers the plant will have no alternative but to strive to produce another flower and so on throughout the summer. Let the flower die and the seed-making mechanism takes over. The whole chemistry of the plant changes from one geared up to producing flowers to one that is concerned with the successful completion of the final stage of the reproductive process. But as soon as you remove the seed head then once again the plant produces flowers. In practical terms this means that for a continual show you must remove the flowering heads as soon as they die, a process known as dead-heading.

In addition to the provision of nutrients that you made prior to planting, the soil will need regular topping up throughout the season. Give a foliar feed every fortnight.

Winter and spring bedding displays

As autumn approaches, the summer bedding gradually becomes more bedraggled. Cold weather or a wet summer will see the beds finished by mid-September – with an Indian summer it may well last a month longer. Even if the plants have not burnt themselves out and come to the end of their natural cycle, the first frosts will destroy most of them.

There is a temptation to allow the bedding to remain in position long after it is past its best, a reluctance to admit that summer is over. Avoid this at all costs. The gardener must always look to the future and seek to get the winter and spring bedding established. With these the fundamental difference is that from now on you will be planting subjects that are frost-hardy. However, the rules governing plant growth still apply. Plants will grow faster the higher the temperature and it is particularly important that they have the opportunity to become established before the cold weather sets in. While the air will be becoming colder, the soil temperature will be changing much more slowly, and during October it will still be warm enough to allow root development to take place and for the plants to become established. The earlier in October that your winter and spring bedding is in position the better will be the display.

Do not add any fertiliser at this time of the year. The excess of nitrogen that general fertilisers provide will result in large amounts of lush growth that will be incapable of withstanding the harsh times ahead. There will still be sufficient potash and phosphates remaining in the soil from the summer feeding to maintain the far slower rates of blooming, which in many cases is restricted to just one crop of flowers. The choice of plants for winter and spring bedding displays is far more limited than for the summer, but nevertheless it is still possible to produce breath-taking layouts that will be the envy of all who see them.

SPRING BEDDING PLANTS

Wallflower

Double daisy

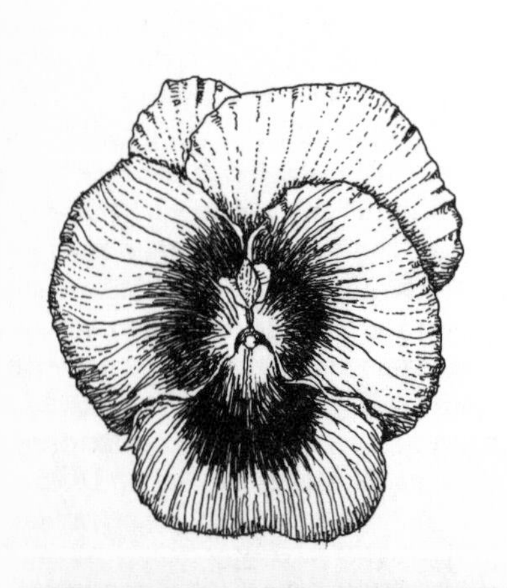

Winter pansy

Polyanthus

Spring bedding plants

Double daisies (Bellis perennis hybrids)

Sometimes called button daisies, these 10 cm (4 in) plants are hardy biennials that come in red, rose or white. Among the better known varieties are 'Dresden China' and 'Rob Roy'. Sow them out of doors during April or May and transfer them to the front of the bedding display during October.

Plant them 20 cm (8 in) apart, perhaps to form an edging to the flower beds. They will bloom freely throughout the spring period.

Forget-me-nots (Myosotis alpestris and varieties)

This old-fashioned cottage garden favourite is effective planted as the sole subject in a bed where it has a charm of its own, forming carpets of blue (the original form) or pink and white (more recent introductions). In addition, it can be grown with wallflowers or bulbs in a formal bedding display, or be used at the front of a herbaceous bedding scheme where the plants may be left to seed themselves.

The seed can be scattered in any well drained sunny location during April. Leave the young plants undisturbed until the autumn and then transplant them to their final bed 15 cm (6 in) apart. Forget-me-nots are one of the first plants of the year to be attacked by powdery mildew, but not until they have finished flowering. Spray with fungicide if necessary.

Pansies (Viola hybrids)

These are short-lived perennials usually grown as annuals or biennials. Winter pansies are the only true bedding plants that will flower continuously from October through to May.

Pansies are easily raised from seed. In July, sow them either outdoors in a damp, shady site or in seed pans in a coldframe or well ventilated greenhouse. Cover pansy seeds well as they require darkness to germinate. When seedlings raised under glass are large enough to handle, transfer each to a 7.5 cm (3 in) pot. Providing the plants are protected by slug pellets they may then be allowed to stand out of doors until required for bedding out. Set them out 23–30 cm (9–12 in) apart in their final positions.

My advice is to buy the more expensive Universal or other F1 type hybrids as these are generally far superior to pansies from cheaper seeds. Also, when purchasing pansy plants, enquire whether they are the F1 type hybrids, for in spite of the very high price they could well be grown from the cheaper, inferior seed that produces plants not capable of the continual production of flowers that is desired.

Polyanthus (Primula hybrids)

Polyanthus is the name for primulas derived from the common primrose (*P. vulgaris*) crossed with the cowslip (*P. veris*) and other species. Their flowers are carried well above the leaves in trusses on stout stems. Modern varieties will flower throughout the winter and occur in shades of red, yellow, white and blue. The more expensive varieties, such as 'Crescendo', give far better results.

Polyanthus have been bred from plants whose natural habitat is damp shady areas and this must be reflected in the method of germinating the seeds. Sow the seeds in a pan of moist compost during May, insert it in a polythene bag and cover the top with paper to exclude the light. When the seeds have germinated the pan may be removed from the plastic container, but the seedlings must be kept moist at all times. Unlike many other plants they will not recover should they dry out. They must also be kept in a shaded part of the greenhouse.

As soon as the seedlings are large enough to handle transfer them to individual 7.5 cm (3 in) pots filled with a peat-based compost. They may be grown on in a cold frame with the glass cover replaced with translucent white plastic to provide the necessary shading, taking care that at no time are they subjected to the direct rays of the sun.

When planting into a bedding display, allow 40 cm (15 in) between individual plants.

Polyanthus are hardy perennials that with care can be used again in future years. The secret of successfully over-summering the mature plants, just like that of the seedlings, depends upon providing them with a damp, shady environment throughout the hottest and driest part of the year. For a nursery bed, seek out a position under a tree, behind a wall or to the side of a shrub where they will be both sheltered from the sun and visually unobtrusive.

Dig out the polyanthus when it is time to replace them with the summer bedding. Carefully pull apart the crowns and plant them in the nursery bed. Do not provide any fertiliser but inspect them regularly, checking that they have sufficient moisture.

Wallflowers (Cheiranthus cheiri)

Every spring garden should contain a bed of wallflowers, grown as much for their seductive perfume as their colourful flowers.

Wallflowers are members of the same family as cabbages and are one of the easiest of all plants to grow. Nevertheless, they still manage to command a very high price during October. Even if you do not normally grow any of your own bedding plants from seed, you really should try this one and save yourself pounds.

The plants should be grown completely out of doors. Sow the seed in drills 15 cm (6 in) apart during May to mid-June. Keep the seedlings watered during prolonged dry spells. When they are 10 cm (4 in) high the plants will require extra space and should be transplanted into nursery beds 10 cm apart in rows 30 cm apart. Once the plants have re-established themselves the centres should be pinched out. This will cause them to become bushy.

Every year millions of wallflowers go on sale, but very few of these are in prime condition. For the best results, wallflowers should be out of the ground for the minimum period of time. Only buy plants showing no sign of wilt. Standing out of water for only short periods will cause the plants to droop, though they will fully recover if placed in a bucket of water for a few hours before planting. Retailers often stand wallflowers in water to make them appear fresh. For a short time this does no harm but if they are left there for several days gradually the bottom leaves turn yellow and then fall off. So avoid buying any plants that have lost several leaves or ones with yellow leaves.

As the plants get older they are sold off cheaper, but this can be a false economy as wallflowers planted out in November seldom do as well as those planted earlier. Set them out 20–30 cm (8–12 in) apart during mid-October.

Wallflowers are perennials whose seeds may be bought as single colours or pastel mixtures. It is usual to discard them immediately after they have flowered as from then on they form straggly plants not worth keeping in a prime position for a whole year for little more than three weeks' flowers. You may find that there are special colours that you wish to keep rather than discard the plants entirely. Wallflowers are easy to grow from cuttings and this can represent a good alternative to seeds. After flowering, take shoots about 7–8 cm (3 in) long, with a heel, from the parent plant and place in a nursery bed about 10 cm apart. As soon as they become established the growing points should be nipped out. Extra bushy plants are obtained by removing the growing centres again during the beginning of August. The plants are then set out in the same way as seedlings during October.

Blooming from May to July, the Siberian wallflower (*Erysimum hieraciifolium*) occurs only in orange shades but when grown *en masse* forms a bright carpet. Slightly shorter than ordinary wallflowers at 40–45 cm (15–18 in), they may be planted closer together with only 30 cm between individual plants.

Spring bulbs

There is a wide range of bulbs that will help provide a colourful garden from late winter to early summer (see pp. 80–90).

ANNUALS FOR SUMMER BEDDING

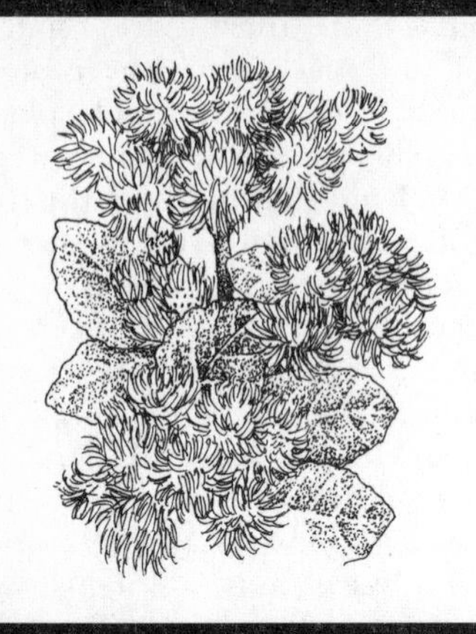

Ageratum

Candytuft

Begonia

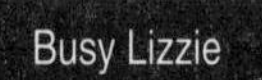

Busy Lizzie

Calendula

Nasturtium

Petunia

Lobelia

French marigold *(Tagetes patula)*

Love-in-a-mist

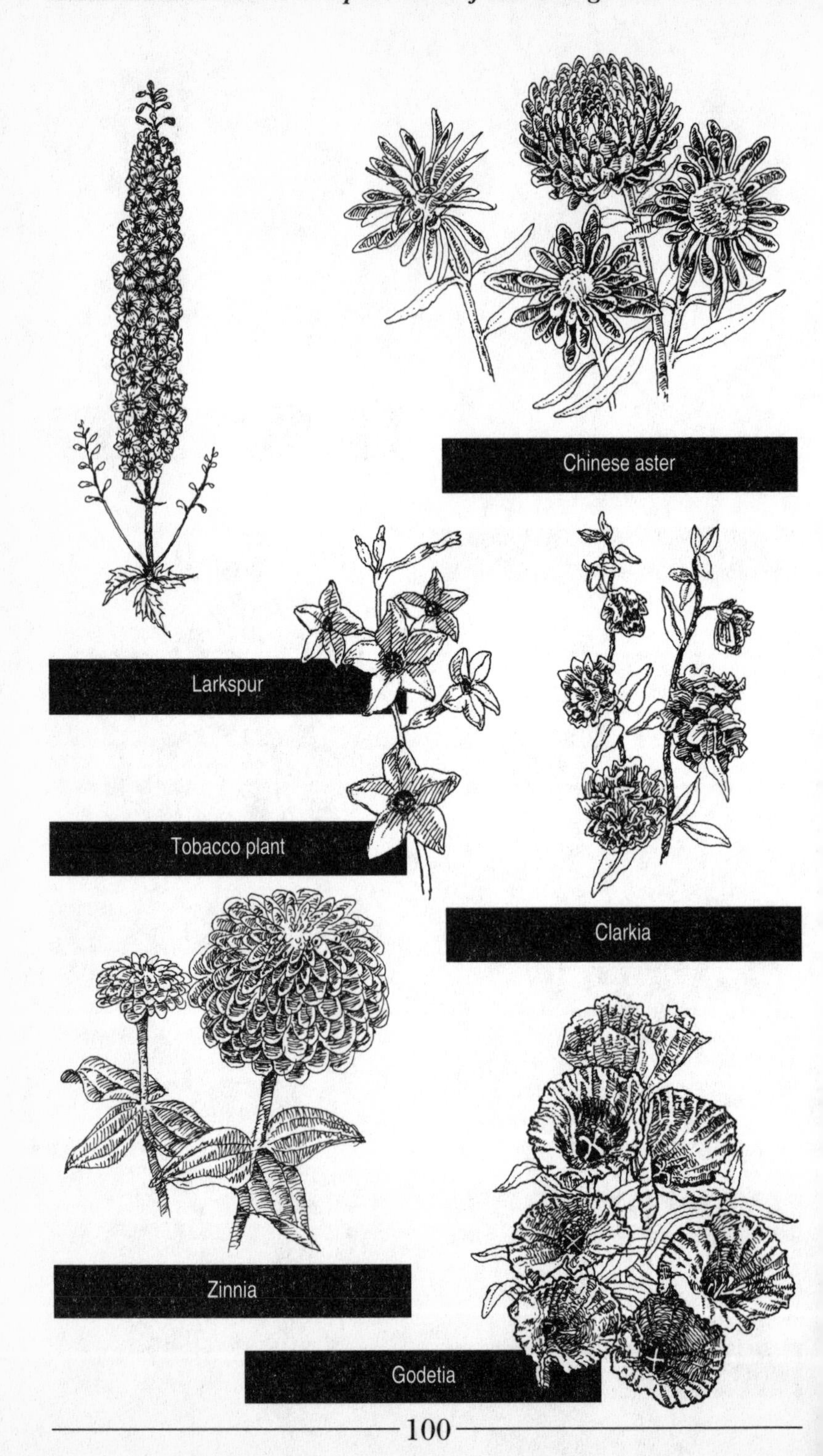
Chinese aster
Larkspur
Tobacco plant
Clarkia
Zinnia
Godetia

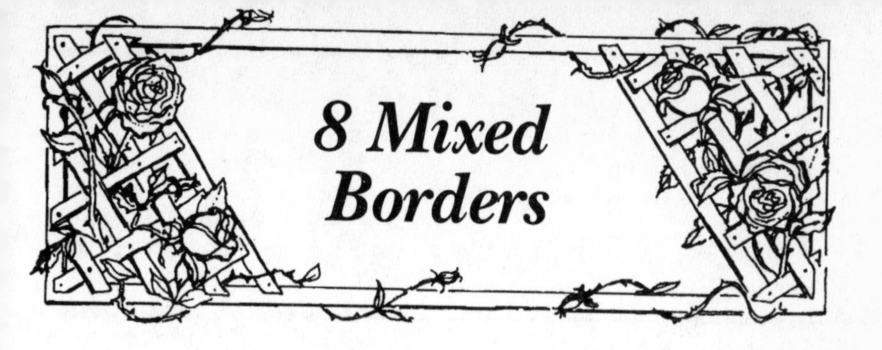

8 Mixed Borders

While the showy colours of the summer bedding catch the eye, its use is only appropriate to small gardens or limited areas of larger sites. It would be impractical to cover a really large area with this type of display, and anyway the effect would be overpowering. Gardens should have restful areas, particularly those at the back of the house. Some people will wish for a more subdued or subtle area in the front garden. This can be provided by a mixed border.

The modern mixed border is the direct descendent of the cottage garden, in which many examples of the plant kingdom coexist together. The layouts of mixed borders vary enormously according to the personal preference of the gardener. The most popular approaches are:

1 Grouping together a collection of plants from the same genus.
2 Collecting plants from a particular genus, as above, but distributing them throughout the garden.
3 Distributing plants among the borders in such a way that there is an item of interest to catch the eye in every area, and in each season of the year.
4 Grouping together several items to create a number of small gardens, each of which takes centre stage during a particular season.

Usually mixed beds surround a lawn, which will have sharp edges. The shape of these borders must be carefully planned. Straight-edged lawns have an unnatural appearance and while they may be appropriate for formal summer bedding displays they are out of place as a boundary to the mixed border. Gentle curves will be far more in keeping with the ambience of the beds and could allow a greater area to be given over to planting. The other advantage is that if 'tongues' of beds intrude into the lawn you can work from the grassed area without stepping onto the cultivated surface. The shape of the borders should provide interest as well as the plants.

The backcloth of a traditional herbaceous border may be a wall, fence, shrubs or a clipped hedge. If it is a fence or a wall, shrubs can be planted in front of it, or climbers grown against it. The herbaceous plants are then arranged in front in tiers. At the back are the tallest, at least a metre (3 ft) in height. The middle distance is occupied by plants 30–100 cm (1–3 ft) in height, and the foreground by low-growing subjects. Nowadays many gardeners plant perennials in island beds, cut out of the lawn with access right round the bed.

Mixed beds and borders should be designed to involve the minimum amount of work. With a few exceptions, unlike formal bedding displays, the plants should not be dug up and disturbed once they have been planted. Dead annuals must be removed and normally these will be replaced with self-sown seedlings (the soil must be weed free for successful germination and subsequent growth).

Soil preparation is very important. If you do not lay a sound foundation you will never achieve good results. Once the site for the mixed bed has been marked out it must be dug over and well rotted manure worked into the ground. This will be your final chance of working texture-improving material straight into the ground. Remove all traces of perennial weeds as you dig, and then rake the soil over.

The plants you choose will depend on whether the bed is in full sun, part-shade or complete shade for most of the day. But before anything is planted it is important to have an overall idea of what the finished bed will look like. Even if you do not possess all the plants that you finally intend to grow you should at least be aware of where you intend putting them. Be sure to leave some space to allow you the opportunity to add extra plants, for as the years go by you will want to acquire a number of different ones, whose existence you may not now be aware of as you start building your garden. One of the great joys of gardening is finding new plants to take home and cultivate.

Annuals for the mixed border

As well as the true annuals gardeners grow many perennials as annuals because the plants in their first year have stronger growth, better form, or else they are not worth retaining in the ground throughout the year for their relatively short flowering period. All true annuals are grown from seed – there is no other way of propagating them. Hardy annuals may be sown directly in the ground either in their final flowering position or in a nursery bed. Usually once they are established in a border they are left to seed themselves. The half-hardy annuals are sown in the warmth of a greenhouse or on a window-sill and brought on in seed boxes (see pp. 40–42).

Biennials for the mixed border

For growing outdoors biennials must be frost-hardy. Though they may be cut down by the severe weather, the root will remain alive to re-emerge the following spring. This means that in general they will not require artificial heat for germination and can usually be sown directly out of doors either in their final position or in a nursery bed. As they do not flower during the first season, sowing may be delayed until May or June.

SOME BIENNIALS FOR MIXED BEDS

Sweet William *(Dianthus barbatus)*

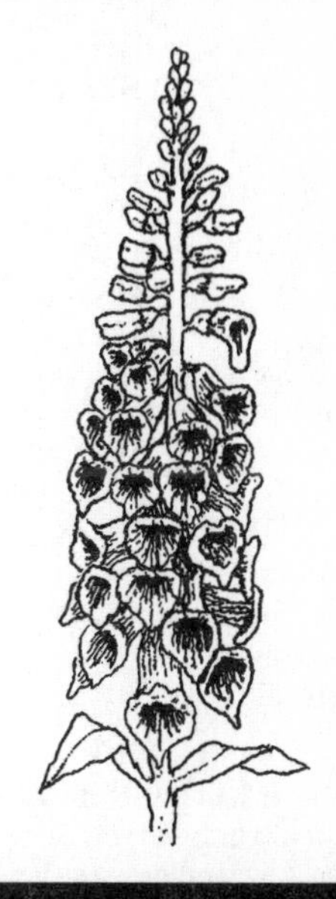

Foxglove *(Digitalis purpurea)*

Canterbury bell
(Campanula medium)

Chinese pink *(Dianthus chinensis)*

Annuals for mixed beds

Name	Status	How to sow	Colours	Distance apart cm	in
Candytuft	HA	Direct	P,W,B	22	9
California poppy	HA	Direct	R,Y,W,P,O	30	12
Chinese aster	HHA	In warmth	Var	45	18
Chrysanthemum	HHA	Direct	Y,W	45	18
Clarkia	HA	Direct	P,R,W	15	6
Cosmos	HHA	In warmth	R,P,W	30	12
Flax	HA	Direct	R,W	15	6
Godetia	HA	Direct	Var.	45	18
Gypsophila	HA	Direct	W,P	45	18
Larkspur	HA	Direct	B,R,W	30	12
Livingstone daisy	HHA	In warmth	Var	30	12
Love-in-a-mist	HA	Direct	R,W,B	30	12
Mallow	HA	Direct	P,W	60	24
Morning glory	HA	Direct	B,P,W	30	12
Nasturtium	HA	Direct	O,Y	22	9
Rudbeckia	HA	Direct	Y	30	12
Strawflower	HHA	In warmth	Var	30	12
Stock	HHA	In warmth	Var	30	12
Sunflower	HHA	In warmth	Y	75	30
Sun plant (portulaca)	HHA	In warmth	Var	15	6
Sweet scabious	HHA	In warmth	Var	30	12
Tobacco plant	HHA	In warmth	Var	30	12

HA: grow as hardy annuals
HHA: grow as half-hardy annuals
Direct: sow direct into their flowering positions
In warmth: sow seed in warmth and transplant out into their final positions
Colours: B, Blue; R, Red; O. Orange; P. Pink; W, White; Y, Yellow; Var, Various.

It is possible to allow biennials to remain virtually undisturbed apart from removing the spent specimens. Some may set seed and the self-sown seedlings will emerge the following year.

Sweet Williams and biennial carnations will both continue to flower if dead-headed. Other biennials, especially foxgloves, produce secondary spikes to the main flowering spike, but these never reach the size of the primary stalk.

Perennials for the mixed border

Perennials will continue to grow for many years, in theory lasting for ever once they are established, but most of them tend to lose their vigour as they age. All perennials can be regenerated by vegetative propagation. The majority of perennials are best planted during either early November or the beginning of March. First make sure there are no roots of perennial weeds in the ground. It is just as necessary to maintain soil quality as it is with those beds that can be dug over every year. Fork in some compost, and each spring scatter a quantity of Growmore around the plants.

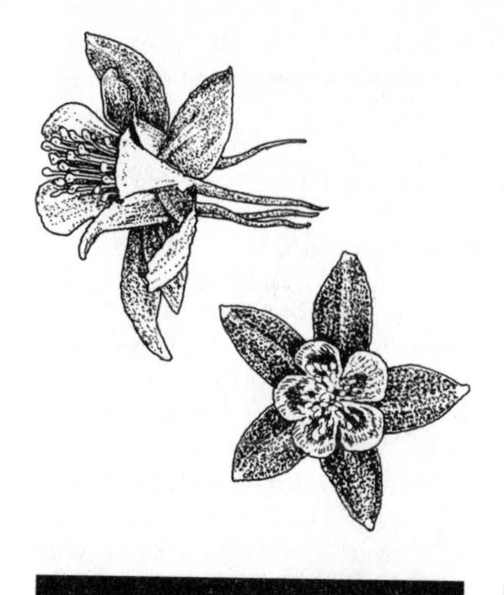

Aquilegia

Lily of the valley (convallaria)

Bergenia

Grow some perennial plants for cut flowers in a spare plot (see pp. 203-211).

In the following pages are some of the most popular kinds of herbaceous perennial, and some late-flowering bulbous plants. In large gardens some of them would look most effective planted together in groups of two or three, perhaps more. The really large species can be grown on their own as statuesque specimen plants.

Achillea (yarrow)

A range of plants that vary from 10 cm (4 in) to 2 m (6 ft). The flowers consist of large flat heads carried on tall stems. The yellow, red or white flowers are borne mainly in June and July. Propagate by root division during early spring.

Agapanthus (African lily)

Height 30–60 cm (1–2 ft). Blue or white flowers are borne in an umbrella-shaped arrangement during July and August. Slightly tender, the plants should be given some protection during the winter months. Propagate by division in March. Agapanthus may also be grown in pots in the greenhouse.

Alchemilla (lady's mantle)

Height 30 cm (1 ft). Grown mainly for its foliage. The green to pale yellow flowers are individually insignificant, but grouped together they give a delicate appearance to the plant.

Anemone x *hybrida, syn. A. japonica (Japanese anemone)*

Height 1 m (3 ft). Open dish-shaped pink or white flowers are carried on the tall grey-green foliage during August and September. This is a good flower for cutting. Propagate by root division or root cuttings during March. It usually takes two years for plants from root cuttings to bloom.

Aquilegia (columbine)

Height 30–60 cm (1–2 ft). The 2 cm long flower consists of five petals making a funnel shape, each outer petal having a swept-back tail. The leaves are similar to those of the maidenhair fern. Border species and their hybrids bloom throughout the late spring and summer. Columbines are not long-lived but seed freely. Old plants should be periodically discarded and replaced with seedlings, which flower the year after they are sown.

Armeria (thrift)

Height 30–45 cm (6–9 in). Forms hummocks of grass-like leaves. In summer, they are covered with globular pink flowerheads about 1 cm in diameter, carried on thin stalks. Armeria likes a well drained, sunny site. Propagate by division during March.

Aster (Michaelmas daisy)

Asters are a large group containing the familiar Michaelmas daisy. This is the name given to two aster species, *A. novae angliae* and *A. novi belgii*. There are a number of varieties, which are more frequently grown than the species. They occur in several shades of violet-

Anenome japonica

Armeria maritima

Michaelmas daisy

blue and red with yellow centres. Most grow to 1 m (3 ft) or more, but there are varieties at 22–38 cm (9–15 in) that are suitable for the front of the border.

Asters are a must for any mixed border as they flower from early September to mid-October at a time when most plants are beginning to cease blooming. Propagate by root division during the early spring.

Bergenia (elephant's ears)

Height up to 30 cm (1 ft). Depending on the species, these bloom from January to late spring, with a long flowering period. Bergenia have large roughly heart-shaped leaves, growing direct from the crown. In some species they acquire a reddish tinge. The flowers, which may be red, white, pink or magenta, resemble hyacinths except that they are grouped on side-stems from the main flowering stalk. Grow in sun or partial shade. Propagate by division during October or after flowering is complete.

Brunnera (perennial forget-me-not)

Height 30–45 cm (1–1½ ft). The plant has large heart-shaped leaves and small blue flowers like forget-me-nots (during May). They prefer a moist, shady location. Propagate by root cuttings or division in late October.

Campanula

A large group in which the height varies from a few centimetres to up to 1.5 m (5 ft). These plants take their name from their bell-like flowers, which occur in light and dark shades of blue, and sometimes white or pink. Most species flower throughout the summer. Tall border species include *campanula persicifolia, C. latifolia* and *C. lactiflora.* Slightly less tall is *C. glomerata,* at 30–45 cm (1–1½ ft).

Depending upon type they may be propagated from seed, root division in the spring or from cuttings taken during May and June.

Chrysanthemum

This is a large genus belonging to the daisy family and includes annual varieties, but the name chrysanthemum is usually applied to the kinds sold in florists, which are half-hardy perennials and hardy greenhouse types.

Chrysanthemums can be divided according to their hardiness: the outdoor, completely hardy ones (the earlies) and those which must finish their growth and flower in a greenhouse (the lates).

Only fully hardy plants should be grown in the border where they will produce flowers in reds, bronzes, yellows, whites and pinks. Chrysanthemums grown in borders require staking as they often grow 150 cm (5 ft). The flowering period is from August through until October.

For details of propagation and raising chrysanthemums for cut flowers, see p. 203–204.

Convallaria (lily of the valley)

Height 15 cm (6 in). A plant

for cool, shady places, the broad leaves providing good ground cover. During late spring white bell-shaped flowers are carried on 22 cm (9 in) stems. They have one of the sweetest of all flower scents. A rarity worth looking out for is the pink form, 'Rosea'. Unless restrained, the rhizomes are invasive and will colonise large areas. Propagate by transplanting rhizomes in October or immediately after the plants have flowered.

Coreopsis

Height 45 cm (18 in). A member of the daisy family with bright golden-yellow flowers through most of the summer. These are quite long lasting when cut. Propagation is by division of the roots during March.

Cortaderia (pampas grass)

Given a good rich soil and an annual mulch pampas grass can reach a height of 3 m (10 ft) and a spread of 2 m (6 ft). Often grown as the focal point of a lawn, it is only really in its glory during October and November when carrying feathery plumes. The plant must be cut right back and the dead leaves removed in March. Propagate by digging up and dividing the plants during the spring.

Crinum

Height 60 cm (2 ft). Suitable only for sheltered positions, in milder areas. Grow it in well-drained soil at the foot of a south-facing wall. In colder areas it may be grown in the greenhouse border. The plant, which is a bulb, has strap-shaped leaves. Long pinkish-white trumpet-like flowers are borne during August and September. Propagate by removing the small offsets during the spring.

Crocosmia (montbretia)

Height 60 cm (2 ft). The plant grows from corms similar to those of gladiolus and possesses the same swordlike leaves. Orange trumpet-like flowers open along the stem during mid-to-late summer. Crocosmia make excellent cut flowers. To propagate, divide the clumps after flowering.

Curtonus

Height 1 m (3 ft). Closely related to crocosmia. The description and cultivation are similar.

Cyclamen

Height 10 cm (4 in). Most people think of cyclamen as pot plants, but a few species are fully hardy. One of the most readily obtainable is *C. hederifolium*, (formerly called *C. neapolitanum*). This grows well in humus-rich soil in part-shade. The small swept-back flowers, typical of the genus, are either pink or white and borne throughout the autumn. Essentially a woodland plant, it is long-lived and with time will form a large tuber up to 7.5 cm (3 in) in diameter. Plant tubers in April or May. Propagation is by seed only, as the tubers do not divide or form offsets.

Dahlias

Several types are available. As with chrysanthemums, there is a classification system for exhibition purposes, but in addition they may be divided into two kinds. First of all there are the bedding dahlias, which grow to just a little over 30 cm (1 ft). These can be grown from seed sown in warmth during March. There are single, semi-double or fully double forms. They are treated as annuals and discarded at the end of the year. The other type are known as the border dahlias, which range from 45 cm to 1.5 m (1½–5 ft). For a description of the various border dahlia types and full cultural details, see pp. 204–09.

Delphinium

Height 1.3 m (4 ft). Tall spikes of bell-shaped flowers in various shades of blue and pink and also white are borne during early summer. The plant requires a sunny position and good rich soil. It also needs staking. If the spike is cut out when the flowers have finished but before they can set seed, secondary smaller stems of flowers are produced late in the season. Delphiniums may be propagated from seeds or root division. The best method is to allow the root to shoot and during April to take cuttings 10 cm (4 in) in length from the base of the crown.

Dianthus (carnations and pinks)

Crosses involving the individual members of the genus *Dianthus* has led to the emergence of two main groups, the pinks and the carnations.

Pinks are about 25 cm (10 in) tall with blooms 2.5 cm (1 in)

Dianthus 'Doris'

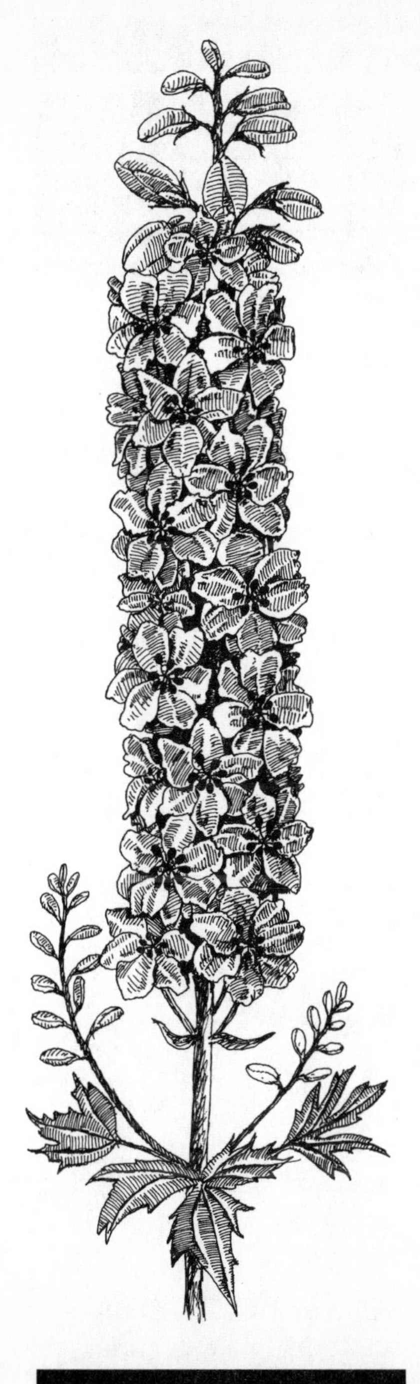

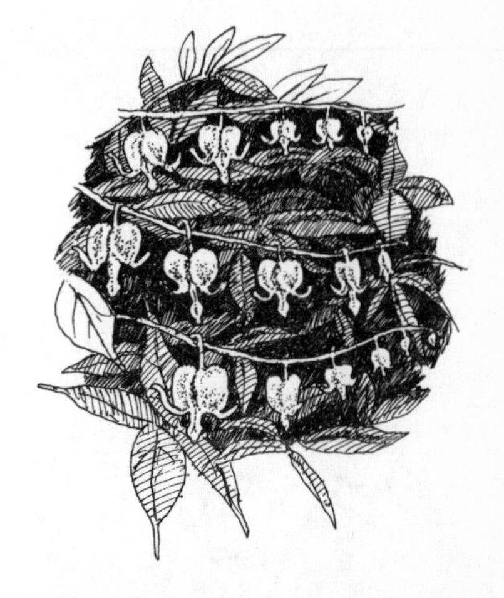

Dicentra spectabile

Delphinium

Globe thistle (echinops)

PROPAGATION OF CARNATIONS AND PINKS

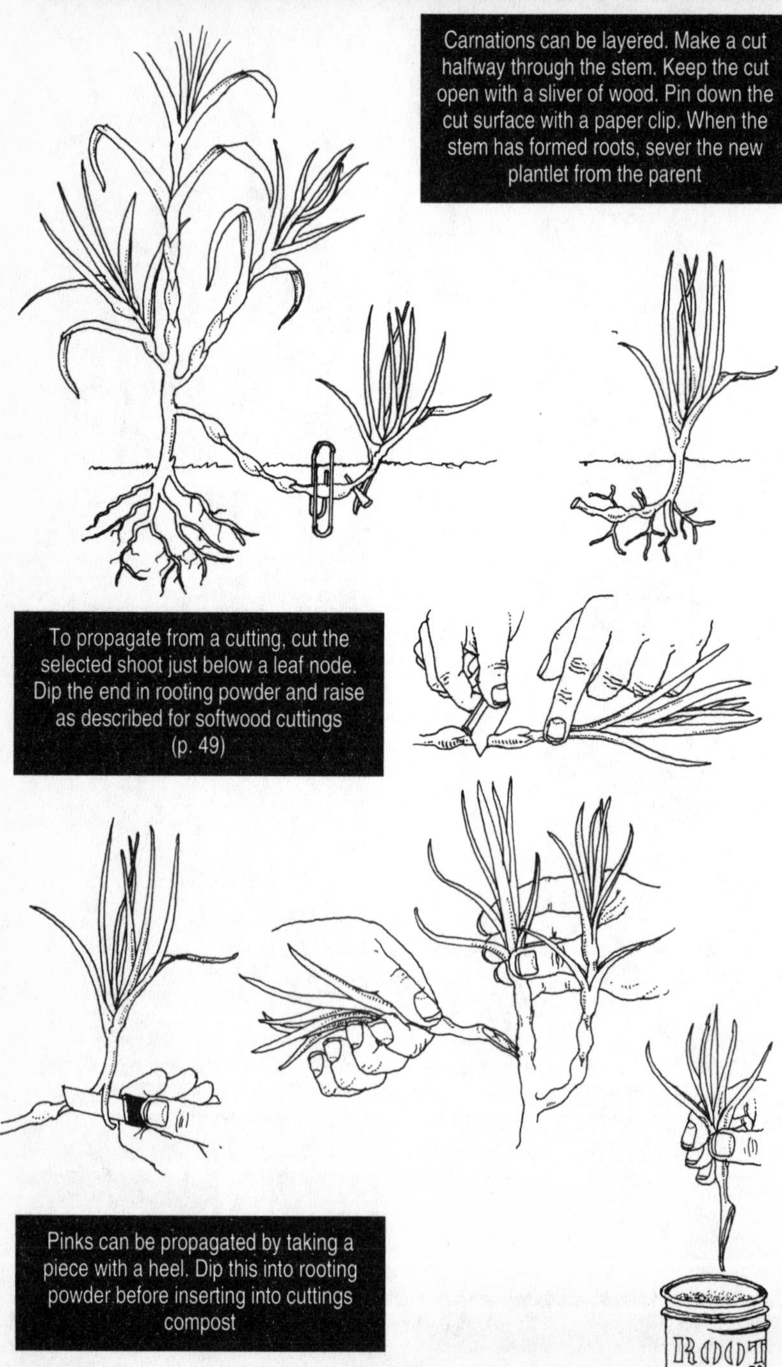

Carnations can be layered. Make a cut halfway through the stem. Keep the cut open with a sliver of wood. Pin down the cut surface with a paper clip. When the stem has formed roots, sever the new plantlet from the parent

To propagate from a cutting, cut the selected shoot just below a leaf node. Dip the end in rooting powder and raise as described for softwood cuttings (p. 49)

Pinks can be propagated by taking a piece with a heel. Dip this into rooting powder before inserting into cuttings compost

across. They all have a very pronounced clovelike scent. There are two types: the old fashioned pinks, and the more vigorous growing modern pinks which produce many more blooms. They bloom from May until July and the modern pinks often flower again in the autumn when they are stopped by the onset of the frosts. Modern pinks should be propagated every two years, but old fashioned pinks only need regenerating every four years, by taking cuttings during July.

The carnations are basically the same as double pinks, but larger. They grow 60 cm (2 ft) tall and have blooms 5 cm (2 in) across. The stalks are amongst the most brittle in the plant kingdom and will require staking. Carnations usually flower only once in a season. To obtain really big blooms on long stems, the flower stems must be disbudded in June, leaving the topmost bud on the main stem and side shoots. Carnations are best regenerated every two years. Propagate by layering, using a variation of the technique used for shrubs. During July, take a long young shoot and with a sharp knife make a cut in the underside of the tissue. Pin it down to the ground with a bent paper clip. At the end of September, sever the new plant which should then be allowed to grow undisturbed. It can be moved to another location during the spring. Alternatively the parent plant, which may now look old and straggly, can be removed and discarded.

All members of the genus *Dianthus* root readily from cuttings. You may be fortunate enough to receive a bouquet of carnations. When the flowers have finished blooming, it is often possible to root a piece providing it still retains some leaves on the stalk. It may be grown out of doors even though the plant from which it originated was almost certainly raised in a greenhouse. Sever a piece of the flowering stalk just below a node that has a pair of leaves still attached. Dip it in rooting powder, place it in moist compost in a pot and cover with a polythene bag. Placed in a sunny position on a window-sill, the cuttings almost invariably root, giving you plants for free and a memento of a very happy occasion. Dianthus, which are fully hardy and include sweet Williams, appreciate a well drained sunny position. They will not tolerate acid soils.

Dicentra (bleeding heart)

D. spectabilis is the form most commonly grown and is 60–90 cm (2–3 ft) in height. In July, it has flowers consisting of rosy red heart-shaped petals with a white inner petal extending below the tip, giving the impression that it is falling from the centre of the bloom. Up to 20 of these flowers are carried on the stalk which curves over the foliage. A pure white variety is obtainable. Propagate dicentra by division during the autumn.

Dierama (wand flower, angel's fishing rod)

Height 1–1.5 m (3–5 ft) depending on the species. The

Helenium

Geum

Helianthus decapetalus

pink, red or white flowers droop from a tall arching stem during June to August giving the impression of a fishing rod.

Propagation is by lifting, dividing and planting the rootstock any time during the dormant season.

Echinops (globe thistle)

Height 1 m (3 ft). Has large blue, spherical flower-heads, which appear during mid-to-late summer. The plant, which is very useful as a cut flower, should be grown at the back of the bed. Propagate by root division during the winter.

Eranthis (winter aconite)

Height 15 cm (6 in). One of the earliest of all spring flowers, its yellow buttercup-like blooms appear during February. Tuberous-rooted, eranthis should be planted 'in the green' in a sunny or partially shaded location, immediately after flowering is over.

They do well planted under deciduous trees or shrubs, but do make sure they have a moisture-retentive soil.

Euphorbia (spurge)

Height various depending upon species. Spurges are mainly grown for their attractive foliage and for the sometimes conspicuous colourful bracts surrounding the flowers, which are themselves small and insignificant. Most require a sunny position, though *E. robbiae* will tolerate shade. Once established spurges tend to propagate themselves by means of self-sown seeds.

Geranium (cranesbill)

Height generally less than 30 cm (1 ft). This must not be confused with the pelargonium hybrids, many of which are being increasingly grown as bedding plants. But even among professional gardeners the term geranium is often used for the plant that is more correctly described as the zonal pelargonium. Since this is now virtually a universal practice the term geranium is used in this way in all other parts of this book.

The white, red, pink and blue cup-like flowers of cranesbill are borne during the summer. The plants like a well drained, sunny position and may be propagated by division or cuttings taken from new growth during April.

Geum (avens)

Height 30 cm (1 ft). A popular cottage garden plant with flowers similar to single roses in shades of red, orange and yellow. The flowering period is from May to August. Geums like an open site with a humus-rich soil. Propagate by seed or by division during spring.

Gypsophila (baby's breath)

Height 1 m (3 ft). There are annual and alpine species, but the well-known border perennial is *G. paniculata* (see under cut flowers, p. 209).

Helenium autumnale

Height, according to variety, is 60–120 cm (2–4 ft). Another of the cottager's favourites, which attracts myriades of butterflies. The flowers, which are borne in

Christmas rose *(Helleborus niger)*

Bearded iris

Hosta sieboldiana

summer, are daisy-like with central discs. Colours range from rich golden yellows to oranges and coppery reds. Propagation is by root division after flowering is complete or during March.

Helianthus (sunflower)

Height 1–2 m (3–6 ft). This is the perennial sunflower, *H. decapetalus* (the better known annual sunflower, *H. annuus,* grows much taller). As well as single versions, there are semi-double and double varieties, which may be red, bronze or yellow. Having a late-season flower, propagation by crown division is best delayed until spring.

Helleborus (Christmas rose, Lenten rose)

Height 30–45 cm (1–1½ ft). Hellebores belong to the buttercup family. The white petalled *H. niger,* the Christmas rose, may bloom in December if protected by cloches, but otherwise it flowers between January and March. *H. orientalis,* the Lenten rose, has flowers of white, pink or purple, sometimes prettily speckled, from February to April. Grow on moist though well-drained soil, preferably humus-rich, in a partially shaded location. Propagate by seed or by root division immediately after flowering.

Hemerocallis (day lily)

Height 75–90 cm (2½–3 ft). Blooming from about June to August, the trumpet-shaped flowers range from yellow through to reddish orange. Although each flower lasts only a day, new buds continually appear to replace the withered ones. Plant in a sunny or slightly shaded position in humus-rich soil. Propagate by root division in October or during April.

Hosta (plantain lily)

Height 30–90 cm (1–3 ft), according to species. A plant at home in sun or part shade so long as there is a moisture-retentive, though well-drained, humus-rich soil. Hostas are grown mainly for their attractive large leaves, which emerge directly from the crown and occur in many shades of green (there are variegated forms too). The white or pale lilac flowers, borne towards the end of the summer, are comparatively insignificant. Providing that the compost is kept sufficiently moist, these plants are ideal for growing in containers. Propagation is by crown division during the autumn.

Irises

Height various depending upon species. One of the most complex of all genera, for convenience irises may be divided into those having rhizomes and those growing from bulbs (these are discussed on p. 84). The rhizomatous irises consist of two main groups: the bearded irises, which take their name from the small hairlike growths on the falls (the outermost petals), and the beardless irises, in which all of the petals are devoid of hairs (there are other minor differences between the two groups).

All rhizomatous irises for the border should be planted in an

Lupin

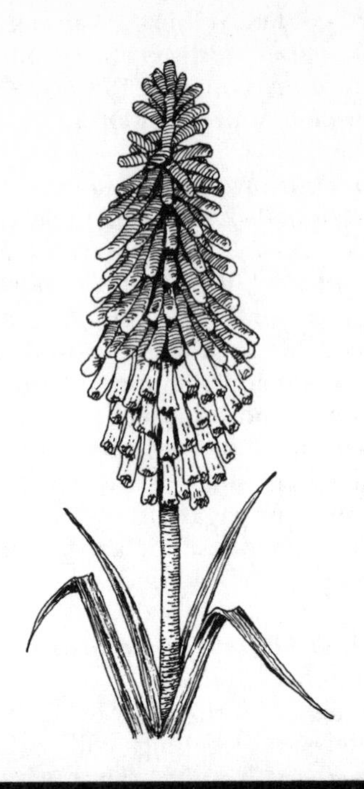

Red hot poker (kniphofia)

Lilium regale

open sunny position in a rich loamy soil. They require dividing from time to time (the special method is described on p. 52–54). The flowers of both groups occur in colours spanning the whole range of the spectrum and appear during early summer.

Kniphofia (red hot pokers)

Height of most species 60–150 cm (2–5 ft). This summer-flowering cottage garden favourite has tall grass-like leaves. The heads of tubular flowers are usually red or orange at the top and the lower portion yellow or cream, though there are some all-red, all-yellow or creamy-white varieties.

Lilies

Height 30–180 cm (1–6 ft), depending on species. This is a very large group. The flowers, orange, yellow, pink or white, are borne on tall stems furnished with long thin leaves. They have six petals which, according to species, either grow forward into a bowl or trumpet shape or are reflexed.

Many possess large hammer-headed stamens covered in golden-yellow or orange pollen. Some have the most exquisite perfumes, and flower size can be as much as 20 cm (8 in) across.

The majority of lilies are hardy and may be grown out of doors in mixed beds. While some species of lily are exacting in their requirements – some demand a lime-free soil, and there are others that need lime – most lilies, particularly modern hybrids, will thrive in a well-drained loam enriched with humus. Heavy soils should have some sand and peat worked into them. Choose a sunny position. Stem-rooting kinds – the majority – need a depth of 15 cm (6 in) of soil over the bulb. The Madonna lily (*L. candidum*) is basal rooting and should be planted with the neck of the bulb only 5 cm (2 in) below the surface of the soil. Tall specimens may need to be staked. Some lilies may easily be propagated by separating large clumps of bulbs and replanting in autumn or spring. Alternatively, grow them from seed, though named varieties will not come true of course.

Lupins

Height 60–120 cm (2–4 ft). A dwarf form is also available. The tall spires of pea-like flowers, which come out in midsummer are in yellows, reds, blues, white and bi-colours. They prefer a neutral or slightly acid soil and appreciate a large amount of well rotted manure mulched round during the spring.

Careful crossing and selecting means one can now obtain from seed top quality lupin plants with flowers in very bright colours. Sow in March or April for flowering the following year. Individual plants may be propagated by crown division during March.

Lysimachia (loosestrife)

Height 1 m (3 ft). *L. clethroides* (Chinese loosestrife) has arching spikes of small white star-shaped flowers during mid-to-late summer.

Paeony

Zonal pelargonium (geranium)

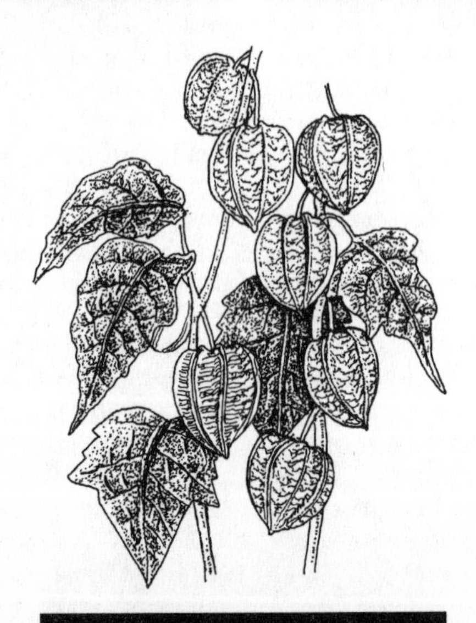

Chinese lantern
(Physalis alkekengi) fruits

L. punctata (yellow loosestrife) bears whorls of yellow cup-shaped flowers from June to August. *L. nummularia* (creeping Jenny) is a popular ground-hugging member of the family with long trailing stems carrying almost round leaves and golden yellow flowers during mid-summer. Propagate lysimachias by division in autumn or spring.

Mimulus (monkey flower)
Height 30–60 cm (1–2 ft). These have large open mouthed flowers reminiscent of some orchids in red, yellow and a combination of the two. They must have a moisture-retentive soil and may also be grown in bog gardens or beside ponds. Propagate by division during late March.

Nepeta (catmint)
Height 37 cm (15 in). Perhaps grown more for the silvery-green foliage than for the spikes of small lavender-blue flowers which are present most of the summer. This is an ideal plant for the front of a display area. Propagate by root division during spring.

Nerine
Height 37 cm (15 in). A very important bulb for the late summer garden, seldom blooming before September and remaining until it is finally destroyed by the persistent bad weather of November. It has narrow pink petals in an open crown shape. The leaves are long and thin. Nerines will grow in most well drained soils and prefer a sunny location. If left, they will develop into a large clump. Propagate by dividing the bulb clumps in April.

Paeonies
Height up to 130 cm (4 ft). Opening from large globular buds during May, the flowers may be either single, with bright yellow stamens, or double. Colours are pink, white or red. Paeonies prefer an open site with rich loamy soil. Once established, they should not be moved as they may be reluctant to recommence flowering. Purchase roots as early in the spring as possible – early establishment may reduce the time taken to flower again by a year. Where lifting or division of the root is unavoidable, this should be performed during September or October. Providing that a large enough piece is transplanted, it may flower the following season.

Pelargoniums (popularly called geraniums)
Do not confuse with the genus *Geranium* (see p. 115).

Height is up to 60 cm (2 ft) but usually half this. There are numerous hybrids available with more being added each year. The most popular types are:

1 *Zonal pelargoniums.* These are the ones most universally known as geraniums. They take their name from the bronze band or zone travelling around the centre of the leaf in many of them (but not all). They have rounded leaves. Forms exist with very fancy leaves, banded or splashed in cream, red, dark green or maroon.

2 *Regal pelargoniums* – the only members commonly referred to as pelargoniums. These have crinkled, saw-edged leaves and flower colours ranging from white and pink through to the deepest shade of carmine. In the light coloured varieties the centres are often blotched with a darker shade. Regal pelargoniums are the most tender of the group and are best grown indoors.

3 Ivy-leafed geraniums (*P. peltatum*). These have rather smooth fleshy leaves. The stems are pendulous, making the plants ideal for hanging baskets and trailing over the sides of containers. Colours are white through to darkest carmine, with red and white bi-colours too.

In addition to the above, scented-leaved species are available, smelling of lemon, peppermint or rose. There are also dwarfs which grow little more than 15 cm (6 in) tall, and slightly larger miniatures.

All pelargoniums may be kept in the greenhouse throughout the year or transferred out of doors as a bedding plant in the summer. Young plants, both cuttings and seedlings, once established should be transferred to 7 cm (3 in) flower pots. On reaching 20–30 cm (8–12 in) they must be transplanted to a 12 cm (5 in) pot in which they should remain. Use a loam or peat-based compost.

Throughout the summer months give them a weekly feed high in potash and phosphates. Avoid fertilisers that have a high nitrogen content, which will only result in a large quantity of sappy growth.

Zonals may be produced from seeds, but for the best results you must buy the expensive modern hybrids. Named forms should be propagated by cuttings, which can be taken at any time between April and the autumn. Cuttings started in the spring will flower late in the season while those taken from August onwards will overwinter and carry flowers at the beginning of the next season.

In time pelargoniums, especially zonals, will grow very straggly unless steps are taken to prevent this. When either seedlings or cuttings have developed four pairs of leaves pinch the centre out. Sometimes the plants will reshoot from beside the previous growing tip. This shoot must also be removed to encourage fresh shoots to emerge from the leaf axils. While long trailing growths are actively sought from ivy-leafed geraniums they also benefit from having their growing tips removed when the shoot is 10 cm (4 in) long. This will allow two stronger but still pendulous stems to develop.

As pelargoniums are tender subjects, hard decisions must be made during October as to whether you intend to keep your plants. They may be over-wintered in different ways. Plants to be saved should be brought inside before the first frosts. Zonals can usually withstand the first frosts – it is only prolonged freezing and wet that destroys them. Regals are effectively killed by the first frost.

Pelargoniums do not require much warmth – they can survive

Solomon's seal (polygonatum)

Pyrethrum

Ornamental rhubarb
(Rheum palmatum)

providing they are kept in frost-free conditions. The lower the temperature the less water you should provide. Where the temperature is kept only just above freezing point, the plants should be allowed to almost dry out. From February onwards the temperature should be raised and more water given to bring the plants back into growth. Where a greenhouse temperature of 15°C (60°F) is maintained, water them regularly and they will then continue to grow throughout the winter. They do need a rest, however, and where plants are kept in bloom for a long period they should be constantly regenerated by means of cuttings.

Stock plants and the previous year's cuttings can be allowed to tick over at 7°C (45°F) throughout the winter, being given just sufficient water to ensure that they do not dry out. They should be brought into a higher temperature during February to produce blooms early in the season. The large pelargoniums may no longer be suitable for containers or bedding purposes, but they should be retained as stock plants to provide cuttings early in the next season.

When overwintering plants, remove all leaves as they die and do not stand the plants close together on clear dry days. If possible, allow some ventilation as this will ensure that the plants are not infected by fungi capable of surviving in low temperatures, especially where there is lack of air circulation.

Physalis (Chinese lantern)

Height 30 cm (1 ft). These have small, insignificant white flowers followed in September by 2 cm (1 in) orange lantern-like structures at the centre of which is a large round fruit containing seed. The plants are undemanding, but prefer an open, well-drained site. Propagate them by root division or by seed sown during the early spring.

Polygonatum (Solomon's seal)

Height 60 cm (2 ft). This plant thrives in damp and shady sites in most garden soils. The arching stems bear broad green leaves below which hang groups of white tubular flowers in May and June. Propagate by root division in autumn or spring.

Potentilla

There are both herbaceous and shrubby forms of potentilla. The herbaceous hybrids grow to 45 cm (1½ ft). Some potentillas produce leaves with a striking resemblance to those of strawberry plants, for which they could be readily mistaken. They require a rich soil and a sunny position. The saucer-shaped flowers, which come in double and semi-double forms as well as single, are carried from June until August and range from deep red through to pink and yellow. Propagate by root division during the autumn or spring.

Primulas

Height 5–15 cm (2–6 in). A very large family of perennials that includes the common primrose (*P. vulgaris*), from which numerous hybrids have been derived, such as the polyanthus (see pp. 95–96). Primulas benefit from a rich loamy soil and carry red, yellow, blue or white flowers from March until May. After they have bloomed the roots may be dug up and divided with a sharp knife. It is important to keep the plants well watered throughout the summer and in partial shade. They may be grown as biennials – sow seeds during one spring to produce plants for flowering during the next. They are then discarded because the blooms gradually become smaller.

There are several other border primulas, all of which require soil that doesn't dry out during the growing period. They include the drumstick primrose, *P. denticulata*, 22 cm (9 in), which has lilac globular flowers, the Japanese primrose, *P. japonica*, which can grow to 60 cm (2 ft) tall and has bright purple-red flowers, and the Himalayan cowslip, *P. sikkimensis*, 45 cm (1½ ft) in height with tall yellow cowslip-like flowers. Sow the seed in a pan of moist compost, which must be kept shaded. When the seedlings are large enough to handle they should be transferred to individual flower pots, grown on and then hardened off – still in a shady position – and transferred to a damp spot in the garden. Many are ideal subjects for growing at the edge of a water garden.

Pyrethrum

Height up to 90 cm (3 ft). Ideal for growing in borders or for cutting, its large daisy flowers, which appear during May to July, are similar to single chrysanthemums. They occur in shades of pink, red and white. Double varieties are also available. After cutting the plants produce a second crop later in the season. They prefer a sunny situation. Propagate by crown division during October.

Ranunculus asiaticus (turban buttercup)

As well as the familiar weed there are several ornamental buttercups which grow to about 30 cm (1 ft). The most spectacular, *R. asiaticus*, produces red, orange, white and yellow flowers during May to June. It is a semi-tender, tuberous-rooted plant that needs lifting in the autumn and storing in frost-free conditions.

Rheum (ornamental rhubarb)

Height up to 250 cm (8 ft). As well as the edible form of rhubarb there are species grown for their decorative value. The tallest is *R. palmatum*, with a pronounced purple tinge to the stalks and deeply cut leaves. Clusters of small red-petalled flowers are borne on a tall central spike during June. It is best in a large garden as it takes up considerable space. A rapid grower, it requires an abundance of nutrients, best provided by mulching with well-rotted manure during the spring. Propagate by digging up the crown in November or December, chopping into pieces and ensuring that each has about three strong buds. The

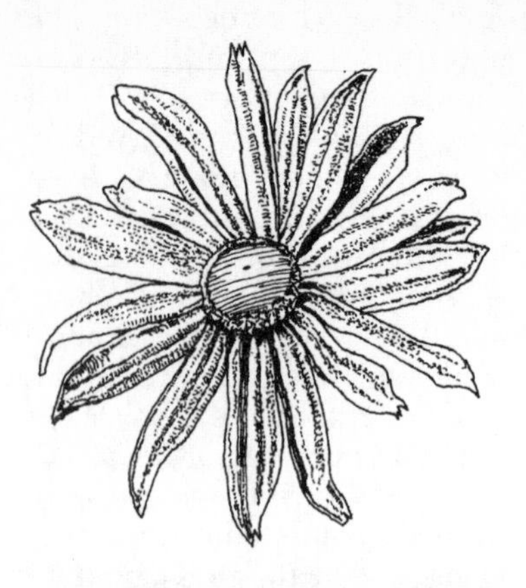

Rudbeckia nitida 'Herbstsonne'

Scabious *(Scabiosa caucasica)*

Salvia nemorosa

pieces may be replanted immediately or allowed to remain on the top of the soil until February.

Rodgersia

Height 100–130 cm (3–4 ft). A useful plant for large borders. It needs light shade, a moist soil and a sheltered position. *R. aesculifolia* has large leaves similar to those of a horse chestnut, and there are other species widely available. Plumes of small flowers on erect stems appear during June or July. Propagation is by division of the rhizomes during autumn.

Rudbeckia (coneflower)

Height 60 cm–2 m (2–6 ft) according to species. The star-shaped daisy-like flowers are generally yellow with a pronounced cone-shaped centre. They are borne from mid-to-late summer. Rudbeckia will grow in most soils but prefers a sunny situation. Propagate by crown division during autumn or spring.

Salvia (sage)

Height up to 1 m (3 ft). A large genus that includes the culinary herbs. As well as the bright red annual bedding plants and some shrubby species, there are herbaceous perennial sages, mostly with purple or blue flowers borne throughout the summer.

The most widely available is *S. superba* and its varieties. Salvias prefer a sunny site and well-drained soil. Propagate by seed or divide clumps in autumn or spring.

Saxifraga (saxifrage)

Most of the saxifrages are rock-garden plants. The best known border saxifrage is London Pride (*s.* x *urbium*), height 25 cm (10 in), which in mid-spring has sprays of tiny pink flowers on tall, slender stems arising from rosettes of leaves. Provide a moisture-retentive soil and some shade. Propagate by dividing the rosettes in spring.

Scabious

Height 45–60 cm (18–24 in). The perennial form is *Scabiosa caucasica,* with large daisy-like flowers, usually blue but sometimes white, carried throughout the summer. Plant in a sunny position in a non-acid, well-drained soil. (Scabious does well in chalky areas.) Propagate by root division during the early spring.

Sedum

Height 30–45 cm (1–1½ ft). The sedums are a large group having thick succulent leaves growing in rosettes. The most widely grown border species is *S. spectabile* (ice plant), which is very useful for the autumn garden. Large, slightly curved flower heads, made up of many tiny rose-pink flowers, appear in September – butterflies love them. As autumn progresses, the flowers gradually turn brown but are still attractive and may be left on the plant throughout the winter. Any well-drained soil will suit sedums, preferably in full sun. Propagate by crown division during March. Many of the smaller species are more suitable for the rock garden, though

Sedum spectabile

London pride

some are ideal for the front of borders. Avoid *S. acre*, a yellow-flowered stonecrop that is highly invasive.

Solidago (golden rod)
Height 75–90 cm (2½–3 ft). Individual tall, stout stems carry long dark green leaves and spikes of frothy golden yellow flowers during late summer. This is a vigorous plant that will grow in most soils in a sunny or part-shade position. Dwarf varieties are available.

Tradescantia (trinity flower)
Height 45–60 cm (18–24 in). Clumps of narrow foliage are topped with clusters of three-petalled flowers, purple, blue, carmine or white, that appear throughout the summer. Plant in well-drained but moisture-retentive soil in sun or partial shade. Propagate by root division in spring or when flowering is over in the autumn.

Trollius (globe flower)
Height up to 60 cm (2 ft). Members of the buttercup family with globe-shaped flowers that occur in shades of yellow and orange during May and June. They require a moisture-retentive soil and may be grown at the edges of the bog garden. Propagate by root division during the autumn.

Dwarf forms of solidago (golden rod) are neat, bushy and most suitable for small gardens

Tradescantia virginiana

9 Container Gardening

Container gardens are attractive features whatever the site. They may be the sole growing area in a town, perhaps on the balcony of a flat, beside a porch, or on a patio. And they can add an extra dimension to a larger garden, a bright jewel of colour, a focal point. The origins of container gardens lie in the window boxes of the city centres, but today virtually any vessel that will hold water is utilised. The only limits as to what you may use for a container are those of your imagination. Wooden wheel-barrows and beer barrels are now well established as plant containers, but even old rowing boats have been used.

The advantage of creating a miniature garden in a vessel is that it produces a completely self-contained environment that allows you to produce ideal conditions for growing near perfect plants.

The first requirement for any container is that it is pleasing to the eye. While it is possible for trailing plants to cover the sides of the container this may take weeks, during which time it is exposed for all to see. Any container must have drainage holes, to stop the build-up of water, which will soon become sour and destroy the roots of the plants. To stop the compost from escaping through the holes each should be covered with a broken piece of flower pot placed so that the convex side is uppermost.

Containers need an open compost, either one that is loam based, such as a John Innes type, or peat mixed with equal parts of sharp sand or fine gravel. A deep vessel will need a large amount of compost to fill it, which will be expensive, and in most instances unnecessary as few of the plants grown in containers are deep rooted. Overcome the problem either by fitting a false bottom or half-filling the container with large pebbles.

Watering

Thoroughly soak the compost before planting – in spite of the relatively small surface area containers tend to dry out very much quicker than flower beds. When wet, soil-based composts acquire a black coloration and as soon as this stage is reached throughout the medium it is sufficiently moist for planting.

It can be more difficult to determine when peat contains the correct amount of moisture as it is naturally of a darker colour. When it is moist enough the individual particles cling

MAKING A PLANT CONTAINER FROM A BEER BARREL

Cut the barrel in half and drill 1 cm (½ in) holes in the bottom for drainage. Additional holes may be drilled in the sides to take trailing plants

Select a site in an open, sunny position and place the tub on blocks

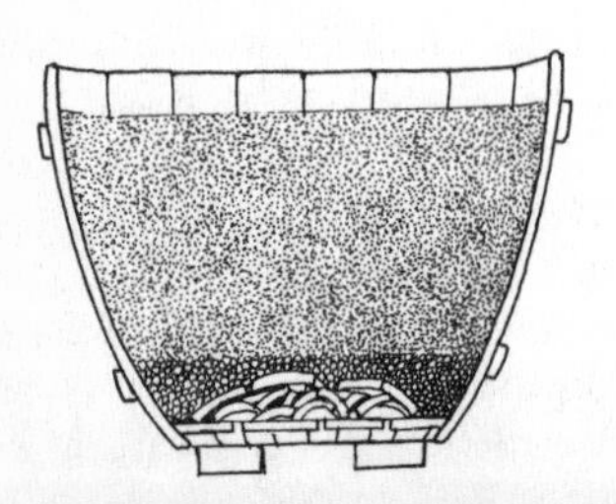

Cover the drainage holes with broken crocks presenting a concave surface to the holes. Then cover the bottom with a layer of pea gravel and finally fill the container with an open compost

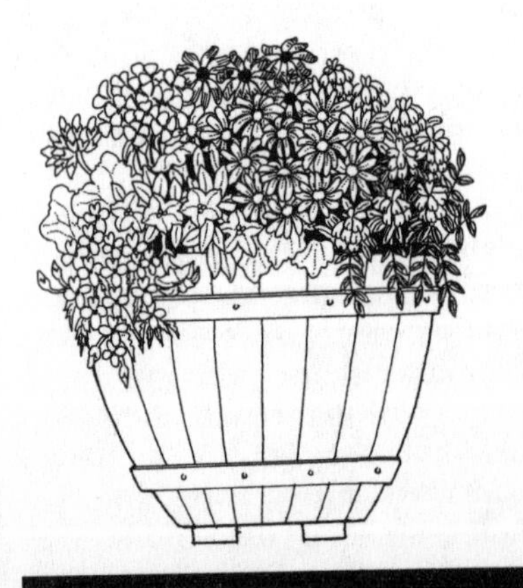

A planted barrel

together, so take a handful and squeeze it in your hand to see if it will form a stable sausage-shaped structure. If it has insufficient moisture it will fall apart, but if there is too much you will see water ousing out. You will soon learn whether the soil requires watering or not simply by inspecting it.

Once your containers are established inspect them every day, even after a shower of rain. While rain showers may be sufficient to sustain the rest of the garden, they are unlikely to have very much effect upon a container. This is partly because the foliage will deflect the water away from the soil. Also water cannot travel through the compost as it does in the ground where, by diffusion, it tends to distribute itself evenly and iron out localised shortages.

Planting

The range of flowers that you can grow in containers is almost as wide as the choice of vessel themselves. But remember, you will require shallow rooted plants and subjects that have very bright foliage or flowers. For summer container displays you will achieve the best results by employing the same plants used for bedding displays together with dramatic central features such as fuchsias and geraniums. Adorn the edges with trailing lobelia and ivy geraniums (these are now available in dramatic colours). Also try to include some foliage plants, such as *Cineraria maritima,* which has silver leaves.

Providing your planted up containers are small enough to handle they can be brought on early in the greenhouse so that when they are finally sited in position they will be just coming into full glory. To achieve a display that is up and running as soon as the last frosts are past, raise your bedding plants at the earliest listed dates (see p. 92). And if you do not have a heated greenhouse you will need to take cuttings of such plants as geraniums and fuchsias in October and overwinter them in a frost-free area. They must be brought into warmth during February to produce the early growth necessary to ensure that they are in full bloom by mid-May.

If you do not intend using the containers during the winter months, cuttings of the main central features such as fuchsias and ivy-leafed geraniums may be planted straight in the container the previous autumn as soon as the current year's display is over. Remember, the seedlings and the rooted cuttings must be hardened off by placing the container out of doors during the daytime and bringing them inside at night for about a week.

Like bedding displays, containers can be changed during October and planted with winter and spring flowering plants. Pansies make a particularly bright show during the early months, along with tulips, daffodils and polyanthus.

For a more stunning display, double bank narcissi and daffodils. Place the first row of bulbs 15 cm (6 in) deep and then place the bulbs of the second layer so that they sit between the necks of the lower group. Shoots from the lower layer will find their way between the bulbs above, and in spite of the difference in the depths of the bulbs the flower buds will all tend to reach the same height, bursting into bloom together.

For your containers, choose spring-flowering bulbs that finish blooming by mid-April, so that you will have sufficient time to replace them with the main summer displays. Bulbs in containers should be treated the same way as those grown in beds and may be transplanted to nursery beds to recuperate for the next year. They will not be exhausted like bulbs that have been forced indoors.

Hanging baskets

These can be hung from porches, walls or any other raised location capable of taking a supporting bracket. The old-fashioned wire baskets are the best.

Line the basket with sphagnum moss, obtainable from florists or garden centres. Pack the moss in carefully, leaving no gaps in the lining.

Place a piece of polythene in the bottom to help retain moisture. Then fill the basket with soil-less compost until it is two-thirds full. Rest it on top of a bucket filled with water to thoroughly soak.

Plant either one tall item, such as a zonal pelagonium or a

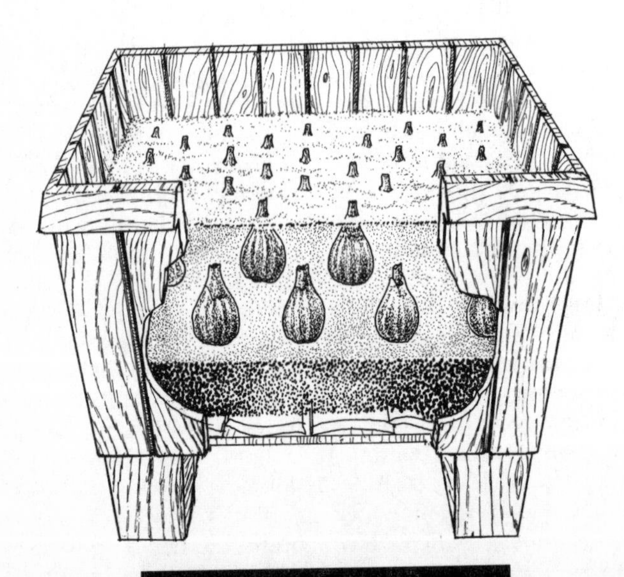

Double-banking daffodils in a container

FILLING A HANGING BASKET

Line the basket with sphagnum moss. Place a piece of polythene in the bottom to help retain moisture

Two-thirds fill the basket with compost and rest it on a bucket of water. Plant the tallest subjects in the centre, shorter ones towards the outside and trailers at the edge. Top up with compost

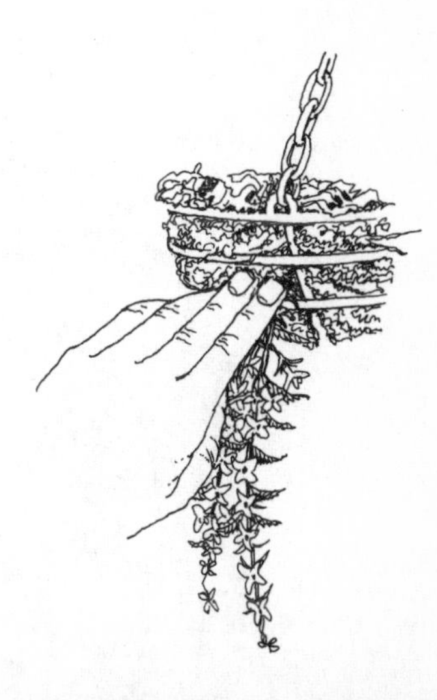

Hang the basket up and push some trailing lobelia through the moss into the compost

fuchsia, in the centre and surround it with three or four medium-sized plants, such as petunias or busy Lizzies. Around the edges place trailing lobelias or ivy-leafed geraniums.

Further trailing plants should be pushed through the moss into the compost from the outside.

Water will be lost from all surfaces of a hanging basket and as a consequence will tend to dry out quicker than any other type of container. Baskets should be inspected and watered at least once daily.

Maintenance

The same principles apply to container plants as to bedding displays. All flowers must be regularly dead-headed. In addition, foliage plants should be periodically stimulated by pruning with a pair of scissors. Give all container plants a foliar feed once a week.

The final result should be a complete ball of colour

10 Shrubs

One of the great advantages of shrubs in the garden is that the majority of them will live for many years and do not require constant regeneration. One important difference between shrubs and herbaceous perennials is that when the latter die back during the winter only the roots stay alive while deciduous shrubs, which also lose their leaves of course, are still alive above ground level. Should you cut any part of a deciduous shrub during the dormant season, the middle of the stem will be green. If it is not then that part at least will be dead. Tender subjects such as certain types of fuchsia are killed by the frost. Where there is dead material then it must be cut back to live tissue as it will never be regenerated.

Ornamental deciduous shrubs should be planted in the dormant season, between November and March, before the buds emerge. Evergreens have a slightly longer planting period, from October until April – still the time of the year when the plant's metabolism is at its lowest. Do not plant when the soil is either frosted or very wet. Unlike fruit trees, ornamental shrubs should generally not be pruned in the year that they were planted. It is important to know the final size a shrub will reach. Indications of size is given against each genus detailed below, but you must remember that within any genus there are usually several species and varieties so the size quoted is no more than a rough guide for planning purposes. Before purchasing a shrub always check with the nurseryman what its eventual size will be.

Because of their size most shrubs will be sited at the back of the border and sufficiently large gaps should be left between them to allow for eventual spread. In the early years the spaces may be filled with annuals and perennials.

Generally, shrubs will keep the areas beneath them weed free. Give an annual mulch with compost during the spring. With frost-tender subjects delay until the autumn (the extra material will act as lagging and protect the roots).

Some popular shrubs

Abelia grandiflora

Height 2 m (6 ft). Grown for its pink trumpet-like flowers borne during the summer. It is a semi-evergreen requiring a sheltered position. There is no need to prune it apart from cutting out dead wood in April. It thrives best in full sun.

Arundinaria japonica (bamboo) – see Pseudosasa japonica

Berberis

A large group of hardy shrubs. Of the many species in cultivation one of the most popular is *B. darwinii* which grows to 2 m (6 ft). It has shiny dark green foliage like small holly leaves which it carries all of the year. The deep yellow flowers appear from mid-to-late spring. These are followed by small oval blue berries with an attractive bloom. The bush can be trained into a dense hedge. Some of the other berberis species have bright red berries and the deciduous varieties have particularly attractive red foliage during mid-autumn. Routine pruning is not necessary. Propagate by hardwood cuttings taken during September.

Buddleia (butterfly bush)

Height 2.5 m (8 ft). By far the most common is *Buddleia davidii.* Its cone-like purple flowerheads secrete large amounts of nectar during August and into September, attracting bees and butterflies such as peacocks, red admirals and tortoiseshells, which are on the wing at this time of the year. Particularly attractive is the very dark purple variety 'Black Knight'. Lilac, burgundy red and white forms are also available. *B. globosa,* which flowers earlier in the year, is covered in spherical clusters of scented orange-yellow flowers.

Buddleias are easily propagated from semi-ripe wood cuttings taken with a heel in July. *B. davidii* flowers on wood produced in the same season. So to maintain a compact structure and retain their vigour, during November the current year's growth should be cut back to the nearest bud beyond the old wood. *B. globosa* carries it flowers on wood produced the previous season. The growths should be slightly trimmed back after the flowers are dead. Any major reductions in size, which are not usually necessary, are also conducted at this time.

Buxus (box)

The common box (*B. sempervirens*) will grow to 2 m (6 ft), but owing to its ability to withstand constant trimming it is usually cultivated as a hedge or a specimen in a tub. It has dense evergreen leaves and the flowers, which appear early in the spring, may not be noticed. For hedging, take hardwood cuttings during September, plant in a nursery bed and move to their permanent positions the following autumn.

Calluna (common heather, ling)

Height 23–30 cm (9–12 in). From the one species, *Calluna vulgaris,* numerous varieties have been bred. Flowering in late summer, it occurs in shades of pink, mauve and violet. Equally important from a design standpoint are the various coloured foliage forms providing low-level ground cover throughout the year and interest during the barren winter months. Callunas must have a well-drained acid soil – they die if any lime is present. They are easily propagated from cuttings taken during September. In early spring, clip back dead flowers. Prune straggly shoots.

Camellia

One of the most popular of all evergreen shrubs. There are several species, but most of the numerous varieties are bred from *C. japonica.* They will reach 2 m (6 ft) in 20 years and acquire a spread of 2.5 m (8 ft). There are singles, semi-doubles and full doubles in white and various shades of pink and red, some with a second colour. Siting of this shrub is very important. It needs a sheltered position where it does not get the sun until late in the morning or the early afternoon, by which time any frosted flowers will have had the chance to thaw out slowly. Camellias should not be planted in the shade. They require a totally lime-free soil and should be mulched with peat or compost (not manure which is too high in nitrogen) every spring. The majority of camellias will flower during their first season. While they are still small they may be grown in tubs and either stood out of doors on the patio or in the cold greenhouse. Pruning is not essential. The flowers are produced on buds that start forming soon after one year's flowers have died. Where it is necessary to restrict the growth this should be done immediately the current season's

Camellia 'Donation'

blooms are over. Propagate by layering.

Cassiope

A type of heather with varieties ranging from 10 to 30 cm (4–12 in), it requires an acid soil and is similar in appearance and cultural requirements to the better known genera *Calluna* and *Erica*.

Ceanothus

Height 2.5 m (8 ft). The most commonly grown form is *C. thyrsiflorus,* an evergreen, free-growing bush with small dark green leaves. During May the shrub appears to be covered with tiny mid-blue balls, giving an overall cloud effect from a distance. Some species dislike soil with a high lime content. Once planted ceanothus requires little attention. Propagate by hardwood cuttings taken in September.

Chaenomeles (Japanese quince, japonica)

Height 1–2 m (3–6 ft). The popularity of this shrub is reflected in the number of popular names, such as 'false quince'. It produces red, pink or white flowers several times a year, including during mild winters when it also carries its yellow quince-type fruits (these may be harvested and made into jelly). No pruning is required where it is grown as a free-standing shrub, but it can be trained against walls and to produce a 'fence'.

Choisya (Mexican orange)

Height 2 m (6 ft). An evergreen grown mainly for the white perfumed flowers produced during the spring. In cold districts it should be planted against a south wall as the leaves are liable to frost damage. A sunny position is best, but partial shade is tolerated. Limit pruning to removing any dead or damaged material.

Cistus (rock rose)

Height 1 m (3 ft). An evergreen shrub which produces large open flowers in white, pink or red with a dense yellow centre sometime between March and July according to species. Some have coloured markings on the petals. Grow in a well-drained soil in a sunny location. Do not prune. Propagate by means of semi-hardwood cuttings taken during July.

Clematis

A climbing shrub which will grow several metres up the available supports. It is very useful for disguising old tree trunks. Different types of clematis are in bloom from May until October. They occur in single and double forms, in a variety of floral shapes, and may be obtained in white, yellow, pink, red, purple and blue. They are followed by very attractive seed-heads, useful in floral decoration.

Clematis prefers an open position with the base of the plant protected from the direct rays of the sun, which can be achieved by underplanting with suitable shrubs. The roots must be kept well watered although they should not be permanently wet.

SOME CLIMBING SHRUBS

Clematis 'Jackmanii Superba'

Clematis tangutica

Passion flower *(Passiflora caerulea)*

Honeysuckle
(Lonicera peryclimenum)

Clematis species that bloom during the spring, e.g. *C. montana*, should be cut back lightly as soon as they have finished flowering simply remove the shoots that carried blooms. The types that bloom during and after August must be cut back hard in February to strong new buds. In the case of mid-season varieties (those blooming between June and August), you must determine whether they flower on the current season's shoots. If so, prune hard back in February. But if the flower buds develop from the previous year's growth, as soon as blooming is over, prune back to a few inches short of that year's growth.

Propagation is by means of internodal cuttings taken during July.

Cornus (dogwood)

C. alba is principally grown for its bright red twigs which dominate from leaf fall until immediately prior to the reappearance of the leaves, providing important colour in the winter garden. It should be situated in a position where it receives direct sunlight to reflect the maximum intensity of colour. The variety 'Sibirica' has the brightest stems. Their height is usually restricted to about 1 m (3 ft) by coppicing. Cut them back to just a few inches above ground level during April. This allows a full, fresh, vigorous season's growth to develop the stem for the following winter. Plant in moist soil in sun or partial shade. Some of the species grown for their flowers, e.g. *C. kousa,* dislike chalky soil.

Cotoneaster

A very large group of evergreen and deciduous shrubs. Some are ground-hugging while others can reach to 3 m (10 ft). They have generally inconspicuous flowers which attract bees in very large numbers so that on sunny days the bush seems to hum. The flowers are followed by bright berries, red, orange or yellow. Birds feed on the berries during winter, making this an important addition to the wildlife garden. The most commonly grown form is *C. horizontalis,* which can be ground-hugging or can ramble over banks and walls. It has very colourful flame-red leaves during the autumn. Because it is so easily propagated by seed, in parts of the country it is beginning to naturalise.

Cytisus (broom)

Height varies from species growing less than 50 cm (18 in) tall to the Moroccan broom, *C. battandieri,* which reaches 4.5 m (15 ft). Our native broom, which grows to over 2 m (6 ft), has many garden varieties. It consists of long whiplike branches supporting leaves for only a few months. The pealike flowers, which occur during mid-spring, come in shades of red and yellow, and also white.

Prune when it is necessary to reduce the size by cutting back immediately flowering is over. Take care, however, not to cut into the old wood.

Plant brooms in full sun in well drained soil (not too rich). Most species are tolerant of lime but live longer on acid soils.

Brooms may be propagated by hardwood cuttings taken during September.

Daphne mezereum

Height up to 1½ m (5 ft). This is the best known of the daphnes, valuable for its early flowers (February to April). Highly scented and purple in colour, they are borne in thick clusters on the previous year's stems. The shrub is deciduous and tolerant of a wide range of soils providing that they are well drained. No pruning is required except removal of straggly shoots. Propagate from semi-ripewood cuttings in July.

Elaeagnus pungens 'Maculata'

Height to 3 m (12 ft), but usually restricted by pruning. This is the most popular member of the genus, having leaves attractively splashed with bright yellow. It is commonly grown for hedging. As with most variegated forms, solid green sports will tend to keep occurring. Immediately these are seen they must be cut out, for if they are allowed to remain they will ultimately take over the shrub. When it is allowed to develop to full size, insignificant flowers are produced which are followed in the autumn by orange berries. This is a resilient bush that will withstand severe pruning, which should be conducted during the spring. Take hardwood cuttings during September.

Erica (heath, heather)

Height 4 cm–6 m (2 in–20 ft). The species *E. arborea* can reach 6 m (20 ft) in favourable localities, and makes a fine specimen plant. For ground cover or rockeries, one of the most popular species with many varieties is *E. carnea*, 15–23 cm (6–9 in). The flowers, in bloom from November to April, are pink, purple or white and the foliage, though usually green, may be golden or bronze. This, and *E.* x *darlyensis*, a cross between *E. carnea* and *E. mediterranea*, growing to 60 cm (2 ft) and another winter flowerer, are both lime-tolerant. If you possess an alkaline soil do not attempt to grow *E. tetralix* or *E. cinerea* and their varieties, all summer blooming (height to 30 cm, 1 ft). Also lime-hating is *E. ciliaris* (Dorset heath), which grows to 25–35 cm (10–14 in), and *E. vagans* (Cornish heath), height 120 cm (4 ft). These species flower from summer to winter, and varieties come in the same flower and foliage shades as *E. carnea*.

Winter flowering heather varieties can be lightly trimmed with scissors during May. The Dorset heath requires no trimming. All ericas can be propagated from 5–7 cm (2–3 in) cuttings taken with a heel and inserted in compost during July.

Escallonia

Average height 2 m (6 ft). Evergreens with small dark green leaves yielding a profusion of red, pink or white flowers from June until September according to the type. 'Apple Blossom' is probably the most popular of varieties. Escallonias require a light trimming after flowering. Avoid hard pruning, which can kill the bush. It may be clipped to form a compact hedge. Hardwood cuttings for hedges should be taken during September.

Forsythia

Height 2.5 m (8 ft). A brittle deciduous shrub that is among the easiest to grow. It can be trained to form a hedge but lacks strength, tending to snap very easily. During April it is covered with a mass of tubular yellow flowers. There is such a profusion of bloom that it tends to dominate the surroundings for a few days. The flowers are followed by light green leaves. The shrub requires annual pruning to keep it tidy. This should be performed immediately after the flowers have died.

Forsythia is one of the easiest of shrubs to propagate. Take cuttings with or without a heel at any time during the summer.

Fothergilla

Height 2 m (6 ft). A shrub related to witch hazel, with sweetly scented white mop-headed flowers about May. A light, lime-free, humus-rich soil in full sun or partial shade is required. Pruning is not necessary. Propagation is by layering long shoots in September, but they can take two years to root.

Fuchsia

Height depending upon variety up to 3 m (10 ft). Fuchsias can be divided into many groups, but for practical purposes the best classification is one based on hardiness.

F. magellanica, with its varieties, are the hardiest of all the fuchsias and is used extensively as hedging in the south-west of England where it may reach 3 m (10 ft). The flowers of the species are slender, with red sepals and purple petals. Pink varieties are obtainable.

Hardy fuchsias should be cut down to ground level in November, March or April.

F. fulgens is a tender shrub but crossing with the hardy *F. magellanica* has resulted in a range of hybrids that are now an important part of the summer gardening scene. Depending upon the mix of genes, there is a whole gradation in the degrees of tenderness. Because much of the showiness comes from the contribution of *F. fulgens,* as a generalisation the most spectacular varieties tend not to survive unprotected out of doors during the winter. But there are exceptions.

Two magnificent singles with rich red sepals and deep purple petals are 'Empress of Prussia' and 'Doctor Foster'. There is a smaller version, 'Mrs Popple'. All these will withstand the winter. The top growth will be cut back by the frosts, but even in the hardest winters the roots survive and they tend to grow as perennials with not more than one year's growth above ground level. Dead wood should be cut out at the base during April or May. As fuchsias grow quickly and flower on wood produced during the current season this is a perfectly satisfactory method of cultivation. The flowers do not appear until July, later than plants raised in the greenhouse.

Tender fuchsias, providing the greenhouse can be kept frost free, can be saved and grown on, getting larger each year. They can be kept in growth by maintaining a winter temperature of 10°C (50°F), but it is far better to allow them to die back and have a rest period. This is achieved by keeping the temperature above freezing point and maintaining the compost just moist. Bring the plants into a temperature of 12°C (54°F) during early March and take the new shoots as cuttings when they are 10 cm (4 in) tall. Place the shoots in a loam or soil-less compost in 8 cm (3 in) pots initially. Later transfer them to 12 cm (5 in) pots. Left to grow undisturbed, the fuchsias will develop into full-size plants.

The production of bushy plants depends upon continually picking out the leader and main side shoots. Allow two to three pairs of leaves to develop, then nip out the growing head. A growing tip will take six to eight weeks to develop flowers and you may control the date at which the blooming commences by ceasing to pinch out the shoots six weeks prior to the time at which they are required. Where it is intended to save the shrubs through the winter, they should be finally transplanted into a 20 cm (8 in) pot which is then buried in the soil with the rim covered over. In spite of their

TYPES OF FUCHSIA FLOWER

F. megellanica (species)

F. 'Thalia' cluster

Single

Semi-double

Double

appearance such fuchsias are still pot plants and they will be totally dependent upon the soil in the container for the provision of both water and nutrients.

Varieties such as 'Swingtime' with their pendulous growth should be restricted to hanging baskets.

A full 'pyramid' can be obtained by simultaneously allowing a plant to develop height and width. Take a cutting in the normal way and stop it when it has reached 20 cm (8 in) tall. Allow the side shoots to develop and stop each at the two-leaf stage. As new leaders develop pinch them out when they reach 20 cm (8 in) and carry the process on indefinitely until the required size is reached.

Standard fuchsias look spectacular and are very expensive to buy, yet extremely easy to produce. Early in the season take a cutting about 15 cm (6 in) long and place it in a 12.5 cm (5 in) flower pot containing a loam-based compost. Place a stake against the cutting and very carefully tie the cutting to the stake. Then place it in a warm, sunny position and keep well watered. As the leaves begin to grow, side shoots will start to appear at the leaf axils. As soon as the shoots are large enough to handle, pinch them out taking great care not to remove or break any of the leaves. These leaves must be protected at all cost for although they will ultimately die, during the initial training period they alone will be generating the carbohydrates necessary for the fuchsia's development. Continue this process, repotting as necessary until the trunk has reached two thirds of the desired height and then allow all the laterals to develop. A balanced standard consists of two thirds bare trunk with one third canopy. To develop a good head, pinch out the laterals as for a pyramid – after all, a standard is only a pyramid on a pole. Where plants are trained into special forms they must be overwintered in a frost-free greenhouse.

Gaultheria

Some species are less than 30 cm (1 ft), others over 2 m (6 ft). They are in the same family as the heathers, though with much larger flowers, and must be grown in a lime-free soil. Pruning is not necessary. Propagate by semi-ripewood cuttings taken during July.

Genista

Height, according to species, 30 cm (1 ft) to 4 m (12 ft) or more. These shrubs are very similar to broom to which they are related. They are covered with bright yellow flowers, mostly during the summer. Propagate by hardwood cuttings during September.

Hamamelis (witch hazel)

The smaller species grow to about 2.5 m (8 ft), while the larger types can be regarded as small trees. The sweet-smelling flowers consist of mop-like heads of very thin petals in shades of yellow, orange or copper bronze. In the most commonly grown species they occur in January to

March, on leafless branches. Only very light pruning is necessary.

Hebe

Height 30–130 cm (1–4 ft). This is a family of evergreen shrubs, usually with dense cones of small flowers, in white or shades or red, blue and purple. The plant does not require pruning. Some hebes are not very hardy, but they are easily propagated from semi-softwood cuttings taken during July.

Helichrysum splendidum

Height 60 cm (2 ft). A shrub member of the genus *Helichrysum*, which is better known for its everlasting annuals. *H. splendidum* is grown widely for its silver-grey foliage. In spring it carries hemispherical clusters of small yellow flowers. A vigorous grower, it should be cut back to the thick stems just above ground level during March. Propagate by layering.

Hibiscus syriacus

Height 2 m (6 ft). An exotic shrub with dark, shiny leaves and large funnel-shaped flowers, in red, blue or white depending upon variety, produced at the end of the summer and well into the autumn. Slightly tender, it requires full sun and should be planted in a sheltered position. No pruning is necessary. Propagate by means of semi-hardwood cuttings taken in July.

Hydrangea

Height 130–150 cm (4–5 ft). Deciduous shrubs that produce their flowers from buds

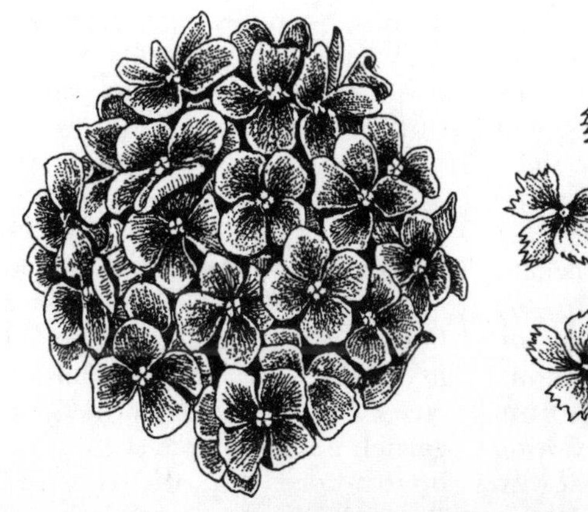

Hydrangeas:
Mop-head (left) and Lacecap

produced in the previous year. As the name implies, they are water-loving subjects and should never be allowed to dry out. They are not suitable for growing in the bog garden, however. Large flowerheads in red or blue appear in late summer. These stay on the bush, changing to green with age and then to a brown colour in which state they will remain throughout the winter. A slightly tender subject, the heads should be allowed to remain on the plant until the following March to afford some protection to the buds.

Because of the need to retain the previous year's growth, only minimal pruning should take place during the pre-growth season. Any wood cut at this stage will produce greenery but will not flower during the current season.

The pH of the soil will affect the flower colour of varieties of *H. macrophylla*. The blue varieties will tend to become reddish when grown in alkaline soil. Pink varieties become purplish in colour when grown in acid soil. To increase the intensity of colour of varieties, give the soil a light dusting with blue aluminium sulphate.

Hydrangeas make excellent pot plants for growing in the greenhouse and bringing indoors when they are in bloom. Take 15 cm (6 in) cuttings from non-flowering growth during August, place in a pot filled with a loam-based compost and keep moist at all times. The cuttings should be grown in a shaded part of the greenhouse.

Hypericum calycinum (rose of Sharon)

Height 30 cm (12 in). This commonly grown plant is on the borderline between perennials and shrubs (a sub-shrub). The five-petalled golden-yellow flowers with conspicuous stamens are borne throughout the summer. They are followed by red berries that later turn black. A vigorous ground-cover plant, it should be cut back almost to ground level during the spring. Propagate by division or softwood cuttings taken in spring.

Kerria (Jew's mallow)

Height 2 m (6 ft). Tall, arching stems carry the bright green leaves and golden-yellow flowers during the spring. The most widely grown is the double form, *K. Japonica* 'Piera' (bachelor's buttons).

The bush should be cut back as soon as flowering is complete. It will tend to shoot from roots that can travel large distances from their origins, and thus becomes invasive unless contained. Propagate by transplanting a small piece of root to which there is a shoot attached.

Laurus (bay laurel, sweet bay)

Height (unrestrained) 3 m (10 ft). Grown for its use as a herb and the decorative effect of its glossy dark green foliage. Need not be pruned in the open garden but tub-grown shrubs can be trimmed into the required shape during the summer.

Lavendula (lavender)

Height 1½–4 ft (45–120 cm)

according to variety. A silver-grey evergreen bush bearing characteristic purple-blue flowers on long thin stems. Old English lavender (*L. angustifolia*, syn. *L. spica)* grows to about 1 m (3 ft). Lower growing, compact varieties of it are 'Hidcote' (deep purple-blue) and 'Munstead' (blue). White and pink varieties are also obtainable.

Lavender responds to hard pruning and should be cut back in September or March. If the plant becomes too straggly it should be replaced. Cuttings can be taken from ripe wood or semi-ripe wood from July onwards. Lavender makes an excellent low level hedge and the clipping necessary to retain the shape constantly causes it to produce fresh dense growth.

Leycesteria

Height 230 cm (7 ft). This deciduous shrub has erect cane-like growths and very complex flowering structures. These consist of white true flowers at the base of which are a series of red bracts that remain to create the illusion of a bloom long after the white structures have been replaced by oval-shaped chocolate-coloured berries. The berries remain on the bush for much of the winter and are enjoyed by birds. During spring cut back the canes that have flowered to ground level. Propagate by taking soft-wood cuttings during June.

Ligustrum (privet)

Height (untrimmed) 3–4 m (10–13 ft). Generally used to form a dense hedge. The species most commonly grown is *L. ovalifolium* which, as the name implies, has oval leaves. The variety 'Aureo-marginatum' is known as golden privet. Privet produces small cones of fragrant white flowers during the summer, which are followed by small black berries.

Clip throughout the summer as required. Cuttings to produce bushes for hedging should be placed in the nursery bed during September. Plant them out in the autumn of the following year.

Lonicera (honeysuckle)

Height several metres, usually only restricted by that of its support. The best known honeysuckles are climbing shrubs with tubular flowers in reds and yellow. They bloom continuously from July until September, and have one of the finest of all garden fragrances – particularly enjoyable on a late summer's evening. They will tolerate most soils but must be grown against a support. Prune as necessary to restrict their size, thinning out old wood. Propagate by pinning a branch to the soil where it will readily form roots.

There are shrubby species too. *L. nitida*, which has very small evergreen leaves and grows to just over a metre high, can be used for making a dense hedge. Clip it when necessary in the summer. Cuttings for hedge-making should be taken in September. Grow them on in the nursery bed to the following October when they may be planted out into their final positions.

Mahonia

Height (3–10 ft) according to species. Has stalks carrying several small bell-shaped light yellow flowers originating from the crowns of leaves which make up the growing part of the plant *M. bealei* and *M. japonica* are particularly useful shrubs as they bloom during the middle of winter, *M. aquifolium* (Oregon grape) blooms a little later, in March and April. Mahonias have tough, leathery dark green leaves similar to those of holly. They prefer a rich loamy soil and should not be allowed to dry out during the summer. Pruning is unnecessary. Propagate by placing hardwood cuttings in the nursery bed during late summer.

Philadelphus (mock orange)

Average height 2 m (6 ft). The white flowers of this deciduous shrub, open in June or July, have a scent reminiscent of orange blossom. The plant will grow on any garden soil.

To restrict the size, pruning should be undertaken immediately the flowers die. Thin out the old stalks to prevent overcrowding. Retain the young shoots, which will flower next year. Propagate from cuttings taken throughout the summer.

Pieris

Height 2–4 m (6–12 ft), depending on species. Related to the heathers, it requires a lime-free soil. Clusters of small heather-like flowers appear during the spring. Most striking, however, is the bright red new foliage, making it one of the most colourful bushes in spring. The leaves gradually turn to a light green shade. One of the best is 'Forest Flame'.

Pieris is slow-growing and does not require pruning apart from removal of straggly growth.

Potentilla

(For details of the herbaceous forms see p. 124.)

Height up to 180 cm (5 ft). A deciduous shrub carrying plentiful open-cupped rose-like flowers throughout the summer in white, yellow and orange. This is a very useful mid-border plant due to the length of the flowering season. Plant in full sun or partial shade. Any well-drained soil is suitable. No pruning is necessary. Propagate by semi-hardwood cuttings during July or hardwood cuttings taken in September.

Pseudosasa japonica, syn. Arundinaria japonica (bamboo)

Height 3 m (10 ft). Provides thick cover and can take over if left undisturbed. It very rarely flowers, although claims of only once in a hundred years are exaggerated. A bamboo crop can be periodically harvested for use around the garden at which time the plant should be generally tidied up. The plant does not require mulching.

Pyracantha (firethorn)

Height up to 5 m (17 ft). Ideal for training against the side of a wall. Large white clusters of flowers in June are followed by profuse red, orange or yellow berries. Birds are very fond of them – if uneaten they will

Rhododendron hybrid 'Damaris'

Deciduous azalea 'Berryrose'

remain on the bushes for much of the winter.

Growth is vigorous. Remove surplus shoots in the spring. After too drastic trimming they tend not to bloom for a year.

Rhododendrons

This family includes the azaleas, which were once regarded as a separate genus. Dwarf azaleas and rhododendrons proper may be as short as 30 cm (12 in). The tallest azaleas can reach 3 m (10 ft), but there are rhododendrons that will attain 18 m (60 ft) if left unpruned. The flowers, which occur mainly in the spring and early summer, are white, pink, cream, yellow, red or purple. Most true rhododendrons are evergreen with some species having attractive new foliage that has a bronze red tinge, but some azaleas are deciduous. The natural habitat of the larger species is woodland and they grow well in partial, but not total, shade.

Many species, particularly the smaller ones, thrive in full sun provided the roots do not dry out. They require a permanently damp soil and will not tolerate lime.

They also benefit from large quantities of leaf mould – the most practical way of providing this is to use it as a mulch each spring. Wood bark is also a very useful mulch.

Many of the hybrid rhododendrons are grafted onto a more vigorous rootstock. A constant check should be maintained to ensure that the rootstock does not take over from the graft. Large rhododendrons can be cut back immediately after flowering to restrict their size.

The strong-growing purple shrub *R. ponticum*, which was introduced into this country during the eighteenth century, has adapted so well that it has now naturalised and it would be taking over much of our lime-free areas if not checked.

Azaleas are grown under the same conditions as true rhododendrons. The more tender evergreen azaleas should not be placed in any position where they are liable to receive the rays of the early morning sun, which would cause the petals to brown after a frost.

The larger species of rhododendron and azaleas can be propagated by layering, the smaller ones by cuttings.

Rhus typhina (stag's-horn sumach)

Height and spread to 3 m (10 ft) or more. On the border between a tree and a shrub, this member of the genus *Rhus* is widely grown for the very large pinnate leaves that turn a spectacular orange-red during the autumn. In addition, the minute flowers on female plants, clustered densely in cones, give rise to striking deep red fruits.

This shrub is undemanding in its soil requirements, prospering on thin sandy soils. There is a belief that the poorer the soil the better it performs. It does not require pruning, but it can be cut close to the ground in early spring to obtain abundant foliage (but no flowers).

Ribes sanguineum
(flowering currant)

Height 2–2.5 m (6–8 ft). Although this species is a member of the same family as the edible currants and gooseberries, its small blue-black fruits should not be eaten. During spring, the rose-red flowers are particularly attractive to bumble bees. The plant will grow in sun or partial shade, and in any reasonable garden soil.

As with blackcurrants, the next year's flowers are borne on new wood and the old wood should be cut out as soon as flowering is over. Propagate by taking hardwood cuttings and planting in a nursery bed in September.

Roses

There can hardly be a garden in the country that does not contain at least one member of the rose family. Several wild species of the rose are grown. These are all single flowered, though double forms, sports and natural crosses occur in nature – the group readily hybridises. What man has done is to bring together roses from all the parts of the world where they occur and, initially by trial and error and more recently using a knowledge of genetics, sought to create improved forms. The early hybrids of species are referred to as 'Old Roses'. They include, among others, the Damasks (derived from *Rosa damascena*), the Bourbons (from *R.* x *odorata* and *R. damascena*), Gallicas (from *R. gallica*), Portland Roses (Damask-type, with *R. chinensis*) and Moss Roses (derived from sports of *R. centifolia* 'Muscosa' and their hybrids). Fortunately these Old Roses are once again being grown and they are worthy of a place in any garden.

A disadvantage of Old Roses, however, is that they only flower for a very short period. Early in the last century the Bourbons and Portlands were crossed with the China rose (*R. chinensis*) to produce Hybrid Perpetuals, roses that would go on producing blooms throughout the summer. Further crosses followed, this time with the tea rose to yield the Hybrid Tea Roses which during this century became increasingly popular. In one sense HTRs have everything – form, large size, scent, fine colour, and they flower from late May with the last roses hanging on stubbornly until Christmas and even beyond. But this has not come without a price and that is the loss of the inborn resistance to disease.

The most debilitating rose disease is black spot. This starts as a small spot of fungal infection, which spreads throughout the leaf until it turns yellow and falls. Soon the whole bush is denuded and is useless for producing blooms and could ultimately die. Black spot is the only minus about clean air. The fungus is destroyed by sulphur compounds in the atmosphere and since these emissions have been strictly controlled the problem has become worse.

Mildew is another fungal infection of roses. The grey powder coats the leaves, sometimes distorting them. Both

SOME POPULAR ROSES

'Fantin Latour' (Bourbon)

'Lili Marlene' (Floribunda)

'Chicago Peace' (Hybrid Tea)

'Albertine' (Rambler)

problems can be controlled by spraying with fungicide. Susceptibility to fungal disease varies with variety.

Rose classification is as follows:

Species (wild forms) together with their sports.
Old Roses (see above).
Hybrid Tea Roses, in which the stalks carry only one flower.
Floribundas, in which there are several blooms at the head of one stem (crossing with HTRs has resulted in the modern large flowered Floribunda varieties).
Shrub Roses, hybrids between species and Old Roses that are suitable for hedging or as specimen shrubs.
Polyantha Roses, which are closely related to the original multi-bloomed roses though they are far smaller bushes in which everything is on a reduced scale resulting in small clusters of flowers.
Miniature Roses, a group of mainly multi-stemmed roses originating from crosses involving the polyantha roses.
Climbers, vigorous strong-stemmed varieties that can be trained against arches, up walls and over doors (again, crosses with HTRs have produced large climbers).
Ramblers, old varieties with lax stems incapable of supporting themselves that can be trained over fences, etc. and also allowed to cascade over banks and low walls.

Roses require an open, well-drained site although climbers can spend part of the day in the shade (but even these should not be planted against north-facing walls). The best soil is a loam that is rich in humus and it should be constantly maintained by mulching each spring with compost or well rotted manure. Feed regularly with a proprietory rose fertiliser. The best method of obtaining roses is to purchase them bare-rooted and unwrapped from November until March. Failing this, bare-rooted plants are available wrapped in plastic bags from department stores and some garden centres. The holes in the bag do not prevent the temperature rising and if the bush is stored for too long a period it will develop long, thin yellow growths. Do not buy such plants. Seek out instead the ones with small pink buds, a sure sign that they have only been out of the ground for a short period of time.

Container-grown roses for planting at any time of the year are available. While they are convenient, they offer no advantages as roses really need planting during the colder months if worthwhile flowers are to be produced in the following season.

Virtually all the more popular bush roses are grafted or budded and should be planted with the graft just below the soil. If it is not visible then plant with little more than the roots themselves buried. Providing there is sufficient anchorage, you may assume that the bushes have been planted deep enough. Roses that form large bushes, including the species types, should be set 120 cm (4 ft) apart.

HTRs must be planted no closer together than 60 cm (2 ft). Standard roses are grafted just below the canopy and should be planted deeper to provide the necessary extra support. They should be supported by a stake on the windward side.

Modern roses require annual pruning (see pp. 67–70).

Rosemary

See p. 239.

Santolina chamaecyparissus (cotton lavender)

Height 60 cm (2 ft). Grown for its silver-grey foliage and suited to the middle or front of beds. It has button-like yellow flowers in July.

In the spring the plant should be cut back very hard to allow the regeneration of fresh vigorous growth. Propagate by means of semi-ripewood cuttings taken during July.

Skimmia

Average height 120–200 cm (4–5 ft). Evergreens with attractive oval leaves and creamy white flowerheads in the spring. *S. japonica* is the most commonly grown. Conspicuous light red berries follow the flowers on female plants in late summer. You must grow a male plant as well to get berries. 'Foremanii' is a female variety, 'Rubella' and 'Fragrans' males. This species is tolerant of most soils but prefers a well drained sunny position without lime. *S. reevesiana* needs lime-free soil but has the advantage of being bisexual. Skimmias do not require pruning.

Spartium (Spanish broom)

Height 2–2.5 m (6–8 ft). Closely resembles the broom *Cytisus* to which it is related, with yellow pea flowers. It has a long flowering season, commencing in the spring and finishing during the autumn. It needs a light, well-drained soil and full sun.

Prune lightly during November to restrict size and stimulate new growth. Propagate by means of hardwood cuttings taken during September.

Symphoricarpos alba (snowberry)

Height 1.5–2 m (5–6 ft). Evergreen shrubs grown for their large white berries which occur during late summer and autumn. They are very hardy, tolerant of virtually all conditions and soils and grow happily close to fences. They have oval leaves and pink flowers, which appear during midsummer. (*S. orbiculatus*, coral berry, is similar but with pink or purple berries.) There is no need to prune. Propagation is from hardwood cuttings taken during September.

Syringa (lilac)

Height 2–4 m (6–12 ft). This popular shrub needs little introduction. Its beautiful scented blossoms, carried during May, come in white as well as all shades of lilac and mauve, and even pink is known. A sunny site is best. Lilacs will grow in any reasonable soil, including those containing chalk.

Most lilacs are grafted and suckers emerge each year from the vigorous growing rootstocks.

Yucca filamentosa

These will be no use for propagation purposes and should be cut out each March. Failure to do so may result in strong plants producing a few very small flowers taking over from the desired form. Pruning tends to reduce flowering, and should be restricted to just a few branches each year, concentrating on those branches which are weak growing, too large, or mishapen.

Viburnum tinus (laurustinus)

Height 2–3 m (6–10 ft). There are many species of *Viburnum*, and *V. tinus* is one of the most commonly grown. It is an evergreen with flat heads of small white flowers carried throughout the winter.

In April, remove old and damaged wood. Propagate from hardwood cuttings taken during September.

Vinca (periwinkle)

Height 30–45 cm (12–18 in). A sub-shrub. Long thin stems carry dark green leaves and blue flowers throughout the spring. A form with variegated leaves is obtainable. Propagate by pinning down one of the stems, which will easily root. When established, sever from the parent and transplant.

Weigela

Height about 2 m (6 ft). A deciduous shrub whose attractive pink tubular flowers appear during May and June. It prefers an open, well-drained but moisture-retentive soil and thrives in sun or partial shade.

Prune to restrict size immediately after flowering. Avoid cutting back the whole of the bush during one year. Propagate by semi-ripewood cuttings taken during July.

Yucca

Height 1–2 m (3–6 ft). A hardy plant with a basal rosette of stiff, narrow straplike leaves. During the summer a tall stem or trunk is produced which carries many creamy-white bell-shaped flowers. The plant is ideal as the central feature in a bed or lawn. Plant in any well-drained soil – even a poor sandy one is suitable – in a sunny position. Do not prune. The method of propagation is novel. Pieces of stem sealed with wax may be purchased through the post and at exhibitions. After sawing or scraping away the ends to expose the live tissue, the miniature logs are inserted in compost where, left in a warm environment, they will root. Yucca is currently popular as a pot plant.

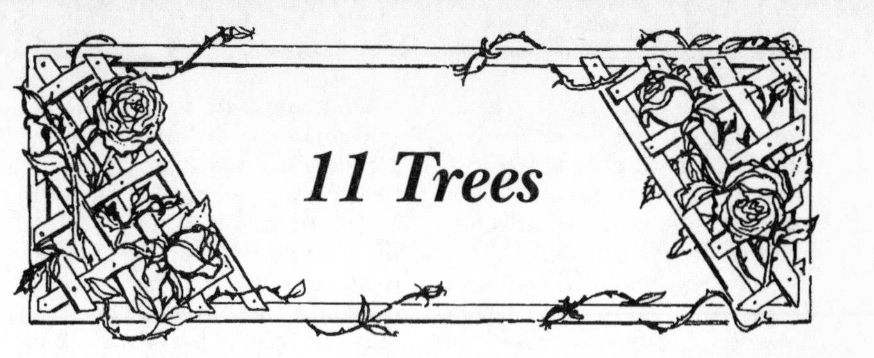

11 Trees

Botanically there is very little difference between trees and shrubs. Both have woody growths, the result of a single season's development adding to those of previous years. As with the distinction between shrubs and perennials, the dividing line is extremely blurred. One commonly held opinion is that trees are tall and shrubs are relatively low-growing. But today the term 'tree' is frequently used to describe those plants which have a solitary main growth with a well defined shape and with little or no tendency to spread. This allows for the inclusion of some species that are only a few inches in height.

If space allows every garden should include at least one tree, to give a sensation of mass. Without them a garden will seem a flat, two-dimensional structure. Few people would disagree that we need to plant more trees, both for their environmental effect and their individual and collective beauty.

Before buying any trees there are several factors to be taken into consideration. A cedar is an elegant tree grown in open parkland but is totally out of keeping in an urban situation. Moreover, the roots of large trees can cause damage to buildings, especially those on clay soils which tend to dry out during periods of prolonged drought. Also, placed in front of a window a large tree increasingly blocks out the light.

This does not mean that you should not plant a tree near to a house, but be very careful in the positioning and your selection of species. Tall trees can always be sited at the furthest distance from the house. Fairly short species can be planted relatively close to the building, as can others which are very slow growing. With all other plants it is an easy matter to replace them if after a year or two you wish to reconsider your initial choice. This is by no means easy with trees, which by their very nature have an air of eternity about them. It is often said that we plant trees not for ourselves but for future generations. This should be borne in mind when planning their purchase and positioning.

One of the fundamental decisions is whether to choose deciduous or evergreen. Should you opt for a deciduous tree, you must be prepared to cope with the falling leaves during the autumn. Such a tree must not be sited near to a pond as the leaves may poison the water. On the plus side, however, you may naturalise bulbs around their base and also place there any other spring flowers that complete their flowering before the tree excludes the light.

As a generalisation, deciduous trees have more spectacular flowers. Evergreens have the advantage that they do not lose all of their leaves at once and become bare. They maintain interest throughout the year but those with a broad canopy effectively sterilise the ground beneath for the whole 12 months.

Confusion can exist about the terms evergreens and conifers. Evergreens, as the word implies, remain green throughout the year and do not lose all of their leaves in the autumn. Conifers are cone-bearing trees and most, but not all, are evergreens.

Where space inhibits the growing of as many trees as you would like, you can always establish a bed of dwarf conifers. For example, there is the slow-growing, ground-hugging *Juniperus horizontalis*, reaching a height of 60 cm (2 ft) and spread of about 180 cm (6 ft) after several years. The columnar *J. communis* 'Compressa' is perfect for a rock garden, reaching little more than 45 cm ($1\frac{1}{2}$ ft) in 10 years. There are many other conifers, with pleasing shapes, brightly coloured shoots in winter or attractive cones. Usually they are grafted onto dwarfing rootstocks. Before buying a conifer at a garden centre, if you are not sure about its eventual size make enquiries first.

Planting trees

Container-grown trees can be planted any time of the year. Before planting, carefully loosen and unwind the exposed outer roots of the root ball, to prevent them growing in circles and crowding each other. The tree must be planted at the same level it grew in the pot.

Bare-rooted trees may be purchased from November through to March. It is better to plant the tree either near to the beginning or the end of this period when the ground is less likely to become frozen or waterlogged. Providing neither of these conditions prevail, dig a hole deep enough for the tree's taproot and about twice the size of the root-ball, place two handfuls of bonemeal into the gap and spread the roots out evenly.

Place a strong stake on the windward side of the tree, then fix the stake to its side by means of an adjustable tie. Fill in the hole, firming down the soil with your feet to complete the process. At this stage restrict the pruning of ornamental trees to the removal of weak branches and any growing in towards the centre of the tree or across other stronger growths.

Moving trees

When moving house there is usually a desire to take your favourite plants with you and trees are no exception. Trees up to 3.5 m (10 ft) can be moved and transplanted. The root-ball that you excavate must be sufficiently large for there to be enough of the fine hairlike roots

PLANTING A BARE-ROOTED TREE

Fork over the planting hole, adding one or two handfuls of bonemeal

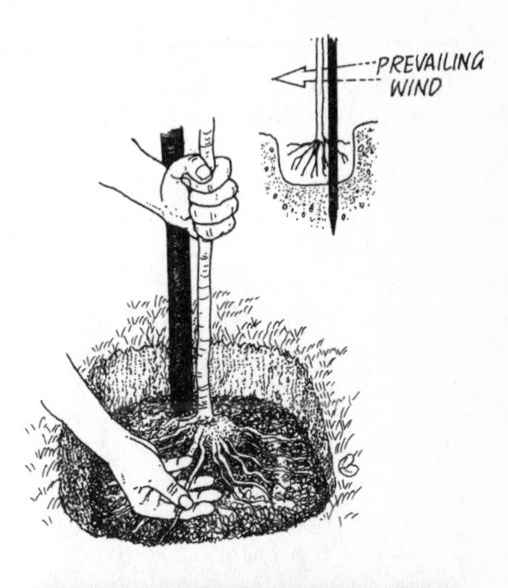

Place the stake so that it will be on the windward side of the tree. Spread the tree roots evenly around the hole

Scoop the soil around and between the roots, firming it well to make sure there are no air pockets

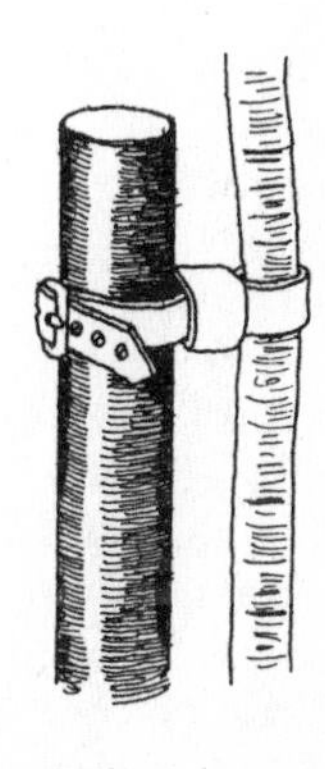

Fasten the tree to the stake using an adjustable tree tie

remaining underground to take up the tree's water and nutrient requirements. The larger the tree, the larger the root-ball must be. Ideally you should only attempt to move a tree during the dormant days of winter.

Pruning

Much of the beauty of a tree lies in its natural shape which often contains its own symmetry. Unlike fruit trees it is certainly not necessary or desirable to prune ornamental trees every year as a matter of routine. Some shaping can be performed if considered desirable. Usually all that is necessary is to prune deciduous trees in March, removing any branches that are weak, damaged, inward-growing or suffering from disease. The same process is conducted on evergreen trees during April.

Guide to popular ornamental trees

In most genera there are several different species and varieties. The descriptions below are of some of the most commonly grown.

Abies (silver fir)

A genus of evergreen conifers, some very tall, and many with brightly coloured cones standing above the foliage. They make excellent specimen trees when grown in lawns. Place in a sunny position. Most do not grow on chalky soils. *A. koreana*, which grows only to 10 m (33 ft), has dark green upper leaves, silvery white beneath, and blue cones. The golden leaved variety of it, 'Aurea', is very slow-growing.

Acer (maples)

A group ranging from large trees to small, shrubby kinds. They are deciduous with characteristic deeply lobed leaves whose autumn colour can be spectacular. The Japanese maple (*A. palmatum*), one of the smallest species, has almost fern-like leaves. It will grow well on most soils so long as they are moisture-retentive with good drainage, with shelter from wind and frost. In design terms, it is ideal with rocks and water.

Arbutus unedo (strawberry tree)

Height up to 4 m (12 ft). Has evergreen foliage and white bell-shaped flowers. The strawberry-like fruits, though edible, are dry and tasteless. Although related to the heathers, this tree can tolerate some lime.

Betula (birch)

Height range from dwarf species to trees of 25 m (80 ft). The silver birch (*B. pendula*), a deciduous native tree of heathland soils, is prized for its graceful form, good autumn colour and silvery white bark. It does not do well on heavy, poorly drained soils. Other good species are available, such as the Chinese red birch (*B. albo-sinensis*), which is less tall and has attractive orange peeling bark.

Cedrus (cedar)

A genus of conifers in which there are only four species. The most familiar cedar, *C. libani* (cedar of Lebanon), has a broad crown and massive horizontal branches. In the British Isles it can grow to 40 m (130 ft). One of the most magnificent of all trees, it is really only suitable for parks or the very largest gardens.

Chamaecyparis (false cypress)

The best known member of this genus is *C. lawsoniana* (Lawson's cypress). It is a conical tree usually growing to 15–20 m (50–65 ft). Very often it is grown to form a screen rather than as a specimen tree. It stands clipping and makes a good hedge. Several cultivars are available.

Cryptomeria japonica (Japanese cedar)

Height 15 m (50 ft). An evergreen conifer which thrives in most soils.

Cupressus

C. macrocarpa, the form most frequently grown, is 30 m (100 ft) tall. A long-lived evergreen conifer, it has an interesting peeling bark.

x *Cupressocyparis leylandii (Leyland cypress)*

Height 15 m (50 ft). A hybrid between *Chamaecyparis nootkatensis* and *Cupressus macrocarpa,* it is columnar in shape and grows extremely rapidly.

Eucalyptus

A large genus of evergreens, some of them small trees, others very tall. They grow very rapidly but many are somewhat tender. The most commonly grown eucalyptus is *E. gunnii,* which is hardy and reaches 20–30 m

Strawberry tree *(Arbutus unedo)*

(65–100 ft). The leaves of young plants are glaucus blue, but the adult leaves are darker and greener. The flowers, opening late summer, are creamy white.

Fagus sylvaticus (beech)

Height 12 m (40 ft). This is our native woodland species, which is only suitable for very large gardens as a specimen tree. It casts dense shade and takes a good deal of moisture and nutrients from the soil, so little else can grow beneath it. But it can be clipped throughout the summer and is ideal for hedging. Heavy soils are unsuitable.

Ilex aquifolium (common holly)

Height to 25 m (80 ft). There are several varieties of this holly, some with variegated leaves and others with yellow berries. If you want berries do be sure you have a female variety, because the name can be misleading. 'Golden King' is a berry-bearing female while 'Golden Queen' is a male and so has no berries. Poor crops of berries from a female may be due to the absence of a male tree to pollinate it. Holly can be cut back to form a dense animal-proof hedge. It grows well on all soils including chalk.

Juniperus (juniper)

Apart from the low-growing junipers (see p. 160), there are taller species of height up to 15 m (50 ft), making fine specimen trees. Some have blue-grey leaves and cones resembling blue berries, such as *J. scopularium.*

Junipers are slow-growing and tolerate most soils, providing they are well drained.

Laburnum

Height 5 m (15 ft). Deciduous with conspicuous sprays of yellow pea-type flowers, which are so much a feature of early summer gardens. Unfortunately the seeds and all other parts of the tree are poisonous, making it unwise to plant a laburnum if you have young children.

Magnolia

Height to 6 m (20 ft) according to species. All the best known garden species are deciduous. This is probably the most spectacular flowering tree of all, with enormous tulip-like pink or white flowers. *M. grandiflora* flowers in late summer. *M. soulangiana* and *M. stellata* bloom in spring and with these it is important to get the siting correct. The flowers are very delicate and liable to turn brown with wind burn or frost damage. Plant the tree where it will receive the full afternoon sun but not that of the early morning.

Malus (crab apple)

Height 2–9 m (6–30 ft), according to species or hybrid. They are grown mainly for the beauty of their flowers and the colour of the leaves and fruit in the autumn. Some, such as the hybrid *M.* 'John Downie', make excellent crab apple jelly. The trees prosper in most soils and only the minimal amount of pruning is required.

Picea (spruce or fir)

The familiar Christmas tree, the Norway spruce, is *P. abies.* It is advisable to purchase a container-grown specimen as very often the bare-rooted trees are damaged when you receive them and are only suitable for one season.

Christmas trees can be kept alive for several years providing that they are maintained in cool conditions. Having evolved in bitter cold regions where the air is often moisture laden they are incapable of withstanding the warm dry air of the lounge. Check daily over the Christmas period that the soil in the container is moist. When the tree is no longer required indoors, it should immediately be taken out of its container and placed in an open, well drained site. When required the following year, it may be lifted, potted up in a container and brought indoors again. The process may be repeated every year until the tree has become too large. Allowed to grow undisturbed in the garden, it could grow to 30 m (100 ft). However, there are less tall, slow-growing forms more suitable for the garden, such as *P. pungens* 'Glauca' which has silvery blue foliage.

Pinus (pines)

The tallest species grow to about 15 m (50 ft), but there are others of medium height and dwarf forms. They are similar to the spruces but have longer needles. Pines need a site in full sun to grow satisfactorily.

Populus (poplar)

Height to 30 m (100 ft) or more and not a tree for the small garden. Poplars should certainly

Magnolia soulangeana

be kept well away from the house. They are fast-growing and deciduous. The leaves of *P. balsamifera,* the balsam poplar, give off a lovely scent when unfolding.

Prunus (ornamental plum, cherry, peach and almond)

A very large family of deciduous trees with some members growing well over 12 m (40 ft), but most of the more popular species reach little more than 3 m (10 ft) and can be restricted if necessary. The genus consists of trees bearing well-known fruits and nuts, but they are not all edible. The majority of the trees are grown for their spectacular flowers, pink or white, which they carry during April. Unfortunately the blossom tends to be very short lived and the ground beneath becomes covered in fallen petals. Where there is a need to restrict a tree it is best achieved by root pruning.

Pyrus salicifolia 'Pendula' (ornamental pear)

Height to 10 m (35 ft). This small tree with weeping branches and willow-like leaves, silvery grey when new, deserves to be more widely grown. Masses of white flowers appear in spring but the pears that follow are inedible.

Salix (willow)

Salix 'Chrysocoma' (golden weeping willow) looks wonderful trailing its branches in a pond,

Picea pungens 'Glauca'

Rowan foliage and berries

but it is not for the small garden, growing to a height of 15 m (50 ft). There are many other willows, however, some of them quite dwarf. An alternative weeping form is *S. caprea* 'Pendula' (Kilmarnock willow) of height 2 m (10 ft). Slightly taller is *S. matsudana* 'Pendula', and its non-weeping variety 'Tortuosa' which has contorted branches. All willows are fast growing, hardy and do best on moist soil in full sun. Their catkins can be very decorative in spring.

Sorbus aucuparia (rowan, mountain ash)

Height 5–6 m (15–20 ft). A native deciduous tree with feathery leaves and white flowerheads, which open in May or June. These are followed by bunches of berries that by August have turned yellow-orange in colour. By October, both the berries and leaves are fiery orange red.

This tree is unfussy about soil and thrives in both sun and partial shade.

Taxus baccata (yew)

Height about 10 m (30 ft). A native conifer evergreen with poisonous red berries and short dark green needles. It can be clipped at any time of the year and is ideal for hedges. 'Aurea', which has golden-yellow foliage, will only reach 3 m (10 ft). It is erect with small needles and similar in many respects to cypresses.

12 Lawns

A well cultivated lawn never passes unnoticed – it is the sign of a master gardener. Grass is used for lawns because it can be walked on, cut and ill-treated in a variety of ways yet still continues to grow. This is possible because it grows not from the tips like many plants but from the base of the stalk.

There are many different species of grass and a lawn will be a mixture of several. Even if they were not in the original mixture, seed will land and germinate on an established patch. Basically there are two types of grass: fine and coarse. Grass seed is sold as mixtures of varieties in the correct amounts to do a specific job. A lawn made mainly of fine grasses will be capable of being brought up to the highest standard but will be unable to withstand a great deal of wear and tear. One made up of coarser grasses will be able to take much rougher treatment but will never possess the visual excellence of the former. For most lawns there needs to be a balance between quality of sward and the ability to withstand sustained usage. Where the area is likely to have above average use, such as being regularly walked on or used as a children's play area, the seed mixture should be selected accordingly.

Within an established lawn there will be a constant battle for survival between the finer types and the coarser varieties of grass. Cutting tends to damage coarser types far more than the fine varieties with the result that the more you mow the better the quality of the lawn. Even if the lawn has to withstand a great deal of rough treatment you should still mow it regularly. If you do not, the coarser grass varieties will dominate and spoil the quality of the lawn.

When you move to a new house you may well inherit a lawn. By the time you have settled in it will probably be overgrown and even on its way to becoming a jungle. But all is not necessarily lost providing there is a foundation of good varieties among the grasses. Regular cutting will ensure that they return to dominate the lawn. Always try to save a lawn before digging it up and relaying, which is a long and laborious task and it will be at least 12 months before you see any worthwhile results from your efforts.

Creating a lawn

To create a new lawn, first dig over the whole of the site taking care to remove both stones and the roots of perennial weeds. Couch-grass with its creeping stolons, if allowed to remain, gradually will take over. Once established it is virtually impossible to remove by hand. Being a grass it will survive the action of any selective weedkiller that you put on the lawn. Where couch-grass is a major problem it should be removed by using a systemic weedkiller, such as glyphosate, before digging the area over.

September and April are the best months for sowing seed or laying turf and the ground should be prepared at least three months before it is required. This will help to break the soil up and allow you to remove any weeds that escaped the first clearance.

The most critical part of laying out a lawn is making the site flat. On level sites this presents no problem. First rake the dug soil and lay a flat plank across the surface. Place a spirit level on the plank and add or remove soil until the ground itself is level. On sloping sites there are two approaches. The whole site could be raised by the addition of soil to that of the highest point – this is a useful approach with small areas or sites that are poorly drained. Alternatively, you could level out the whole area.

The first method involves driving a peg into the ground flush with the surface at the higher level. A second peg is driven into the lower level and allowed to protrude to the point where a plank resting on the two pegs is shown to be absolutely flat with the spirit level. The lower area can then be raised by the addition of soil to that of the high ground.

If levelling the whole area, find the mid-point of the slope. Treat the lower area by the method described above, removing soil from the higher ground. The level to which soil can be removed from the higher ground can be ascertained by driving a peg into it once soil has been removed and checking with the spirit level. Continue until what was originally the higher area is now level with the previous lower part. Rake over and check the levels again making any final adjustments until the site is flat.

Flattening the surface is achieved by 'walking the lawn', slowly covering every part of the surface. Do this by placing the whole of the foot firmly down on the ground, then bring the heel of the second foot up to touch the tip of the toe of the first and place that foot firmly on the ground, then bring the first foot in front of the second and so on. Continue the process until the whole of the area has been covered. Check again your levels and rake the surface again.

The choice now confronting the gardener is whether to use seed or turf. Seed is the cheaper, but it is slower to establish and you must take precautions to prevent it being consumed by birds or the area being walked on by cats, at least until the seed has germinated.

A lawn from seed

It is possible to produce the

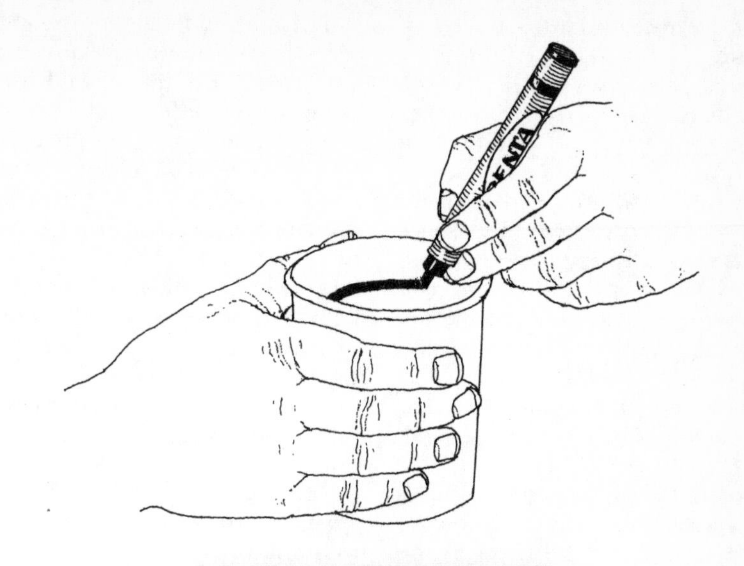

Use a plastic pot as a grass seed measure

Sowing grass seed

highest quality lawn from seed. After all, turf is only produced by sowing seed onto soil. Before purchasing seed, decide whether you want a fine or hard-wearing mixture. You will need to sow at the rate of 45 grams per square metre (1½ oz/sq yd). To ensure an even distribution of seed, mark the lawn out in a grid with divisions a metre apart before sowing. Weigh the seed and place it in a container marked so you know what volume 45 grams occupies. Having sown the seed, just cover with finely sifted soil. Protect the grass seed from birds by creating a meshwork of cotton tied to pegs at the edge of the lawn.

Allow the grass to grow until it is 7–10 cm (3–4 in) in height before making the first cut, which should be on a dry day. If you attempt to cut the lawn when the soil is wet the mower may well pull the young blades of grass, which will have very little root, out of the ground. Adjust the mower to its highest setting and continue at this level for a further two months.

Laying turf

Turf is more robust than freshly germinated seed, but until the root system of the grass has bonded with the topsoil it still has only a very precarious hold on life. In times of drought, unlike the topsoil, the turf will not have its water supply augmented by moisture rising from below by capillary action.

When you receive the turf, which will come wound in rolls, aim to lay it immediately. If this is not possible the turves must be stored and laid flat to stop the grass from yellowing. Every day the turves are left unlaid the system is effectively dying without it making any progress towards producing a lawn.

Ensure that the bed is fully prepared before you receive the turves. Mark out a level position by setting out a line between two pegs. The siting of the line must be established as being square by reference to the house, the path or a wall or fence. All turves will be laid relative to this and if it is out of true then the whole lawn will appear to be askew. When laying the turves the aim must be to form complete bonds in all directions as quickly as possible. Not only must a turf marry with the ground below, it must form a bond with its neighbours. Begin by laying the first row of turves against the reference line. To avoid spoiling the levels, kneel on a wooden board or plank as you work forward on subsequent rows. Tamp the turves down with the back of a rake to get good contact with the soil below. Stagger the turves so the joints in one row come halfway along that of the next, in a brick-laying pattern.

In practice, the rows are unlikely to end with exactly one whole or half turf and you will need to cut turves to size. You may be left with relatively small pieces. Any piece less than half a turf will be insecure at the edge of the lawn and may well fail to bond. Small pieces should be worked into the centre of rows rather than left at the edges, but continue to ensure that the joints are in such positions as to allow maximum bonding. Try to avoid leaving large joints between the individual turves. Where any sizeable joints do exist, fill them with sifted soil.

Depending upon the time of the year the turves usually take about two months to fully integrate with the soil beneath. During this period it will be necessary to water the lawn regularly. Consider each turf to be an independent system similar to a container and treat it accordingly. The best time for turf laying is the autumn. If you lay it in spring you may have to water frequently. Summer is not a good time to establish turf because of the hot, dry conditions.

The edges

Razor-sharp, clear-cut edges are the hallmark of a well cared for lawn. To achieve these you will need a half-moon grass cutter, which unlike a spade will not leave join marks corresponding to the edges of the blade. Set out the edge of the lawn by means of a taut line, making sure that it is related to a point of reference such as a path. Then cut the shape with the edging tool.

Most curves can be related to a circle. First mark out the piece of the circle that you require by placing a stake at its centre of curvature. Then attach a piece of string to the stake and at the other end a cold chisel or a

Laying turves

similar piece of metal. Swing the piece of metal on its pivot so that it cuts an arc in the turf.

Any curve that is not part of a true circle can be marked out by eye using a piece of pliable material such as a length of hose pipe. When the shape has been formed, the pliable material should be held in position by means of wooden pegs. Again cut out the shape with the edging tool.

To avoid having to constantly true up the edges of the lawn, place strips of lawn edging plastic against the sharp cut edge and keep it in position by means of pegs.

Lawn maintenance

Lawns need constant attention. During the summer they should be cut at least once a week, preferably twice. The very highest quality lawns need cutting more frequently even than that. Grass also needs cutting during the winter, but here timing is far less critical. The weather rather than the date that the lawn was last cut should be the deciding factor. Never cut a lawn when it is thoroughly soaked as a result of heavy or prolonged rainfall and never while it is frosted. Apart from this you should not miss any opportunity to mow the lawn.

Choice of lawn mower

Today there is the widest possible choice of lawn mowers, which can be confusing. They may be divided into two groups: cylinder mowers, which consist of about three curved blades

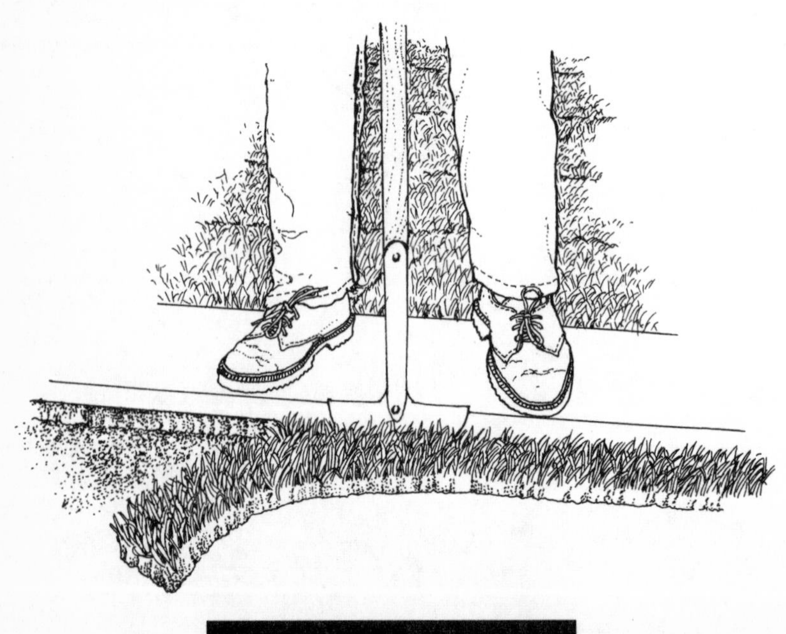

Cutting a curved edge

attached to a spindle rotating in a vertical plane, and rotary mowers, which consist of one blade rotating in a horizontal plane. Both have their advantages and disadvantages. Cylinder mowers fitted with a roller will often give better looking results, but they can only achieve their true potential when used on top quality lawns. Rotary mowers with their ability to glide over irregularities in the surface are better on lawns that tend to take a lot of wear and tear. They are also far better suited for use during the winter and spring when the lawn is liable to retain more moisture.

There are three methods of propulsion: mains electricity, battery and petrol. If you have a small lawn only a short distance from the house or an electrical point, mains electricity is the most convenient. The problem is the cable. This will greatly restrict the movement of the mower and if there are shrubs and obstacles between the point and the extremities of the lawn it may be difficult to manoeuvre. Where an electric cable is involved it is wise to include a circuit breaker in the system as there is always the possibility of cutting the wire.

For greater distances from the house and for larger lawns there is a choice between petrol and battery driven mowers. For very large lawns petrol is really the only practical option.

The lawn year

When winter is over, even having had occasional mowing the lawn will be in need of some attention. On a fine day when the grass has had an opportunity to dry out it should be scarified, a process that consists of firmly raking over the surface to disperse any worm casts and remove the detritus that has collected during the winter. Next follows the very important but often neglected task of aeration. Constant walking on the surface leads to the soil becoming compacted, which inhibits drainage and stops essential air from reaching the roots of the grass. An effective method of aerating a lawn is to make a series of insertions in rows 30 cm (1 ft) apart with a fork to a depth of about 10 cm (4 in). Move the fork backwards and forwards so that the prongs produce a series of reasonably large holes.

The first mowing of the new season in March should be with the mower still at its highest setting. Providing the lawn is reasonably dry the mower can be lowered a setting at each successive cut until it is cutting the lawn as short as you want. A top quality lawn should be no taller than 1–2 cm (½ in) whereas a hard-wearing lawn that has to work for its living should be allowed to grow to 2–4 cm (1–1½ in). When cutting a lawn always fit a box to catch the uprisings. If the cuttings are allowed to remain they will choke the roots and the lawn will rapidly begin to deteriorate.

Over the year, a lawn produces an enormous amount of green material which will drain the nutritional reserves of the soil. A top quality lawn demands feeding. Two dressings with proprietory lawn fertilisers a year will suffice. Never feed before April, as the temperature will not be high enough for the lawn to take full advantage of it. Much of the fertiliser that is not taken up will be wasted. From the moment it is dissolved by rainwater it starts diffusing away from the roots of the plants, ultimately travelling beyond their reach.

It is important to ensure an even distribution of the fertiliser, as any build-up of the particles may be sufficient to withdraw the water from the grass by osmosis and kill it, resulting in burnt patches. Fertilisers are best distributed by means of special spreaders which when wheeled across the surface deposit an even layer throughout the lawn. But the fertiliser that boosts the grass will also stimulate the weeds into growth, so unless you use a combined fertiliser and weedkiller apply a selective lawn weedkiller a week after feeding.

The only weeds that are likely to prosper in a lawn are those such as daisies, dandelions and plantains, which have crowns remaining close to the surface of the soil – the mower passes over them without disturbing the buds. These will grow quite quickly and even when the lawn has been treated with weedkiller they tend to reappear. Remove the weeds by digging out the crowns with a penknife, making sure that you remove all pieces of the root.

Throughout the summer the lawn should be cut regularly and the edges trimmed. There should be no need for any additional treatment. Even using a box, by the end of the season there will be a large quantity of dead grass, moss and other material. The lawn should again be scarified and then fed during September. This is an important part of lawn hygiene and will go a long way to ensuring that problems do not build up.

From mid-October onwards the lawn should be cut when the weather allows, with the mower on its highest setting. This treatment must be continued until early March.

Repairs

Wear and tear takes its toll on lawns and, just as for sowing, April and September are the best times for effecting repairs.

Bare patches

Where an area has been worn bare, the hard compacted soil should be thoroughly loosened with a fork, any deficit made up with sifted soil and the area densely sown with seed.

Humps and depressions

Occasionally as a result of subsidence or other minor earth movements small areas appear that are above or below the level of the rest of the lawn. These should be treated by cutting an 'H' in the turf, lifting the two flaps formed and adding or removing soil to restore the level.

Where a large area deviates from the level it should be dug up and then relaid, after levelling and treating by the method given for new lawns (pp. 170–173).

LAWN REPAIRS

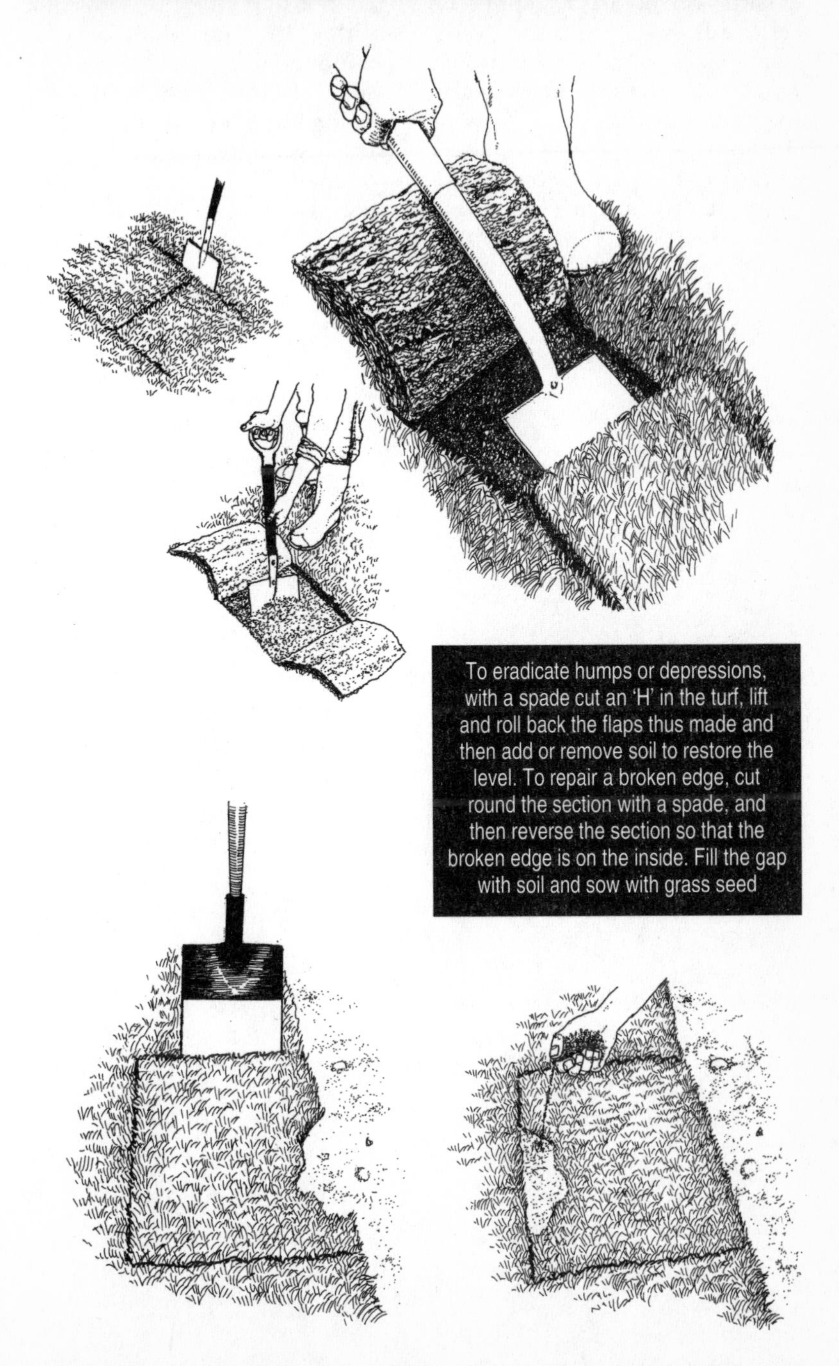

To eradicate humps or depressions, with a spade cut an 'H' in the turf, lift and roll back the flaps thus made and then add or remove soil to restore the level. To repair a broken edge, cut round the section with a spade, and then reverse the section so that the broken edge is on the inside. Fill the gap with soil and sow with grass seed

Broken edges

From time to time the edge of a lawn will break. It cannot be repaired by replacement of a small piece of turf as it would quickly dry out and never marry together with the main body of the lawn.

Effect a repair by cutting a piece of turf 30 cm (1 ft) along the edge and 60 cm (2 ft) into the lawn. Remove the turf taking care not to damage it. Reverse it so that the square-cut edge is positioned as the new part of the edge of the lawn with the missing area now occurring in the body of the lawn as a hole.

Repair the hole as described previously.

13 Water Gardens

For most people the greatest delight of the whole garden is the pond and thanks to modern moulds and liners no garden need be without a water feature. It simultaneously combines movement, through the darting forms of fishes and the visits of various forms of life, such as birds, frogs, toads and dragonflies, with the peace and tranquillity of still water. The visiting fauna provide the pond with much of its interest while they receive in return a place in which they can feed, drink and breed.

There are three main types of material used in pond construction. Concrete once had no competitors but is not a popular material now. It is the most difficult to use and the walls need to be sufficiently thick to ensure that they are not cracked by frost, but once established there is not much danger of accidental piercing.

Preformed glass-fibre pools are fairly expensive and the sizes and shapes available are limited. Nevertheless they are practical, easily installed and provide probably the best solution for the majority of urban ponds.

A liner made of flexible plastic sheeting allows you to construct a pond as large as you like and in any shape you desire. If you wish to construct a medium-sized or large pond this is the most suitable material to use. Polythene is not suitable as it has a very limited life. Reinforced PVC is stronger, but even better is butyl rubber which should last very many years.

Unlike some garden features, it is not possible to alter a pond at a later stage, so construct the largest one you can afford both in terms of space and cash, even if this means delaying its construction for some time. More than any other item of the landscape it is necessary to plan a pond carefully and to be absolutely clear in your mind what exactly you are seeking to achieve. The ideal depth is about 45–60 cm (1½–2 ft).

The pond should be sited in a sunny, open position, with no overhanging trees or shrubs. Leaves that drop into the water decay and pollute.

To maintain both interest and clear water it is necessary to have both animal and plant life. The types of aquatic plants you can choose will depend upon the depth of water. Water lilies grow at varying depths, from 30 cm to 2 m (1–6 ft), according to species and variety. The plants that grow in the shallower areas around the edges of a pond are termed marginals. A pond must be constructed with differing depths to reflect the plants' varying depth requirements. Fibreglass shells are moulded to include shelves.

Laying a preformed pond

When laying a glass-fibre pond it is important to be accurate with your levelling. The surface of the water will always be level, but unless the shell is laid absolutely flat uneven stress will be created throughout the structure. This combined with the different water pressure could in time cause stress fractures to develop.

Dig out a hole slightly larger than the shell. Check that there are no flints or other stones in any of the surfaces, then place a layer of sand at the bottom of the hole. Before lowering the shell in the hole check with a spirit level on a straight-edge that the bottom of the hole is absolutely level. After the shell has been lowered and is lying absolutely flat, gradually work sand or sifted soil down the gap between the shell and the edge of the hole – checking constantly that the shell remains level. When the shell is finally locked in position make a final check with the spirit level and allow the water to slowly enter the pond.

Laying a pond liner

A flexible pond liner acts as a membrane between the soil and the water. Although it is a flat sheet the weight of the water will ensure that it moulds itself to the contours of the hole. When calculating the area of sheeting allow for an overlap of 20 cm (8 in) at all positions. A liner should not be subjected to sudden changes of depth. Where these occur the membrane will become over-stretched, making it more likely to tear. Dig out the hole with gentle sloping sides and the depth varying from about 1.25 cm (4 ft) at the centre to zero at its edge. Check that there are no stones at the surface. Should any remain the weight of water pressing down on the membrane will almost certainly result in a puncture.

Lay the liner over the surface of the hole, then allow water to very slowly enter the hole from a hose pipe. Check continuously that the sheet is filling evenly and that there is always adequate sheeting available at all positions so that it does not suffer localised stretching. Be prepared to turn off the water supply and gently adjust the sheet if necessary. Allow the pond to continue to fill slowly until it is within a few centimetres of the top. Weigh down the overlaps with soil and place pieces of rock around the sides for a natural effect.

Filling and stocking a pond

Whatever method of construction you use, the water should be allowed to stand for at least a week before adding plants or fish. This gives a chance for chlorine and other chemicals in the water to disperse. Fresh concrete releases chemicals poisonous to plants and fish, but there are proprietary preparations to paint on that

INSTALLING A PREFORMED POND

Ensure the pit is level

Gradually work sand or soil between the shell and the edge of the hole

USING A LINER

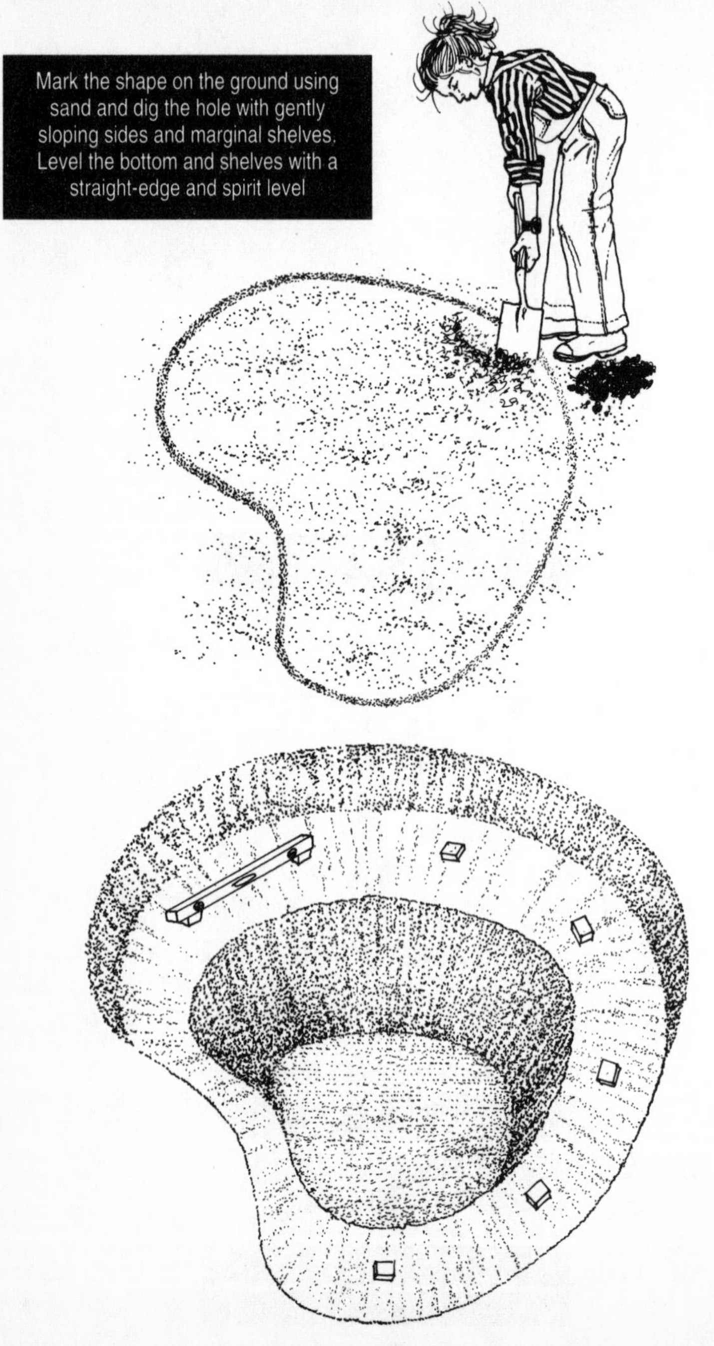

Mark the shape on the ground using sand and dig the hole with gently sloping sides and marginal shelves. Level the bottom and shelves with a straight-edge and spirit level

Lay the liner over the pool and fill with water very slowly

Place paving stones around the edges

neutralise the lime and seal the concrete – otherwise you will have to wait a few weeks after filling before you can safely introduce any pond life.

A healthy pond is a balanced system supporting many types of life. To achieve such a balance, aim to include as great a variety of plants and animals as space allows. Most important are the oxygenating plants. You will also need floating aquatics, plants for the shallower areas of the margins and others for the deeper water, plus a few water snails.

Resist the temptation to keep too many fish. By artificial feeding it is possible for a pond to sustain more than would occur in the wild. But they still need adequate oxygen and space to swim, otherwise they will never reach full size. Avoid over-feeding, which will simply pollute the water.

Goldfish will breed in modest sized pools. Success in rearing them will depend on there being sufficient cover (pond plants and submerged pots) in which the fry can hide from their cannibalistic parents. If you want a wildlife pond where frogs, toads and newts can breed, it is not a good idea to keep goldfish as they will eat the tadpoles.

Oxygenating plants

The roots, leaves and stems are completely submerged, though some have flowers above the surface. The oxygen they generate by photosynthesis dissolves in the water as soon as it escapes from the leaves. Dissolved oxygen is needed by fish for respiration.

Another important function of oxygenating plants is to keep the water clear of algae, which are the cause of green water (see pp. 188–89).

One of the best oxygenators is *Lagarosiphon major,* sometimes called *Elodea crispa.* It has long stems and curled leaves and is widely available at garden centres. The Canadian pondweed (*Elodea canadensis*) is an excellent oxygenator but unfortunately extremely vigorous – it will rapidly clog up your pond. Less rampant, more attractive in appearance and also good oxygenators are some of our native species, including the hornwort (*Ceratophyllum demersum*), water milfoil (*Myriophyllum spicatum*) and water starwort (*Callitriche palustris*).

Aquatics for deeper water

These are water plants with submerged roots and leaves, and flowers on the surface or just above it.

The only really deep water aquatics are the water lilies, which are mostly *Nymphaea* species. However, many of the water lilies and their cultivars are only suitable for relatively shallow water. The very dwarf varieties, such as *N. pygmaea,* need as little as 15–30 cm (6–12 in) depth of water between crown and surface. There are intermediate kinds, and also some very vigorous growers requiring a depth of nearly 1 m (3 ft). So it is important to make your selection from types suitable for the depth of your pond. Purchase them from a water lily specialist supplier or a garden centre prepared to guarantee the correctness of their labels and able to state the depths of water required. Aim to have a maximum of one variety per 5 square metres (6 square yards) of surface area.

Water lily flowers come in both singles and doubles, some with pleasant perfumes. They occur in white and shades of pink, red and yellow, and often have striking stamens.

The water hawthorn (*Aponogeton distachylus*) is a very attractive plant for depths of 30–60 cm (1–2 ft) and may be grown as an alternative to a water lily in a small pond. It has oval-shaped floating leaves and intriguing flowers (white with black anthers) that smell like may blossom.

Nymphoides peltata, which has round floating leaves like those of water lilies but smaller, has fringed yellow flowers and needs a minimum depth of 30 cm (1 ft).

Floating plants

These have leaves, stems and flowers on the surface, or just below it.

The duckweeds (*Lemna* species) are unwelcome as they can smother the surface of a pond, especially when the water is rich in nutrients. They are difficult to get rid of, especially on large ponds where it cannot be reached by a rake. Before placing any new plant in the pond, make sure there is no duckweed clinging to it. The tiniest amount can spread very quickly. Only the ivy-leaved duckweed (*Lemna trisulca*) is safe to introduce. The delicate leaves float just under the surface (it is a useful oxygenator).

The fairy fern (*Azolla caroliniana*) can choke large ponds but is quite easily controlled in smaller ones. In winter it turns an attractive red.

Frogbit (*Hydrocharis morsus-ranae*) has no vices. It has smallish rounded leaves and occasional white flowers.

The water soldier (*Stratiotes aloides*) consists of spiny rosettes. It sinks to the bottom of the pond in the winter.

Marginal plants

Marginal plants can either grow in permanently damp soil at the water's edge or they can have their roots submerged with the leaves and flowers above the surface (the shelves around your pool are provided for them). Though mainly of ornamental value, marginals help provide some shade for the fish. There are a good many to choose from but beware of the vigorous kinds if you have a small pond.

The arrowheads (*Sagittaria* spp.) are handsome but invasive plants growing to about 40–45 cm (15–18 in), with oval floating leaves and arrow-shaped aerial leaves.

From the buttercup family is the greater spearwort (*Ranunculus lingua*). Its height is about 60 cm (2 ft), and it has yellow flowers in July and August. It must be firmly controlled, however, for given a free root run it will spread rapidly. And then there is that great favourite *Caltha palustris* (kingcup, marsh marigold), which flowers in March. The double variety is particularly good, and so is the single white form.

An easy-to-grow marginal for very shallow water is the water forget-me-not (*Myosotis palustris*). Its height is about 23 cm (9 in). Also with small blue flowers is the brooklime speedwell (*Veronica beccabunga*).

Among the irises, *I. ensata* (formerly called *I. kaempferi*) and the similar species *I. laevigata* are the most popular for garden ponds. There are many cultivars of these, in purple, pink, lavender and white, some with variegated leaves. The blue flag iris (*I. versicolor*), available in blue, reddish-purple and lavender shades, is also a good choice for shallow water or moist soil. Its height is 45 cm (1 ft), and it prefers semi-shade, as does our native species the yellow flag (*I. pseudacorus*). The latter grows to 1 m (3 ft) tall and needs firm control. There is a form with variegated leaves.

The water mint (*Mentha aquatica*), like its dry-land relatives, spreads by underground stolons. Like them it can be planted in an earthenware pot to keep it under control. Submerge it to a depth of 5–10 cm (2–4 in). To stimulate growth, repot every year. *Typha latifolia*, the greater reedmace – what some people call bulrush – has brown furry heads and grows to about 150 cm (5 ft). But it is much too invasive for garden ponds. The more slender *T. angustifolia* is a little less aggressive. *T. minima* would be the best choice.

Bog plants

Bog plants can be grown

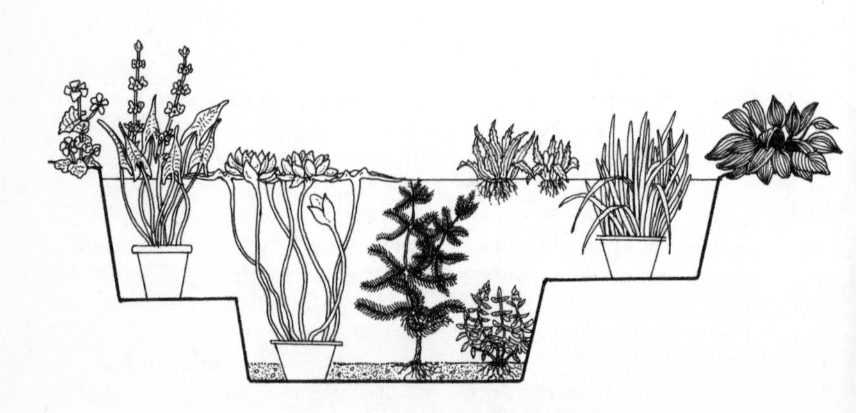

Cross-section of a garden pond

PLANTS FOR PERMANENTLY MOIST SOIL

Musk *(Mimulus luteus)*

Skunk cabbage
(Lysichiton americanus)

Globe flower *(Trollius x hybridus)*

where the soil is permanently moist. Some of the plants listed under marginals are also suitable for these conditions, such as the kingcup. Trollius, the globe flower (see p. 129), is another member of the buttercup family that is suited to bog gardens.

A striking bog arum is the skunk cabbage (*Lysichiton americanus*). About 60 cm (2 ft) tall, it has bright yellow flowers in mid-spring and large fleshy leaves. If grown as a marginal, the maximum depth of water above the roots should be 5 cm (2 in).

The rhubarb-leaved *Gunnera manicata,* which towers to more than 2.5 m (8 ft), is obviously only for the very largest gardens. A semi-tender plant, it requires some protection throughout the winter.

Mimulus are excellent subjects for growing beside ponds (see p. 121).

Planting aquatics

The best planting time is between April and September. Most water plants will colonise the whole pond in a single season if given the chance. They will do this if you cover the base of your pond with soil for direct planting. It is easier to keep them in check by planting in plastic baskets sold specifically for the purpose. Baskets restrict the growth of the roots, and they are easily lifted out should you need to divide the plants or clean out the pond.

The baskets come in different slzes and the more open type require liners before they are filled (a piece of hessian will do). Use soil mixed with well rotted manure, or a good quality loam. Too rich a compost will encourage algae. Place only one type of plant in each container, wet the soil well and top it with gravel. Oxygenating plants, marginals and deep water plants such as water lilies can all be planted this way.

Water snails can now be added. They are useful scavengers that feed on algae and the decaying vegetable matter that develops in a pond. Ramshorns are particularly recommended for this cleaning up job. They will not feed on your water plants – some species do, especially the greater pond snail (this has a large, pointed shell).

Allow the pond plants to settle before putting in any fish.

Not long after planting, the water is likely to become green with algae. This happens partly because the plants are not fully settled and partly because of the profusion of minerals in the new water (some will seep out of the planting soil too). However, the water should soon clear itself.

Before placing the fish in the pond, check that the temperature of the water in their container and the pond is the same. If there is a noticeable difference, allow the container of fish to stand by the pond until the water is of equal temperature. The fish will then not be subjected to stress.

Pond problems

Green water

A proliferation of the microscopic free-floating algae

that make the water look like green pea soup comes about through a lack of balance between the various forms of life in the pond. Balance is more difficult to achieve the smaller the pond.

The problem tends to appear in the spring and early summer when temperatures are rising and the days are lengthening. Having sufficient oxygenating weed is one way to combat these algae. The explanation is as follows. Fish and other aquatic creatures produce waste products that accumulate and form the toxic chemical ammonia, which is broken down by bacteria into nitrates (also toxic). Water plants absorb the nitrates from the water and use them to build up their proteins. So do the algae, but the oxygenators absorb more and thus tend to starve the algae out.

Like any other green plant, algae need sunlight. Deny it to them by having up to 70 per cent of the surface covered by water lily leaves and/or floating leaves (e.g. frogbit).

The tiny crustaceans daphnia and cyclops, which are often present in a well balanced pond, feed on algae and eliminate the problem. Tadpoles do the same. Unfortunately these small creatures will be eaten when there are fish in the pond.

Green water is generally a temporary, seasonal problem that usually sorts itself out. If it happens, avoid changing your pool water because you will upset the balance of life that has been built up. If you refill from the tap, you may be creating ideal conditions for fresh algal growth as most tap water is rich in minerals. Take out excess aquatic plants at the end of the summer, which will help to reduce rotting and an accumulation of excess nitrates.

Blanket weed

Blanket weed, a form of alga that looks like a tangle of green filaments, is most likely to be a problem in spring – before the other plants have started to grow and compete with it. A good method of control is to wind the blanket weed around a strong stick and then lift it out of the water. Pond snails will munch away any that remains.

Leaves in the water

Even when there are no trees in close proximity to the pond, strong winds in autumn may deposit fallen leaves in the water. Bacteria will bring about their decay, using up the water's oxygen in the process. Furthermore, leaves contain tannins and other chemicals which discolour the water. If leaves and debris accumulate too much your fish will die, and the time may come when you will need to drain the pond to clean it out.

The best season for the clean-out is early summer, when the water has warmed up. This is also a good time to replace or divide plants. Be ruthless with any of the aggressive species that are ousting the choicer plants. When replanting, use fresh compost.

Catch the fish and place them in the largest container you possess. Keep them in a cool place and aim to return them in a matter of hours. Kept overnight they could suffocate from lack of oxygen in the water. Put pond snails in a bucket.

Lift out the aquatic plants in their baskets and drain the pond, though if you have a really large pond it will be impractical to empty it completely. You will have to clean out the bottom with your hands. If the pond has a liner, avoid walking on it if possible. Stepping on stones will damage it. After removing the muck and scrubbing the sides with a brush, replace the plants and refill with clean water.

Ice

Even in the hardest winter, ice does not usually exceed a thickness of 15 cm (6 in). Fish can still survive underneath, especially if part of the pool is kept free from ice to allow exchange of gases. In respiration, the fish expire carbon dioxide which, together with methane from rotting vegetation, gets trapped under the ice and the fish can suffocate.

When temperatures are dropping to zero, place a medium-sized rubber ball in the water. The slightest wind will cause the ball to move and may be enough to prevent ice forming in that area.

However, after a very hard frost you will wake to find the pond completely frozen over. Never attempt to break the ice with a hammer as the shock waves could kill the fish. You can create an airhole by placing a large tin can on the ice and pouring very hot water into it. The area of ice that subsequently melts will be sufficient to allow toxic gases to escape and some oxygen to dissolve in the water.

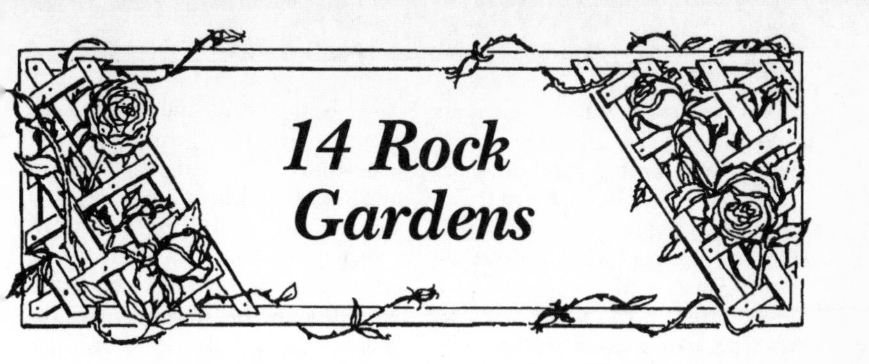

14 Rock Gardens

A garden should be far more than just a collection of plants – it needs to be a complete landscape in which the items are all interrelated, where the setting is as important as the plants themselves. Such an approach requires the use of non-living accessories – in particular, rocks. The use of rocks does not have to be restricted to alpine gardens. They may be used to good effect with the widest possible range of plants, from annuals to dwarf trees.

What is the difference between rock gardens and simply rocks in the garden? It has become fashionable to create winter gardens with heathers and dwarf conifers interspersed between rocks. While the visual effect is pleasing to the eye and this is perfectly justifiable in landscaping terms, from a cultivation point of view the stones might just as well not be there. In the true rock garden the rocks are the dominant feature with the plants growing in the soil in the space between the stones which supplies and maintains the necessary moisture.

Constructing a rock garden

Choose rocks from your own locality as they will blend better with the surroundings. Also, they are usually cheaper if obtained direct from a nearby quarry. Choose a south-facing site if possible, as most alpines demand plenty of sun. Avoid a north-facing situation, or one under the drip of trees.

The first step is to create an artificial slope. To provide the necessary drainage lay a foundation of brick rubble, which can provide up to one third of the height. The soil for the slope needs to be of an open consistency, achieved by mixing equal parts of loam and grit.

When placing the rocks aim to mimic a mountain landscape. The pieces of stone must appear as natural outcrops in a series of steps. Extremely dramatic in large gardens, the same illusion can be achieved in the smallest of areas.

The secret is to use for the main framework rocks at least 30 cm (1 ft) in width and depth and 15 cm (6 in) height. You will not be able to achieve a natural look with pieces smaller than this. In nature, rocks are often found in layers or strata and in many types there are distinctive layers within the mineral. Where these occur it is important that the stone is laid so that the layering effect occurs in the horizontal plane.

To avoid water pockets collecting beneath the rocks, place them with a slight forward tilt (20 degrees from the horizontal will be sufficient). The step effect is achieved by placing succeeding rows of rock behind that of the lower level. In the true rock garden the roots of the plants must struggle for their existence amongst the crevices. This can only be achieved by ramming the soil and grit mixture between every gap in the rock.

Alpine plants

The majority of plants included under this heading originate from mountain regions (not necessarily the Alps). Such species require a well drained soil, but, being shallow rooted, deep cultivated ground is not essential for them. Strong mountain winds encourage a low-growing habit, as the wind simply sheers over them. Mountain habitats can be quite hot during the daytime and yet freezing cold at night. Alpines are able to withstand these extremes of temperature.

While a well constructed rock garden provides the best possible habit for true alpines it is possible to grow a number of species in close association with rocks that would be equally at home in a conventional bed. Excluded are plants which need damp conditions or shade. Also avoid tall plants and those that grow too vigorously.

Step effect and positioning of stones to aid drainage

Some rock garden plants

Alyssum saxatile

Height 15 cm (6 in), spread of 45 cm (1½ ft). The plant has grey leaves and is covered with clusters of small yellow flowers from April to June. It can also be planted at the front of a border and may be left for several years without attention. Propagate by division or root cuttings taken during July.

Aubreta (Aubretia)

Height 10 cm (4 in), spread 60 cm (2 ft). This low-growing evergreen needs full sun and a well-drained, non-acid soil. It is at its best amongst rocks or cascading over walls. The four-petalled flowers, which appear during April, occur in all shades of blue, purple and magenta. It should be cut hard back after flowering is over. Propagate named varieties by taking 5 cm cuttings and placing them in a flower pot containing peat and sand during August. Aubreta may be raised from seed sown during the spring. To encourage it to grow in walls, find a gap that can be filled with soil and place a seed in the medium. Then keep it watered until it has germinated and the seedling has become established.

Edraianthus

Height 7–10 cm (3 in). A group of low-growing plants, ideally suited to growing in rock gardens and needing a sunny position. They form a carpet of blue-to-purple bell-shaped flowers during May. Propagation is by seed, which may be

Build a natural-looking rocky outcrop

gathered in June or July, or from cuttings taken directly from the crown of the plant during August.

Gentian

Height 15–30 cm (6–12 in). Famous for the electric blue flowers of many of the species. Though well suited to the alpine garden, they need a water-retentive soil. Flowering time ranges from late spring to the autumn according to species. Gentian may be propagated from seed, root division during the spring or cuttings in May and June.

Primula

Alpine primulas require a well-drained soil rich in humus and can tolerate full sunlight. They may be raised in a similar manner to the border varieties but do not need as much moisture. It is not necessary to keep the seedlings shaded once they have germinated.

Saxifraga (saxifrage)

Most of the saxifrages are rock-garden plants. The best known border saxifrage is London Pride (*S.* x *urbium*), height 25 cm (10 in), which in mid-spring has sprays of tiny pink flowers on tall slender stems arising from rosettes of leaves. Provide a moisture-retentive soil and some shade. Propagate by dividing the rosettes in spring.

Sempervivum (houseleek)

Height 3–4 cm (1½–2 in) with flowers 20 cm (8 in) tall. The genus is closely related to the sedums to which some species bear a very close resemblence. The plants consist of rosettes of modified leaves radiating from a central crown. They are low-growing and many of them are also ideal for the front of borders. A thick spike of red or pink flowers appears in midsummer. Sempervivums will grow in any dry, well drained location. At one time they were planted in dry walls or even stone roofs where it was thought they would bring good luck for the household. Propagate by removing the offsets and replanting in a new position at any time except midsummer.

Sowing and planting alpines

Much of the attraction of the rock garden lies in the interrelationships between plants and rocks, with some of the flowers seeming to grow almost out of the stones themselves. One cannot place a growing rock plant in a narrow crevice and expect it to 'take'. There will be insufficient moisture to satisfy its needs, for there has to be a well established root system capable of clinging to the rocks and extracting the film of water adhering to them. However, a seed which lands on what appears to be no more than the merest speck of soil will in many cases grab a foothold and survive.

Sow the seeds during spring or autumn where you wish to site plants. Items such as aubreta and alyssum can be sown in the same way in dry walls or any place where there are holes which

Grow alpines in the crevices

have collected soil or are capable of being filled with it. The success with which such plants germinate and cling to life is all around to see – many old walls support a variety of self-sown plants.

In addition to the crevices within your rock garden there will be some areas of soil without rock. In these, plant out species that are either difficult or impractical to grow from seed.

Paving plants

Old paved paths with cracks look untidy and spoil the look of the garden, quickly becoming homes for weeds. But the cracks in paving stones are very similar to fissures in a rock and can be utilised in the same way. So instead of replacing the path, spray the weeds in it with herbicide and after all traces of them have been removed fill the gaps with soil if necessary and sow with aubreta, alyssum or thyme. What was once an eyesore will soon become an enchanting feature.

Scree gardens

Scree is the mass of loose rock fragments that collect at the bottoms of mountain slopes. Quite an assortment of plants can germinate and actually survive in this most hostile environment. Like rock plants they thrive in cold, dry conditions where there is good drainage. Imitation scree is particularly suited to small gardens that have no room for

Gentiana septemfida (left) is an easy growing gentian. The maiden pink *(Dianthus deltoides)* will grow in most soils. Both plants flower during the summer

a rockery.

Again create the garden on a well drained site with a brick rubble foundation if necessary. Cover the surface either with 5 cm (2 in) of rubble from a quarry or pea gravel. A scree area is the only part of the garden not likely to become afflicted with weeds and is among the easiest to maintain.

The planting is restricted to alpines, dwarf trees and a few of the shorter growing resilient herbaceous perennials. Avoid tall growing plants, which look out of place in such settings.

Sink gardens

Sink gardens were the original container gardens and are still a useful way to include a collection of alpines or even herbs where space is limited. You will need to get hold of an old-fashioned ceramic sink, but unfortunately these are becoming increasingly scarce (they are sometimes obtainable from demolition sites).

Carefully remove all of the glaze. This often leaves a pleasing sandstone appearance. If it does not, use a mixture of one part of cement to two parts

A sink garden is an attractive way to grow alpines where space is limited

sifted peat and spread the thick paste over the surface of the sink. When it dries the container should have an almost natural rough-cast effect.

Set the sink on four bricks or flattened rocks, leaving the drainage hole unblocked but covered with a piece of broken crock so that it retains the compost yet allows water to escape. Fill the sink with a mixture of equal parts loam and grit to within 5 cm (2 in) of the top. Spread gravel on the surface and add some small pieces of rock to improve the visual effect.

Remember, before making any plantings, that if you have used limestone for your rocks that the lime will slowly be leached out by rainfall and kill any plants which are not lime-tolerant.

15 Winter Gardens

Most gardens are designed with spring, summer and autumn in mind. From mid-February until mid-November there is no problem in maintaining both colour and interest, but for a truly complete landscape, a garden for all seasons, find a space to plant a winter's bed – an area which will remove the depression of the cold, dark days of December and January. Select an open site in full sun near the house – you will not wish to walk long distances during the cold wet weather.

Lay the bed out in the usual way with tall subjects at the back, medium height plants in the middle and the shorter ones in the front. For the main backdrop choose from the shrubs in the table below.

The flowers of a number of winter shrubs have beautiful perfumes which cannot help but remind you of the spring flowers that are just around the corner. In front of these plant white Christmas roses (*Helleborous niger*) and *Bergenia crassifolia* (elephant's ears), a species which can bloom as early as January. In the foreground place corms of the light purple *Crocus imperati* and the golden yellow *C. chrysanthus,* both winter flowering.

Additional winter colour can be provided by a mixed display of dwarf conifers and heathers. Seek out the winter-flowering heathers, the many varieties and cultivars of the *Erica* genus. In addition, plant cultivars of the heather *Calluna vulgaris* for their leaf colour. Among the dwarf conifers you will find varieties with eye-catching coloured needles, including variegated forms, often with very brightly coloured winter shoots and interestingly shaped cones.

All winter gardens should contain groups of snowdrops. Not only are these bulbs in flower for

Some winter shrubs

Name	**Colour**	**Maximum height**
Mahonia spp.	Primrose yellow	2.5 m (8 ft)
Viburnum tinus	White, pink buds	2 m (6 ft)
Viburnum bodnantense	White flushed pink	3 m (10 ft)
Jasminum nudiflorum (winter jasmine)	Yellow	3 m (10 ft)

a relatively long period, their white colour lightens the beds and adds interest. The arrival of snowdrops, more than any other plant, heralds the start of a new garden season. They are the transition between one gardening year and the next.

Next to the snowdrops plant their little companion, the ground-hugging winter aconite whose bright yellow flowers will begin to take over from February onwards.

In the largest gardens use can be made of shrubs or trees with coloured barks – the dogwood (*Cornus* species) and some of the willows (e.g. *Salix alba* 'Chermesina') – more readily apparent when they are not carrying any leaves. The greatest intensity of colour occurs in first season shoots. To keep dogwood shrubs in check and maintain an annual supply of new growth, prune them hard back to ground level during early April.

If space allows, why not include the luxury of the winter-flowering Japanese cherry *Prunus* 'Fudanzakura' or one of the witch hazels (*Hamamelis* species) with their sweetly scented, spidery yellow flowers?

View the winter garden not as a chore but a challenge. With a little careful thought it is possible to maintain interest for 12 months of the year. Colour in December and January is the sign of a well planned garden.

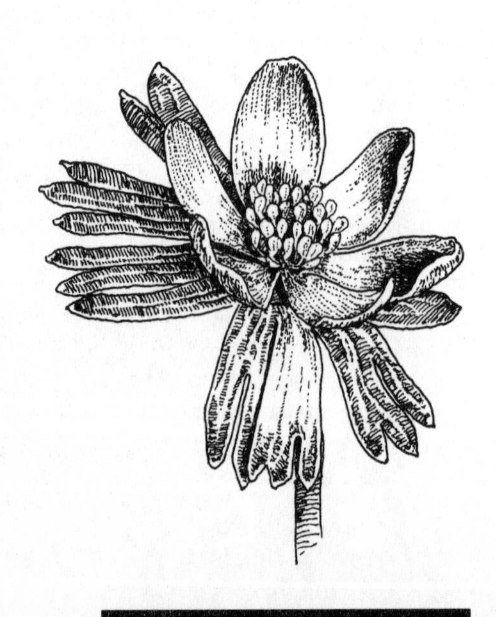

Winter aconite

Mahonia japonica

Viburnum tinus

Winter jasmine

Witch hazel in flower

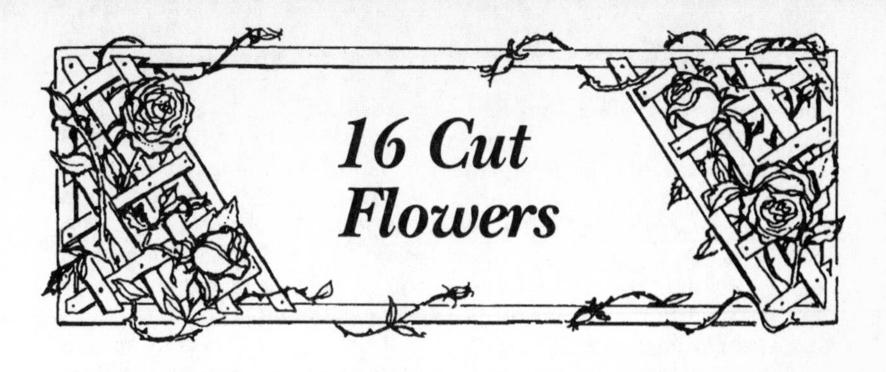

16 Cut Flowers

One of the greatest delights of a garden is to be able to provide a constant supply of cut flowers for the home. Mixed and herbaceous beds will yield a range of suitable material for floral arrangements throughout the year. But you must limit the amount you take, otherwise the display beds will appear decimated. An answer to the problem is to set aside a small area where flowers for cutting may be raised and harvested as crops.

You will require a well drained site that receives maximum sunlight, but above all the soil must be kept in tip-top condition. Remember, *plants grown for a constant supply of cut flowers will make as much demand on the soil as vegetables.*

Some all-time favourites

Anemones

The best anemones for cut flowers are varieties from the 'De Caen' group. These are single cup-shaped flowers and will provide blooms to cut and come again throughout the spring. Their height is about 20–30 cm (8–12 in) and they come in red, blue and white. 'St Brigid' hybrids are doubles or semi-doubles in the same bright colours, but they tend to produce fewer blooms.

Anemones grow best in a sunny site. Plant the tubers about 4 cm (2 in) deep and 10 cm (4 in) apart during September or October. They may also be planted during the spring to give a succession of flowers during the summer.

Chrysanthemums

The chrysanthemum is the queen of the autumn flowers and nothing quite compares with them late in the year. They are often considered as difficult, beyond the ability of amateurs, and requiring a greenhouse for cultivation.

Successful chrysanthemum growing like any aspect of gardening does demand some attention to detail – but difficult? Never! And you only need a greenhouse for late varieties.

The plants are usually purchased as rooted cuttings. These should be potted as soon as they are received. They must be brought inside during the evenings and be hardened off by being left out of doors during the day. Delay planting until the soil and weather conditions are suitable.

Set the plants out in the garden about mid-April in mild areas and early May elsewhere.

They require an open site, free from draughts and protected from the wind which in a bad October can destroy the plants. Since the borders will be past their best and no longer the centre of attention there is no reason why a limited number of chrysanthemums for cutting should not be grown at the back of display areas if there is no other available space.

As border plants they may be grouped together 40 cm (16 in) apart. But if they are to be grown solely for cut flowers, plant them with a distance of at least 60 cm (2 ft) between individual plants. Place a 120 cm (4 ft) high stake beside the chrysanthemum and tie the plant to it as it grows.

About a fortnight after the plant has been set out it must be stopped. This consists of pinching out the growing tip with the forefinger and thumb to encourage the development of side shoots and hence flowers. (Flowering takes place approximately three months from the date that the side shoots first appear.)

Allow no more than six branches to develop. From now on the branches may be grown to produce sprays, in which case they will need no further attention.

To produce specimen blooms, however, disbud by removing all buds other than the leader as soon as they are large enough to handle. This will direct all of the plant's energy into producing a limited number of top quality blooms. For the largest blooms, allow only three buds to develop.

During July, chrysanthemum plants start forming roots near to the surface. After a heavy rainfall or a thorough soaking with the watering can, mulch with compost. Feed with a light sprinkling of sulphate of potash and repeat the feeding in a month's time.

Propagate chrysanthemums by digging up the roots (termed 'stools') in the early spring and taking the shoots as cuttings when they are 7 cm (3 in) high.

There are several different forms of chrysanthemums. The most popular for individual blooms are the incurves, in which the petals all turn inwards towards the centre, the reflexes, whose petals curve outwards, and the intermediates, which are similar to incurves but their petals do not turn inwards to the same extent.

A common pest of chrysanthemums is the red spider mite, which feeds on both leaves and flowers. At the first sign of damage spray with rotenone or malathion. Another pest is the leaf miner, the tunnelling of which disfigures and weakens the plants. Keep it under control by spraying with malathion.

Dahlias

Border dahlias provide blooms from July until they are cut down by the first frosts of autumn. Their blooms range from 3 cm (1 in) to 15 cm (6 in) in diameter. Dahlias are obtainable in shades of red, yellow, gold, mauve and pink, and also in white and bicolours. In addition to the wide colour range and size, there are diverse forms.

SOME CHRYSANTHEMUM TYPES

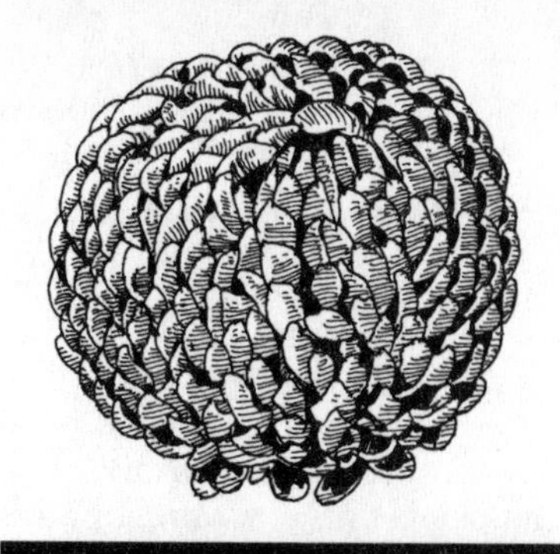

Incurved

Reflexed

Intermediate

Pompon

Single

Some of the types grown are:

1 *Single-flowered.* These consist of a single row of petals surrounding a flat disc.
2 *Anemone-flowered.* Double flowers consisting of short tubular petals in the centre surrounded by a ring of larger, flat petals.
3 *Ball.* Unlike any other dahlia apart from the pompoms, the flower appears to be a round, almost a perfect sphere.
4 *Pompom.* Although there are slight differences, the pompom is less than 5 cm (2 in) in diameter and like a smaller version of the ball.
5 *Collerette.* An intriguing form that at first sight looks like a single. It has a full ring of large, flat single petals surrounding the central disc, but in between is a 'collar' of petals greatly reduced in size.
6 *Decorative.* Fully double blooms without a central disc, and lightly twisted wide petals. These are the monsters of the dahlia world with blooms ranging from 10 to 25 cm (4–10 in) across.
7 *Cactus.* Fully double blooms without a central disc, the petals are curled to form a tube for the majority of the length.
8 *Semi-cactus.* Fully double blooms without a central disc, the petals form a tube for less than half their length.

Aim to grow at least four to six plants to provide a continuous supply of blooms throughout the summer.

Border dahlias are grown from tubers, which should be purchased as soon as they are available (usually in March).

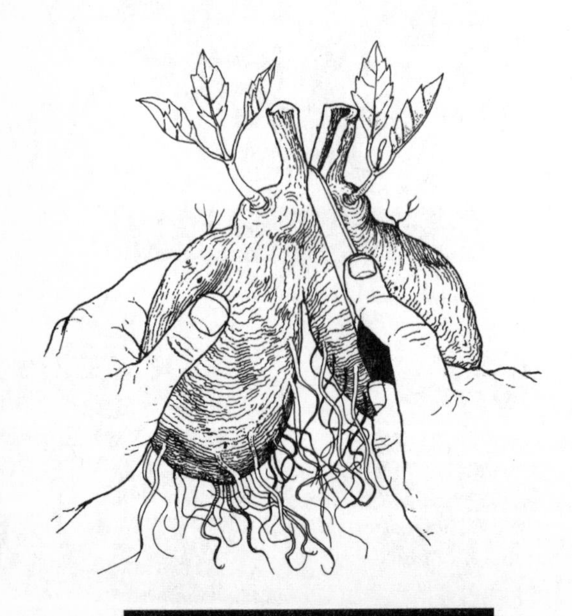

When dividing dahlias, be sure the buds remain attached to the tubers

These tubers were produced from cuttings taken the previous year and grown in pots. The advantage of this method of propagation is that it produces a standard-sized tuber for the following year. Make sure that none of the fingerlike swelling are detached from the main body of the root. Unlike potatoes, whose tubers are complete units individually capable of forming a plant, dahlia tubers are only the food stores – the shoots lie at the base of the previous year's stem. As soon as one of the tubers becomes detached it is simply a lost food source.

After purchase, remove the tubers from their containers and stand them in a cool but dry and frost-free place. Plant the tubers in their flowering positions 15 cm (6 in) deep during the first week in May. Those producing flowers of 5 cm (2 in) diameter should be planted 60 cm (2 ft) apart while those yielding flowers 7–10 cm (3–4 in) in diameter should be placed 75 cm (2½ ft) apart. Larger varieties should be planted 90 cm (3 ft) away from their neighbours.

Place a cane next to the dahlia surmounted by an inverted flower pot filled with dried grass. Earwigs, which might chew and destroy the flower, will use this as a hiding place and they may be removed and destroyed. Tie the plant to the cane.

Earwigs will seek shelter in a flower pot filled with dried grass inverted over the support cane.
Apprehend and destroy

Dahlia buds develop in groups of three with one leader and two secondary buds providing back-up if anything happens to the main bud. For large flowers on long stems, remove both the secondary buds. For twice the number of blooms only slightly smaller and with shorter stems, remove the leading bud and allow the two secondaries to develop together.

Ensure that no flower is allowed to remain on the plant and run to seed. The plant will then continually produce more flowers.

Providing that the soil is not likely to become waterlogged it is perfectly safe to allow dahlia tubers to remain in the ground undisturbed during winter. There will be much less fluctuation of temperature below ground level than above and the frost will only penetrate a few centimetres, providing safe winter storage conditions for the tubers. Before the first frosts, cut back the foliage to 15 cm (6 in) above ground level and mark the position of the tubers with a stick. Early in spring, cover the overlying soil with compost and apply a good general fertiliser.

Where there is danger of waterlogging or the tubers are to be lifted to reduce the size of the plant or for propagation purposes, allow the foliage to be cut down by frost. Lift the tubers with a fork in late October or early November. Take great care not to damage any of the tubers, which will be far greater in number and very much larger than those planted out during the previous spring. Should any tubers become damaged they

Dahlia buds form with one main lead bud backed up by two secondary buds

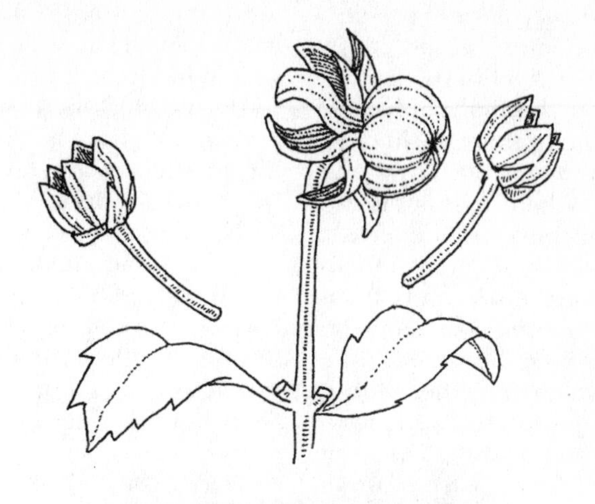

For a small number of large blooms, remove the secondary buds

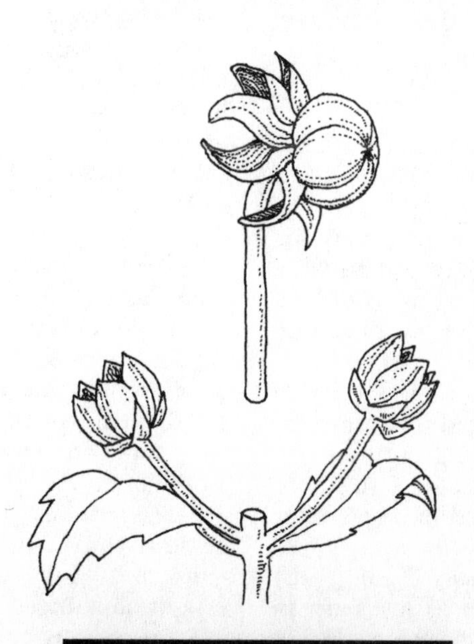

For slightly smaller blooms but twice the number, remove the primary bud

must be cut free at the narrow neck where they are attached to the stem. Dry the cut by dusting with flowers of sulphur or, if this is not available, talcum powder. The tubers must be stored in dry, frost-free conditions.

Propagate border dahlias by allowing lifted tubers to shoot in the greenhouse during March and April. When the shoots are 10 cm (4 in) long, cut them from the tubers and place them individually in flower pots filled with potting compost. Keep the pots in the greenhouse until the shoots have rooted, then either transfer them to a cold frame to harden them off. After all danger of frosts have passed, plant them out in the open ground to provide flowers during the current year.

Bedding dahlias are grown from seed, but they do not yield the long-stemmed flowers needed for cutting.

Gladiolus

Gladioli are among the most expensive of cut flowers at a florists, although they are easy to grow. But they need canes for support and so are not suitable subjects for display borders. Grown in rows they produce one spike per plant per season.

Gladioli like a rich soil, so work well rotted manure or compost into the ground before planting and scatter Growmore or blood, fish and bone fertiliser over the soil.

Plant the corms 7 cm (3 in) deep and 12 cm (5 in) apart in rows 30 cm (1 ft) apart during late March or early April.

Gladioli are generally trouble free but the new growth requires protection from slugs and snails. Tie the spike to the cane as it grows and allow it to develop until the bottom four blooms have opened, at which stage it should be cut.

During October, while the remaining foliage is still attached lift the whole plant and cut back to 5 cm (2 in) beyond the corm.

The original corm will be a pad of dead material below which will be a completely new corm. Surrounding it will be several cormlets, which can be grown on in a nursery bed to form flowering corms for future years.

Place the corms and the cormlets in paper (not plastic) bags marked with the name of the variety and store in a cool but frost-free place.

Gypsophila paniculata

With its cloudlike mass of tiny flowers, gypsophila is a must for flower arrangers. One plant will be sufficient.

It requires an alkaline soil (on acid soils it will be necessary to add lime at a rate of 100 g/sq metre (4 oz/sq yd) prior to planting).

The flowers appear from June until September. Do not gather all of the blooms at once, since unlike many plants cutting will not stimulate further flower production.

The varieties to grow are 'Bristol Fairy', which is pure white, and 'Pink Star', which has a slight pink tinge.

Propagate from seed or from cuttings taken early in the spring.

Annuals and biennials suitable for cut flowers

Name and type	Colour	Height cm	Height in
Aster, HHA	Mixed	30	12
Candytuft, HA	Mixed	25	10
Clarkia, HA	Red, white	45	18
Chrysanthemum carinatum, HA	Multicoloured	60	24
Cornflower, HA	Blue, red, white	30	12
Gypsophila elegans, HA	White	45	18
Larkspur, HA	Blue, red, white	100	40
Marigold, African, HHA	Orange, yellow	45	18
Rudbeckia, HHA	Yellow, orange	60	24
Sweet William, HB	Red, white	30	12
Zinnia, HHA	Mixed	35	14

HA: hardy annual
HHA: half-hardy annual
HB: hardy biennial

Sweet peas

Sweet peas are deliciously scented annuals which climb by means of tendrils and flower in a wide range of colours from June until August. They will grow in virtually any soil but appreciate a humus-rich environment to which a little lime has been added.

The relatively large seeds are surrounded by a tough skin which should be nicked with a sharp knife before sowing. This will enable the seeds to take up water more readily and so trigger the germination process. Sow the seeds individually in pots either in October or late March. Allow the seedlings to remain in the greenhouse until they are about 5 cm (2 in) in height. Harden them off before planting out. If you have no greenhouse, the seeds may be sown directly into the ground but some form of protection is required throughout the winter.

When the main shoot is about 10 cm (4 in) tall and a side shoot has begun to develop, pinch out the main stem just above the side shoot. Cultivating the secondary growth rather than the leader results in a far more vigorous plant. Allow only one side shoot to develop and when this is 10 cm (4 in) high plant the sweet peas out in a drill, placing each plant next to a cane.

To channel all the plants' energy into first producing strong growth and then flowers, remove all tendrils and side shoots. Tie the stems to the canes. Give the plants a weekly feed with liquid fertiliser and water regularly throughout dry spells. Do not allow any blooms to run to seed as this will stop flower production.

Sweet peas are often infected with greenfly though usually they can be ignored. Should they reach epidemic proportions, spray with a pesticide or soft soap solution.

Late-sown sweet peas are liable to be attacked by mildew, which should be sprayed with a fungicide as soon as it is seen.

Everlasting annuals

A small number of annuals are described as everlasting. These are plants that can be dried and used in the preserved state as floral decorations for the winter months. Once considered old-fashioned cottager's subjects, they are becoming very popular again. Cut the flowers just before the blossoms are fully opened. Hang them upside down in bunches to dry in a greenhouse or conservatory. It is possible to buy packets of mixed everlasting flowers as well as individual species.

Perennials suitable for cut flowers

Name	Flowering period	Height cm	Height in	Colours
Achillea	Jun–Aug	100	40	Yellow, white
Aquilegia	Jun	60	24	Various
Coreopsis	Jul–Aug	100	40	Yellow
Delphinium	Jun	100	40	Blue, pink, white
Echinops	Jun–Aug	100	40	Blueish grey
Helenium	Sept–Oct	100	40	Red, orange, yellow
Lupin	Jun	100	40	Various
Michaelmas daisy	Sept–Oct	125	45	Blue, mauve, red, pink, white
Paeony	May–Jun	90	36	Red, pink, white
Physalis	Jul–Aug	60	24	Orange 'lanterns'
Poppy (Iceland)	Jun–Jul	50	20	Orange-yellow
Pyrethrum	Jun	50	20	Red, pink, white
Scabious	Jun–Aug	60	24	Blue, white, mauve, pink, red
Sedum spectabile	Sept–Oct	30	12	Pink, red
Statice (*Limonium latifolia)*	May–Aug	50	20	Blue
Thalictrum	Jul–Sept	100	40	Mauve

17 The Vegetable Garden

Everyone should attempt to grow at least some of their own vegetables in the garden. The size of your plot will limit your activities to some extent, but worthwhile crops can be grown in the tiniest areas. Today the majority of gardens are much smaller than they once were and unless you have plenty of room you will need to plan carefully the use of your available space. For example, potatoes could be given a miss as they take up a lot of space, are cheap to buy and do not display the same improvement in flavour that gathering fresh from the garden does with many other vegetables. Lettuce may be raised in window boxes and tomatoes, probably the most popular of all vegetable crops, can be grown in pots on a balcony or patio – a variety has even been specially bred for hanging baskets. And vegetables with visual appeal such as the red-leafed beetroot, rhubarb chard and 'Salad Bowl' lettuce with its delicate fingerlike leaves are not out of place grown in mixed borders. The majority of gardeners, however, will set aside part of their garden as a conventional vegetable plot or rent an allotment from the local authority.

Whether you have a large or small plot most methods of cultivation are similar, with only slight differences. One of the reasons for leaving large spaces between rows of vegetables is to enable the gardener to move between the plants. With smaller plots this may not always be necessary as much of the work can be performed from the paths. There are a number of ploys, such as sowing mixed rows.

Vegetable growing is probably more demanding on the ground than any other method of gardening. For success you must get the soil in first rate condition and aim to keep it that way.

Digging

Dig the soil over as soon as it becomes vacant during the autumn. Ideally all available ground should be dug before Christmas. This will give plenty of time for the frost to do its work. During the winter the soil that you've turned over will freeze hard. The expansion of the contained moisture as a result of freezing forces the soil particles apart. So the soil becomes more pliable, enabling you to get a fine tilth. Early digging will also allow you to start sowing and planting without delay immediately the ground is dry and warm enough to work on.

Single digging

To turn over a vegetable plot, dig out the first sod of soil and place it in front of the hole that has been created. Dig out the next sod in the same way until you have formed a line across the plot. You will now have a raised mound and a trench between it and yourself. Start the second row in the same manner, this time placing the soil in the trench left by the first row. In this way the earth is completely rotated.

Double digging

In the method known as double digging, you dig down a second spade's depth once the first trench has been formed, bringing soil from a lower level to the surface. This method, which increases the depth of cultivation, is beneficial for long-rooted vegetables though it is doubtful whether the extra effort involved can be justified in terms of improved crops.

Manuring

Work well rotted animal manure into the soil every three years to simultaneously improve the texture and build up the nutrient levels. Either spread the manure over the ground before digging or place it in the trench during the digging process. If manure is not available, use compost. In the other two years of the three-year cycle scatter either Growmore or blood, fish and bone at the rate of 50 g/sq m (2 oz/sq yd).

The majority of vegetables prefer a slightly alkaline soil. A year before the vegetable plot is due for manuring dress it with lime at the same rate as given for Growmore. Do this in the autumn prior to digging, and add the Growmore the following spring.

Cropping systems

A vegetable garden if not a thing of beauty demonstrates a well ordered mind by the way it is laid out. The conventional way to plant vegetables is in rows. Another way is to space them apart equally in blocks.

Straight rows can be achieved by using a line and a measuring stick. There is no need to buy either. To make a line, take two pieces of wood 1 cm (½ in) thick or metal rods 50 mm (¼ in) in diameter and 30–45 cm (12–18 in) long. Then tie each end of a piece of string slightly longer than the length of the plot to each rod. Prepare a measuring rod by taking a piece of wood 1 cm x 1 cm square and 2 m long and place marks on it denoting every 5 cm. (Should you prefer to work in the Imperial system, use a piece of wood ½ in x ½ in and 6 ft long. Mark off each foot and subdivide it into 3-inch lengths.)

Beans and peas

Broad beans

Unless you are prepared to spray against blackfly stick to the November/December-sown 'Aquadulce', whose seeds are both hardy enough to germinate during the cold part of the year and the young seedlings can withstand the worst of the winter weather. Psychologically it is always a good idea to include early broad beans in the garden as the dark green seedlings, which emerge after about three weeks, remind one that the next season and its crops are only just around the corner. In locations which experience a hard winter the seed should be sown during the first week of November. In milder areas it can be delayed until December.

Unless they are dwarf varieties, broad beans will need some support. This may best be achieved by placing a stake with at least 1 m (3 ft) above ground level at all four corners of the row and then wrap two pieces of string 30 cm (1 ft) apart around the stakes to encase the beans.

During late May and early June blackfly will attack the succulent young growing tips. As soon as the plants are fully in flower or when the blackfly are first seen, the top 10 cm (4 in) of the plant should be removed. These may be boiled and eaten as a vegetable. Usually it is only the tender young shoots that the aphids attack, but if in spite of your treatment they remain to infest the rest of the plant they can be destroyed by spraying with a systemic insecticide. If the blackfly are allowed to remain they will completely destroy the crop.

All beans fix nitrogen from the air by means of pea-shaped growths, termed nodules, which can be seen on their roots. These together with the tops should be placed on the compost heap after the final picking.

Runner beans

These are arguably the most popular of all garden vegetables and if you do not normally grow any food crops it is well worth cultivating runner beans because unless you are very careful those bought in the shop are often tough.

Unlike broad beans, runner beans are not frost-hardy and should not be sown until mid-May.

Set out runner beans either in rows, which requires a line of supports, or against wigwams constructed from bamboo canes. Using either method it is important that the roots have access to moisture throughout the summer which may be very dry. Dig a trench 40 cm (15 in) deep by 30 cm (1 ft) wide and line it with newspaper. Place a layer of manure or compost 7 cm (3 in) deep at the bottom of the trench and cover it with topsoil. Place bamboo canes about 2.5 m (8 ft) tall every 30 cm (1 ft) along the trench and cross over the poles about 2 m (6 ft) above the ground. Lay a pole latitudinally between the Vs where the poles cross over and tie the three poles into place. This creates a row of rigid supports. It is important to create a strong structure as powerful winds can develop during August which will blow any weak supports and the beans over.

One of the big disadvantages with runner beans is that they screen the plants behind them from the sunlight, limiting what may be grown in the area behind. Where possible the runner beans should be sited at the back of the plot. A solution to this problem is to grow the beans up 'wigwams' sited in the corners of the plot or at the edges where light exclusion is likely to be less serious.

To create a wigwam, dig out a 1 m (3 ft) square hole 45 cm (18 in) deep, line it with newspaper and treat it the same way as for the trench. Place nine canes in a circular arrangement, crossing over 2 m (6 ft) from the ground.

The wigwam system is more adaptable, allowing a little-and-often sowing system. Start by providing and sowing two wigwams the first week in May and adding an extra one each fortnight until the beginning of July. This should give you a continuous supply of beans from the beginning of August through until the first frosts.

Whichever method you use, place two bean seeds, one either side of each bamboo cane. Any remaining bean seeds may be planted in a convenient space to provide a back-up should any fail to germinate.

Runner bean seedlings emerge when slugs and snails are most active, so protect them with slug pellets. The other main problem is blackfly. These must be controlled by spraying with a systemic insecticide. Do not attempt to pinch out the growing tips as described for broad beans as the blackfly will be at their most active long before the plants have reached their full height. Occasionally the lower flowers do not set beans, but this

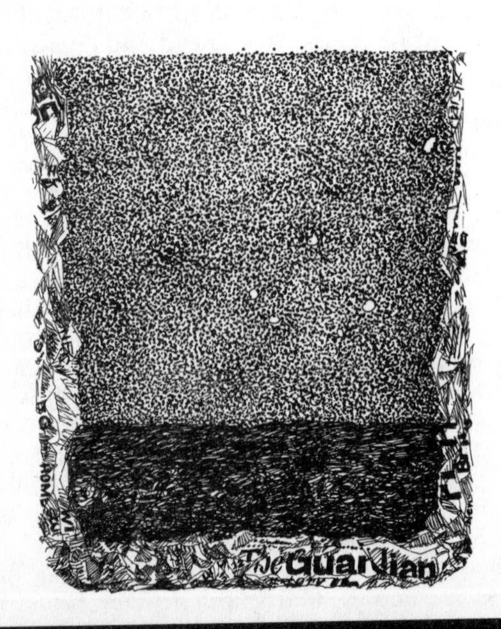

Runner bean trench, lined with newspaper, manure and/or compost

is only a temporary problem which will delay harvesting by just a few days.

French beans

Dwarf French beans do not throw shadows on the crops behind and also have the advantage that they need not be staked. They are ready to be eaten in a shorter period than runner beans, and even earlier crops can be obtained by growing them or at least starting them under glass.

It is not necessary to trench dwarf beans. While they should not be allowed to dry out their roots are not so deep as those of runner beans, and as they carry less foliage they will lose less moisture by transpiration. For a succession, plant a row of dwarf beans during the first week of May, June and July. An earlier crop can be obtained by sowing under cloches during the second week in April. A fortnight before sowing, place the cloches over the soil to raise the temperature – this will aid germination. Providing that the ends of the tunnel of cloches are blocked, the plants are unlikely to be affected by late-season frosts.

Climbing varieties of French beans give excellent crops of a similar quality to the dwarf types but they do require supports. Apart from slugs and snails, dwarf beans are not usually attacked by pest – including aphids.

Peas

Peas picked fresh from the garden are one of the delights of summer and are easily grown

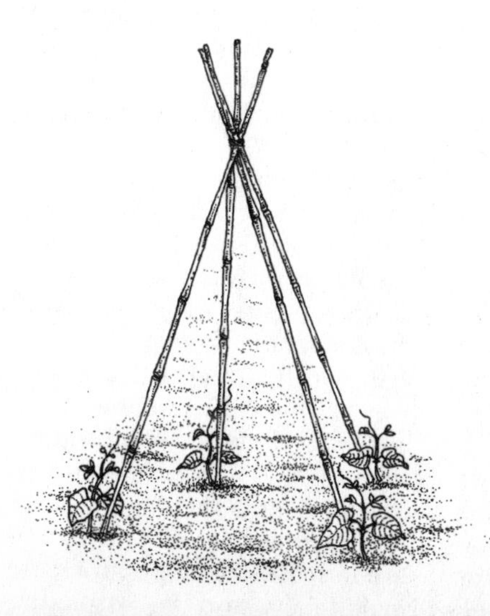

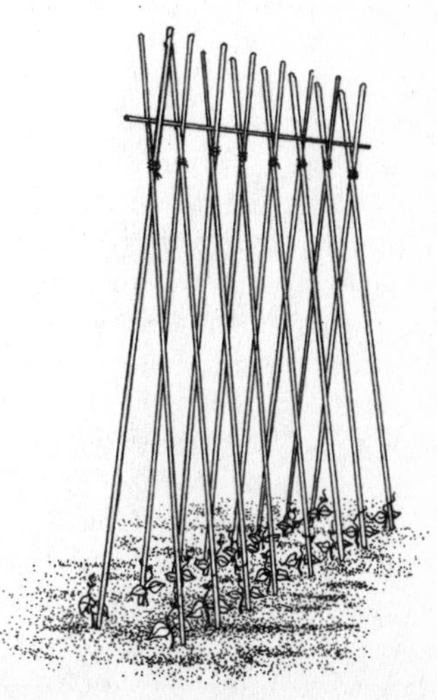

Wigwam runner bean support and traditional cross-cane system

provided that a little care is taken. Peas are classified as first earlies, second earlies and maincrop. While earlies grow quicker and are very much shorter, their crops are only a fraction of those obtained from the maincrop varieties. In a small garden with room for only one sowing, make it a maincrop variety such as 'Alderman'.

All peas require staking. If you live in the country you may still be able to obtain hazel sticks, which is the traditional means of pea support. The modern method is to grow the peas on nylon mesh.

Sow the peas in a drill 30 cm (1 ft) wide and 5 cm (2 in) deep. Scatter them in the drill so that there is about 5 cm between each pea and its nearest neighbour. Cover with soil.

Birds and slugs are attracted to emerging peas. Protect them with slug pellets and cover the drill with wire netting or a meshwork of cotton strands.

Earlies have no problems with maggots of the pea moth. Not so the maincrop. The female moths are on the wing from mid-June to mid-July, laying their eggs on the leaves and newly developing pods. If pea moths are a problem in your area spray with insecticide as soon as the pods have set, before the maggots can get into them. A late crop of peas may be obtained by sowing earlies late in May. Do not attempt this if your garden plants are prone to infection by powdery mildew – peas are highly susceptible to this disease.

Mangetout peas have extra wide, edible pods which are harvested as soon as the peas inside begin to swell. Crisp, sweet and expensive in the shops, they are worth a bit of space in the garden. Grow them exactly in the same way as ordinary garden peas.

Potatoes

Potatoes were once the most important crop in the vegetable garden. Today economics have changed and even if you have a large garden or an allotment you may not bother to grow maincrop potatoes. But earlies remain worthwhile providing you can spare the space. Potatoes are a good source of vitamin C in our diet, but the older they are and the longer they are out of the ground the more the vitamin diminishes. This alone is sufficient reason for growing early potatoes.

The one time you really ought to grow maincrop potatoes is when you have to deal with virgin soil. Nothing quite clears ground like cultivating potatoes on it for a season – this applies whether you are planning a vegetable or an ornamental garden. Potatoes are one of the few vegetable crops that actually prefer an acid soil.

Potatoes are susceptible to several diseases and to avoid problems you should purchase fresh certified seed each season. The term seed potatoes is a misnomer. Potatoes can produce fruits (they look like green tomatoes) and they are used in the development of new varieties. But seed potatoes are small tubers and the vegetative means of propagating them. If you examine seed potatoes you will find that one end is slightly larger and that it has green or purple buds called 'eyes'. Ideal tubers for planting will possess about three buds.

Seed potatoes should be 'chitted', i.e. sprouted, as soon as they are received. Stand them in a wooden apple box with the ends containing the buds uppermost and keep them in a light, frost-free place. In due course each eye will produce a shoot.

Traditionally potatoes were always planted on Good Friday – 'The better the day the better the deed'. But this is a variable date and a very unscientific approach. In mild areas in the south potatoes are best planted during the first week in April while in the north and areas prone to late frosts planting should be delayed until the second or third week of the month.

Examine the sprouted potatoes and discard any that are diseased. Those with four or more shoots should be cut into two halves, each part containing at least two shoots. Space the potatoes 35–40 cm (15 in) apart in rows 60 cm (2 ft) apart. Do not try to place the rows closer together as earthing up will be difficult. Make a hole 15 cm (6 in) deep with a dibber and place the tuber, shoots uppermost, in the hole. Cover with earth, taking care not to damage the growing stems. Alternatively, plant the potatoes in a trench with manure in the bottom. Earthing up tubers prevents them coming out of the soil, where they would become green. Any green coloured potatoes will be poisonous. Start earthing up when the haulm is about 10 cm (4 in) high and draw up about 10 cm (4 in) of soil around them to form a ridge. As the plants become larger draw up more and more earth around them. End the process when the haulms are full grown.

Potatoes are very dependent upon moisture for their development, so water thoroughly throughout dry spells.

Early potatoes mature during July. Only lift these as required. Maincrop potatoes will be ready for harvesting when their haulms have turned yellow and died back, which will be about September or October. When lifting potatoes care must be taken not to pierce them. Push the fork in the side of the ridge about 30 cm (1 ft) from the centre of the plant and at an angle of 45° and then work it right under the tubers. After they are gathered, leave the potatoes on the surface long enough for any soil to dry off. Check them over and remove any showing signs of disease. Then bag them up for storing in a cool but frost-free place.

Growing potatoes under plastic

The modern way to grow small crops of potatoes is under black plastic. There are several advantages. There is no need to earth up. The plastic acts as a mulch, retaining moisture and suppressing weeds. And the earth beneath warms up far more quickly, retains the heat more effectively and yields an earlier crop.

Buy a strip of black

PLANTING POTATOES

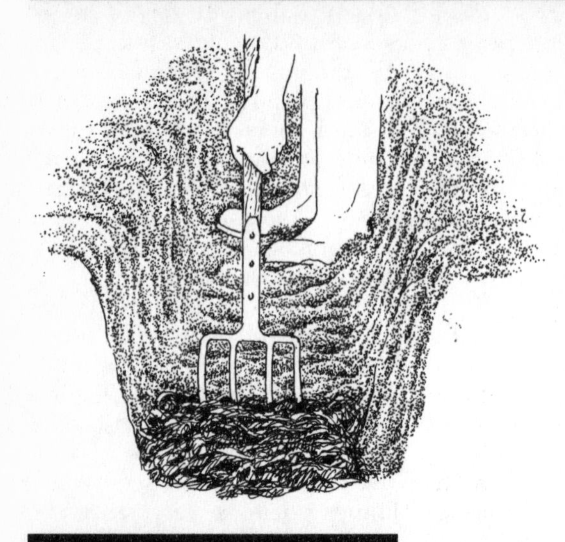

Dig a trench and fork in manure for compost

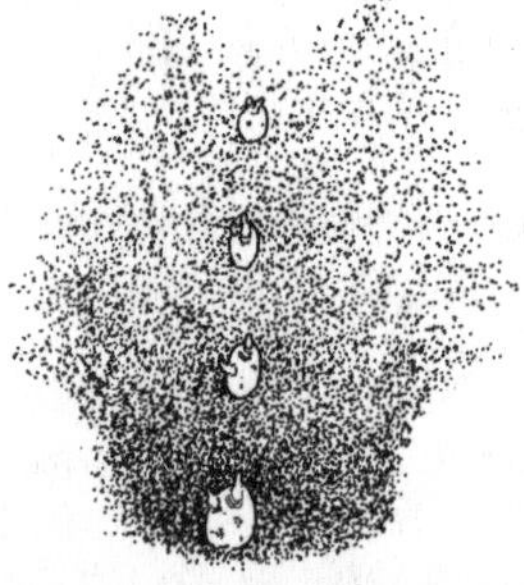

Plant the chitted potatoes, sprouts uppermost, in the trench

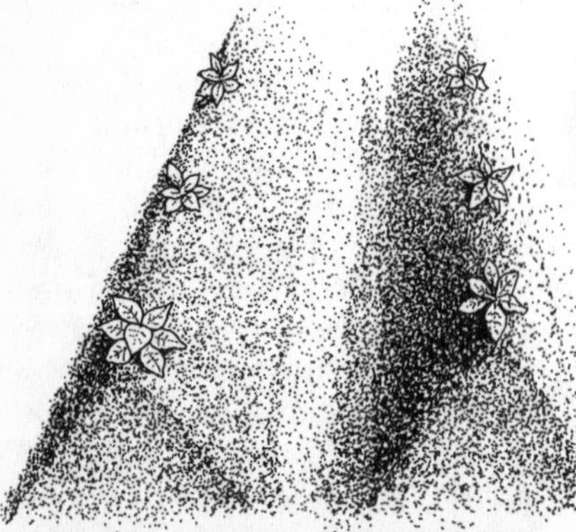

Earth up the plants to prevent developing tubers turning green

horticultural-grade plastic at least 60 cm (2 ft) wide. Make sure that the ground is moist before placing the plastic on the soil. Spread earth over the edges to anchor it down. Then make a cut in the plastic every 30 cm (1 ft) and with a dibber plant a seed potato. When the shoots grow they will push through the slits in the plastic. Apart from checking from time to time that they do not require watering the potatoes may be left undisturbed until they are ready for harvesting.

New potatoes for Christmas

At the end of September take a flower pot or bucket at least 25 cm (10 in) in diameter and fill it with an open rich compost. Plant one chitted seed potato in the container, cover with black plastic and place in the greenhouse. Make a hole through which the potato haulm can emerge. From time to time lift the plastic to water the soil. Allow the potatoes to develop and then die back. Harvest for Christmas.

Root vegetables

The most popular root crops are biennials, which are harvested the year they are sown and before they have had the opportunity to run to seed. As the roots become older they become progressively tougher because the individual cells become increasingly woody. Aim to grow the roots quickly and to eat them while they are still young.

Never grow root vegetables on freshly manured land. Where the soil is rich the roots will fork as they try to take in ever-increasing amounts of the abundant nutrients. Neither do root vegetables prosper in impoverished ground – the ideal condition exists where the soil was manured for the previous year's crops. During autumn, prior to sowing, dig the soil to create a fine tilth and treat with fertiliser (see pp. 213–214). Root vegetables prefer an open situation.

Most root vegetables require a temperature of 7°C (45°F) for germination, and if they are sown too early in soil that is wet they are unlikely to grow. Of the popular vegetables only parsnips require a full season for maturation but even these seeds should be delayed until the last week of March or the beginning of April – the earliest time for planting all root vegetable seeds. Earlier crops of carrots, radishes and beetroot may be obtained by covering the ground with cloches during the first fortnight of March and then sowing early varieties and keeping the glass or plastic over them until the middle of May. A succession of these vegetables can be achieved by first sowing early varieties. These are types that can usually withstand harsher weather conditions, but although they grow much quicker they are invariably smaller than the maincrop varieties.

Follow the earlies with maincrops and then during the first fortnight in July re-sow with earlies, which should reach maturity before the falling temperatures and diminishing length of daylight in the autumn stop all growth.

The Growing of root crops

Name	Sowings	Sowing depth cm	Sowing depth in	Cropping
Beetroot	Mar–Jun	2.5	1	Jun–Oct
Carrot				
Earlies	Mar onwards	1.5	$\frac{3}{4}$	From June
Maincrop	Apr–Jun	1.5	$\frac{3}{4}$	Sept–Oct
Celeriac	Apr	See text		Oct
Kohl-rabi	Apr–ul	2	$\frac{3}{4}$–1	Jun–Winter
Parsnip	Late Mar–Early Apr	1.5	$\frac{3}{4}$	Oct onwards
Radish	Mar–Aug	1	$\frac{1}{2}$	4–8 weeks after sowing
Salsify	Apr–May	1	$\frac{1}{2}$	Sept–Mar
Scorzonera	Apr–May	1	$\frac{1}{2}$	Sept–Mar
Swede	May–Jun	1.5	$\frac{3}{4}$	Oct onwards
Turnip	Mar–Aug	1.5	$\frac{3}{4}$	3 months

A late sowing of carrot seeds is particularly useful where carrot fly is a problem as the mature insects are no longer on the wing when the roots are developing, hence the old saying 'Sow in July avoid the fly'. However, late June is the last date that ensures a worthwhile crop.

Root vegetable seeds are small and must be sown as thinly as possible. When the seedlings are 6–8 cm (3 in) tall they should be thinned out. Take care not to damage the thinnings, and also immediately remove them, as they will omit a strong smell of the vegetable that will attract the egg-laying pests. As soon as the young roots are almost touching they will require thinning out again.

Where the soil is well drained the majority of root vegetables may be left in the ground throughout the winter or they can be lifted and stored in boxes between dry sand or peat.

Beetroot

The relatively large and irregularly shaped beetroot seed actually contains about three seeds inside a hard casing. Consequently, when the seeds germinate clusters of seedlings tend to grow in little groups. Sow the seeds 5 cm (2 in) apart. You must gradually reduce the cluster of seedlings to one, taking care not to dislodge the one you wish to retain. Do not aim for large beetroot (the ideal size is slightly smaller than a tennis ball). When a beetroot is cut it should be a dark crimson colour with only the slightest trace of concentric white rings. The presence of well-pronounced white rings is a sign that the beetroot is tough and past its best.

There are two main types of beetroot: the familiar spherical varieties and long varieties resembling very fat carrots (ideal maincrop roots for storing through the winter). Both golden and white varieties of beetroot exist, providing colour variations for the salad bowl.

Carrots

There are long, short and intermediate varieties. The long-rooted kinds taper to a point, are late maturing and prefer deep, sandy, well-cultivates soil. Short-rooted carrots are best for early crops and are the ones to grow on stony or heavy soils until they have been improved. There are two kinds of short-rooted carrot: the shorthorn, with almost globular roots, and the early stump-rooted type which are cylindrical and blunt-ended. Intermediate varieties are of medium length and may be either tapering or stump-rooted.

Sow early varieties in succession over March to mid-April, then the maincrop sorts up to mid-July. For late July sowings, choose a shorthorn variety.

The maggots of the carrot fly are likely to be the chief problem when growing this crop. They tunnel through the carrot and ruin it. A tell-tale sign of infestation is a reddish discoloration of the leaves. For methods of control, see pp. 263 and 270.

Celeriac

Celeriac has a swollen root about the size of a cricket ball which possess the true flavour of celery, for which it is an excellent substitute in stews and casseroles. It may also be grated on salads, certainly it deserves to be more widely known.

Grow celeriac as a half-hardy annual. It requires a long growing season. Sow the seeds in a greenhouse or indoors during March. When the seedlings are large enough to handle transplant them into boxes of seed compost and grow on under glass until the end of

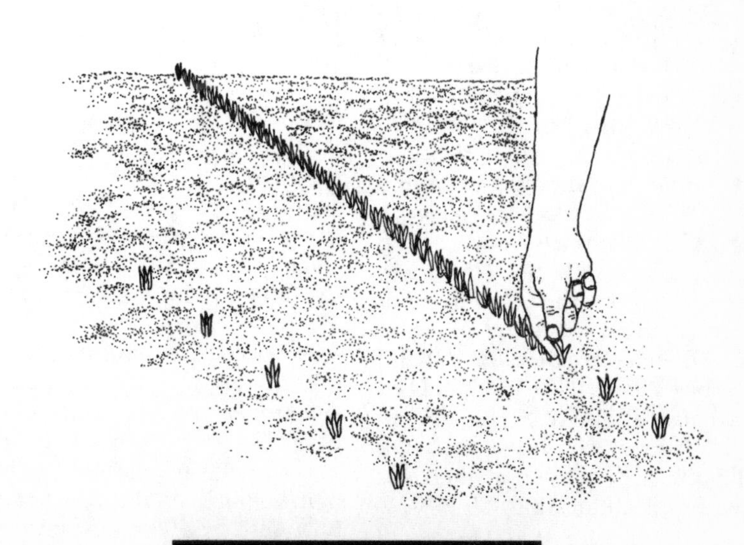

Keep thinning carrot seedlings so that remaining plants have room to develop

April. The seedlings must be hardened off before being transplanted 15 cm (6 in) apart in rows 30 cm (1 ft) apart into a humus-rich soil. Though the seedlings are only half-hardy the mature roots may be left in the ground throughout the winter and cropped as required.

Kohl-rabi

This is a brassica and is not really a root vegetable at all, but it looks and tastes like a turnip and is grown in the same way. The edible part is the globular swelling of the stem which becomes tough and woody unless it is eaten before it exceeds 5 cm (2 in) in diameter. Sow any time between March and August. The crop should be ready to harvest in 2–3 months.

Parsnips

Parsnips require a deep, well cultivated soil. Sow in March 1 cm (½ in) apart. The seed takes five to six weeks to germinate and it can be erratic. As soon as the seedlings have two well developed leaves thin out to 4 cm apart, and when they are 5 cm tall they should be thinned to 10 cm apart. The parsnips should be ready for eating during August, but they are better left in the ground until after the first frosts the action of which helps to develop the full flavour. They can be allowed to remain in the ground until March. Traditionally what remained was used for wine making.

Radishes

There are two types of radish: the familiar red and white summer varieties, and the large-growing winter radishes which may be red, white or black and up to 25 cm (10 in) in length.

Summer radishes must be grown and eaten quickly. They can be ready for harvesting in as little as three weeks, but during spring and autumn they will take up to eight weeks to reach edible size. If they are allowed to remain in the soil too long and get too large they will become hotter to the taste, woody and hollow inside. The secret is to sow little and often. During December, January and February they may be sowed in frames or under cloches.

Winter radishes are sown in July or August. In November and December they will be ready for lifting and may be stored (they keep well). As with all long-rooted vegetables a deep, well-cultivated soil is essential. Garden pests are not much of a problem – it seems they are repelled by the peppery foliage.

Salsify and scorzonera

Although different plants, these long thin-rooted vegetables which grow to about 30 cm (1 ft) may be considered together. They are great favourites in continental Europe where their distinctive sweet flavour, said by some people to resemble fish, is greatly appreciated. Salsify is sometimes called the oyster plant. Scorzonera has a lighter, more delicate flavour. Their cultivation is similar to parsnips. Sow the seed directly into the ground during April. The crop should be ready by mid-October. The roots may be lifted and stored in sand or peat or left in the ground for use as required.

Swedes and turnips

These are both members of the cabbage family. Turnips usually have white flesh (there are some yellow varieties too) and may be eaten cooked or raw. Swedes are yellow, and milder and sweeter in flavour but should always be cooked. Both are fast growing. Turnips are usually sown in the spring and eaten 2–3 months after germination, which only takes a few days. Left too long in the ground they become woody. A late crop of turnips for winter use can be obtained by sowing during the last week in August.

Swedes may be sown in the spring but it is usual to delay until mid-June. The roots will be ready to harvest in late autumn. They are hardier than turnips and may be left in the ground over winter. Keep a few in storage, though, for when the ground is frozen.

Being brassicas, turnips and swedes are susceptible to the pests that attack the cabbage family. The main problem is aphids. The tiny whitish-grey insects are seen inside the leaves which become contorted and whitish-yellow in appearance. Viruses spread by the aphids stunt the growth of the leaves and the roots fail to swell. Aphids should be treated as soon as they are seen by spraying with derris, malathion or a soft soap solution.

Summary of root crop operations

1 Dig the ground during the autumn to aid the breakdown of the soil to produce a fine tilth.
2 Place a line across the plot and make a drill to the required depth.
3 Sow the seed as thinly as possible.
4 When the seeds have germinated, thin out gradually. Do not attempt to complete the task in one operation as plant mortality is at its highest during the seedling stage and there will be no back-up should the young plants die.
5 A rising temperature, fertile soil and moisture will encourage your seeds to germinate, and thousands of weed seeds too. Hoe regularly between the rows and remove by hand the weed seedlings that appear within the row.
6 As roots get older they generally develop a tougher, woodier texture which makes them unpalatable. At the same time the flavour intensifies – there is an optimum time for harvesting all roots. Some root vegetables actually improve with keeping.
7 Do not allow any roots to remain in the ground beyond the March following the year in which they were planted as they will run to seed.

Onions, leeks and garlic

Onions

Onions may be grown either from seed sown during January or August, depending upon variety, or from small immature onions termed sets. A rich medium to light soil is required, and a position in full sun. Scatter

Growmore or blood, fish and bone at the rate of 50 gm/sq m (2 oz/sq yd) prior to planting out. Ideally, beds for spring-sown onions or sets should have been prepared and manured the previous autumn.

Because onions require a long growing season, to obtain the largest possible size the sowings must be made in January or early February in heat, i.e. 7–10°C (45–50°F). The plants are raised indoors until the end of March when they should be transplanted into pots or boxes and thoroughly hardened off in a cold frame prior to planting out in beds during the first week of April.

Alternatively, onions can be sown directly into the ground during March. This will produce small yet still very worthwhile onions. The thinnings may be eaten as spring onions.

Japanese onions are sown during the last two weeks of August. Here the problem is keeping the temperature below 21°C (70°F) during hot weather. While the seeds can be sown out of doors, it will be easier to control the temperature if they are germinated indoors in a seed pan and then transferred to a seed box. The young onions should be transplanted to their growing beds 15 cm (6 in) apart in rows 30 cm (1 ft) apart when they are 15–20 cm (6–8 in) tall.

Most gardeners find growing onions from sets much more convenient than from seed. Sets are partially grown the previous season and then held in a state of suspended growth. They are heat treated and once planted will get away to a flying start. During April, plant the sets with the bulb two thirds buried and the same distance apart as seedlings (see above). Birds quite often remove sets from the ground. They mistake the dead stem for a piece of straw and try to take it for nest building. It will be necessary to inspect the bed daily until the sets have formed roots.

As the bulbs begin to swell, gradually remove the soil from their base with your finger. Pinch out any thick flower stalks that appear in the centre of the greenery as soon as you can identify them.

Providing that the soil is in tip-top condition onions will not require any additional feeding, but if your soil is inclined to be thin give a weekly feed with either liquid manure or a foliar fertiliser.

Autumn-sown onions will be ready for lifting in July, winter or spring sown onions about August. When the onion has completed the current year's growing cycle the leaves naturally die back. Once they are dead the onion should be removed from the soil and allowed to remain on the ground to dry out thoroughly. After a few days turn the onions over. If it is late in the season (a time of heavy dews), place the onions on sacking and take them inside during the night. Also bring them in when there is danger of rain. You will know that the onions are thoroughly ripened when the outer skins are a golden colour.

Rot spreads readily among stored onions. Make sure that air can circulate around them. Store the onions in a net bag suspended from a garage or greenhouse roof.

Spring onions

You can use the thinnings of immature maincrop onions for saladings. But most gardeners grow 'White Lisbon', a special purpose spring onion. It is a quick grower with a good white skin and pleasant flavour. Sow in drills about 2.5 cm (1 in) deep during the early spring. Harvest when they are 30 cm (1 ft) high.

Welsh onions

These are a completely different species of onion which, when picked small, can provide a substitute for spring onions. They are non-bulbous, look like small leeks, and increase rapidly by division to form clumps. Although the rate of growth and division slows down to a virtual standstill during the winter months the foliage does not die back, with the result that they are one of the very few vegetables which may be harvested all the year round.

Plant Welsh onions at any time of the year either in rows of two or in a small block, 15 cm (6 in) apart either way. Alternatively you can sow seed. Do not take any onions during the first year when the plants are still establishing themselves. From the second year onwards harvest by removing a whole clump. Select a pair of onions from the group, taking care not to damage them in any way, and return them to the original site. Feed once a year with a scattering of a general fertiliser. Very occasionally Welsh onions will produce a flowering stalk, which must be removed. Apart from keeping them weed free they require no further attention. They are strong, hardy plants not usually affected by pests.

Shallots

Shallots are a different species from the ordinary onion of the kitchen. They are small, have a milder flavour and are produced in clumps. Having a reduced surface area they are easier to ripen thoroughly, making them far better keepers than the larger onions.

Shallots are grown by planting some of the bulbs from last year's crop 20 cm (8 in) apart in rows 25 cm (10 in) apart during February. Birds tend to tweak them out of the ground, just as they do with onions sets, so it will be necessary to keep an eye on them until they are rooted. As the shallots grow, each bulb will continually divide to form a cluster of up to 10 new shallots. As the foliage dies down, during mid-July, lift them and allow to ripen in the sun as described for onions. When dry, separate the bulbs and store in a cool, frost-free place.

Tradition has it that shallots should be planted on the shortest day and lifted on the longest. Better results are obtained if both dates are delayed by about six weeks.

Garlic

A garlic bulb consists of several cloves or bulblets massed together. Each clove can be grown to form a complete new bulb. A garlic bulb purchased from the greengrocer will provide sufficient cloves for an average sized crop. Separate the cloves and plant them 10–15 cm (4–6 in) apart out of doors during the early spring. These will develop into onion-type plants that will die down by midsummer. The white-skinned bulbs should be dried and stored in a cool dry place.

Leeks

Early leeks are raised by sowing seed inside during January and February for planting out in April. The maincrop is sown out of doors at the end of March. The seedlings are ready for planting out in their final position when they are 20 cm (8 in) long and as thick as a pencil. The best crops are obtained if the leeks are planted out by mid-July at the latest. (It is advisable to grow your own plants as it is often not possible to purchase seedlings until quite late in the season.)

When transplanting leeks, take care not to damage the long roots. With a pair of scissors trim the leaves back to a length of 15 cm (6 in), to reduce the quantity of water lost by transpiration. With a dibber make holes about 2 cm (1 in) in diameter, 15 cm (6 in) deep and 20 cm (8 in) apart in rows 30 cm (1 ft) apart. Place a leek plant in each of the holes and fill with water. Do not fill the holes with soil. If there is no rain, continue to fill the holes with water each day until it is clear that the roots are supporting the plants. The holes will gradually fill with soil but while they remain open they are an excellent aid to watering.

PLANTING LEEKS

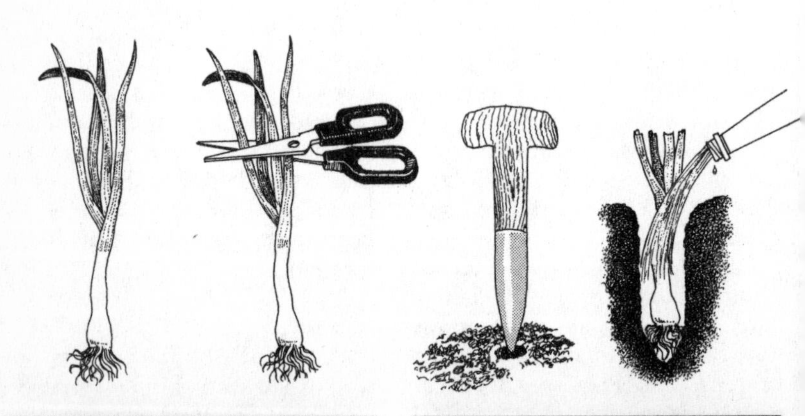

Before planting, trim the leaves to reduce the loss of water by transpiration

Make holes with a dibber. Drop a seedling into each one and water well

Guide to growing the cabbage family

Name	Sowing	Transplanting	Distance apart cm	Distance apart in	Cropping
Cabbage					
summer	Mar–May	May–Jun	30	12	Jul–Oct
spring	Aug	Sept–Oct	30	12	Apr–June
winter	May	Jul	30	12	Oct–Mar
Kale	May	Jul	45	18	Nov–Mar
Brussel sprouts					
early	Mar	May	60	24	Oct–Jan
late	Apr	Jun	60	24	Dec–Mar
Cauliflower					
summer	Jan	Mar	60	24	Jul
autumn	Apr	Jun–Jul	60	24	Sept–Dec
winter	May	Jul	60	24	Dec–Apr
Broccoli					
white-headed	May	Jun–Jul	75	30	Jan–May
purple-headed	May	Jun–Jul	75	30	Dec–May
Calabrese	May	Jun–Jul	60	24	Aug–Sept

To increase the length of the blanched stem, pull the earth up around the leeks when they are 30 cm (1 ft) tall.

Leeks stand the winter in the ground and should be harvested up till April. After this they will start to produce a flower, which will be seen as a spike emerging from the centre of the stem. At this stage the leek will be very hard and must be assigned to the compost heap.

Cabbage family

The brassicas, or cabbage family, include Brussels sprouts, cauliflower, calabrese, broccoli and kale. All succeed best planted in an open sunny location on a rich, moisture-retentive soil. Dig manure or compost into the brassica patch before planting or sowing.

The majority of cabbages can be sown outdoors, in short rows. Only early cauliflowers need sowing inside during the winter. All cabbage plants for transplanting may be raised in the greenhouse, but it is far more time consuming. The only advantage of this method is that cabbages grown individually in pots suffer less root disturbance when they are planted into their permanent positions.

See the table above for cultural information on the various brassicas.

Cabbage pests and diseases.

Cabbages are attacked by the caterpillars of both the large and small white butterflies. The former is the worst, capable of destroying a crop in just a few days. For control, see p. 262–263.

These days, probably more damage is done to brassicas by aphids than any other pest. Greyish in colour, they cause yellowing and distortion of the leaves. As soon as they are seen, spray with a systemic insecticide or soft soap solution. Pay particular attention to the underside of the leaves and the cabbage hearts.

Sowing and harvesting times for lettuces

Sowings	Harvest	Recommended varieties
Mar–early Aug	Jun–Oct	'Baltic' (Iceberg type), 'Little Gem' (cos) 'All the Year Round' (butterhead) 'Salad Bowl' (loose leaf)
Aug	Nov–Dec (From early Oct, under glass)	'Avondefiance' (butterhead)
Aug–Sept	Mar–May (Outside all winter*)	'Winter Gem' (cos) 'All the Year Round' (butterhead)
Nov–Feb	Jan–Mar (Heated greenhouse)	'Winter Gem' (cos) 'Tom Thumb' (butterhead) 'All the Year Round' (butterhead)

For the control of cabbage root fly, see pp. 263 and 270.

Clubroot, a fungus disease, can be serious. See pp. 278–279.

Lettuces

Lettuce is an indispensable ingredient of the salad bowl. With a little bit of planning and the use of glass it is possible to harvest lettuces for most of the year. As lettuces soon run to seed after reaching maturity, sow just a little at a time but often.

The gardener has a far greater choice of varieties than it is possible to buy at a greengrocers. Try them all until you decide which you prefer. There are four basic types.

Butterhead (cabbage) lettuces are round headed with tightly packed hearts of soft leaves. Crispheads – also termed 'Icebergs' after a well-known variety – have dense heads or crisp, curled leaves.

Cos lettuces are tall and upright with a sweet flavour. They are old favourites but grown less frequently than they once were. A small variety that remains very popular is 'Little Gem'.

Loose-leaf lettuces are non-hearting varieties producing bunches of curly leaves. Unlike other varieties of lettuce where the whole plant is pulled, harvesting consists of removing only the outside leaves. The plants may be continually cropped in this way for several weeks, making fewer sowings necessary than with other varieties.

November to February sowings must be conducted in the greenhouse. Other sowings, except those in midsummer, may also be made in the greenhouse. The seedlings should be transferred to their final position outdoors when the leaves are 7–8 cm (3 in) high. Lettuces may also be sown directly into shallow drills where the plants are to grow. Thin out the young plants as soon as they are large enough to handle. Where lettuce are grown in rows they should be 20–22 cm (8–9 in) apart.

During the summer keep lettuces well watered. Drying out will encourage them to 'bolt'. To be crisp and tender they must be grown quickly in a nitrogen-rich soil, except those grown over the winter for use in spring. If there is a deficiency of nitrogen in the soil, give the young plant a light sprinkling of nitrate of soda in a circle radius about 10 cm from the stem.

Protect lettuces from attack by slugs and snails.

Spinach

The name 'spinach' tends to be used for several green leafy vegetables in the plant family Chenopodiaceae. 'True' spinach is the annual grown for either summer or winter use. There is also New Zealand spinach, another annual but only half-hardy and with smaller leaves. Spinach beet or perpetual spinach is a biennial which, as the name implies, will continue cropping for several months from one sowing. And then there is Swiss chard, also known as sea kale beet, which is not usually available in the shops. If you have never tried this vegetable you really should! It is effectively two vegetables in one. The leaf blades can be removed and cooked in a similar manner to ordinary spinach while the broad white stems are cooked like asparagus – delicious when served with melted butter.

Annual spinach should be sown in open ground in succession from March until May for gathering during the summer months. For winter spinach, sow from August to late September.

Sow the seed in drills 1–2 cm (½–1 in) deep. Thin the seedlings to 15 cm (6 in) apart in a series of stages. As with all annuals a lack of water will cause the spinach plants to run to seed.

Spinach beet and Swiss chard are cultivated in a similar way. Between April and July make a single sowing 2–3 cm (1 in) deep. Thin out the seedlings until they are no closer than 20 cm (8 in) apart, to ensure a succession of leaves until the following spring. Swiss chard is particularly useful as it acquires fresh impetus during late winter/early spring, producing another bumper crop of leaves before running to seed.

None of the vegetables in this group are attacked by pests other than slugs and snails.

Tomatoes

Tomatoes range from the small sweet cherry types to the huge 'beefsteak' forms. As well as the usual red varieties there are yellow and orange ones available. Most gardeners choose a standard variety, with fruits up to 5 cm (2 in) across, or one of the cherry types such as 'Gardener's Delight', unsurpassed for flavour.

Greenhouse culture

Sow tomato seeds during late January in pans at a depth of 1 cm (½ in). Many young tomato seedlings retain the seed case on the end of one of the leaves. Those plants seem to perform better, but there is no simple explanation for it. Tomatoes also retain the two seed leaves as a pair of solitary 'wings' long after the second and subsequent pairs of true leaves have formed. Again, retention of these seem to aid the plant.

When the little seedlings are 4 cm (1½ in) long, transplant

them into individual 9 cm (3¹ 2 in) pots filled with John Innes No. 2 potting compost. The seedlings should be kept in their pots until they have reached a height of 22 cm (9 in), at which stage they should be planted into their permanent position.

Tomatoes are vulnerabl to viral infections, and after a year or two you will very likely have disease problems if you continue growing tomatoes in the same border soil. One solution is to remove all of the soil (which may be safely used in another part of the garden) and replace it. But this is arduous and time consuming. An alternative is to use growing bags, which provide an isolated environment for the roots and hence ensure they will not pick up any disease contracted by the previous year's plants. Each growing bag will hold three plants, but care must be taken that the bags do not become broken.

Once the plants have been placed in their final positions they must be supported. In the greenhouse the easiest way to provide support is by means of pieces of soft string suspended from the ceiling. Tie the string in a very loose lop just below the first pair of true leaves and encourage the plants to twist around it. If this is not practical, support them by 2 m (6 ft) canes. Place these behind the growing bags so as not to damage them. From now on it will only be necessary to provide sufficient heat to ensure that the temperature does not drop to freezing point.

As the tomato plants develop, side shoots will be seen growing

Cordon tomato plants should be tied firmly to a bamboo stake

Pinch out side shoots from the leaf axils

out of each leaf joint. Pinch these out with finger and thumb as soon as they are large enough to allow it.

Sometimes the bottom trusses of fruit do not set, owing to poor pollination. When the small yellow flowers are fully open, gently shake them or spray with a water mister to dislodge the pollen and transfer it to other flowers.

When six trusses have formed, pinch out the growing tip at the top of the plant. Remember to water your tomato plants daily. Failure to do this can result in splitting or uneven ripening. And you will only get first rate crops if you provide the necessary nutrients.

A convenient means of feeding is to provide a special tomato fertiliser such as 'Tomorite'. Alternatively you may feed with home-made liquid manure (see p. 25).

Outdoor culture

Tomatoes must not be planted out of doors until all danger of frost has passed. In most areas this will be the first week of June. This effectively reduces the growing season to four months during which time the plants will only be capable of producing and ripening four trusses of tomatoes. Once the fourth truss has set, pinch out the top.

Any green tomatoes on the plants at the end of September should be picked and placed in a drawer to ripen.

Tomatoes grow well out of doors providing that they have a south-facing aspect where they can catch the sun all day. Prepare a trench 35–40 cm (15 in) deep and 30 cm (1 ft) wide, line it with several layers of newspaper and place 10 cm (4 in) of old manure or compost in the bottom. Return the soil to the trench. Plant cordon tomatoes 45 cm (18 in) apart. Remove side shoots as for greenhouse tomatoes.

Place a bamboo cane by each plant and sink a 9 cm (3½ in) flower pot next to its roots. Unless there has been some rainfall, fill the flower pot with water daily. Not only will this provide the correct amount, it will also direct it towards the roots and thus ensure that none is wasted.

Bush varieties should be set 60 cm (2 ft) apart. Their bushy habit means no canes are required, and there is no need to remove side shoots.

Growing bags allow you to make use of walls, balcony, patio or any hard surface that has a south-facing elevation. Once sited you can grow as good a crop as you can in open ground.

The glitzy appearance of growing bags can be improved to such an extent that they become a garden feature. In addition to the holes for the tomatoes, make six smaller holes in the front shoulder of the bag. Into every other hole place a trailing lobelia and in between plant pansies or fibrous-rooted begonias. Very soon these will cover up the bag and give a flowering display similar to a container. Should the appearance of the growing bag not worry you, place lettuce plants in the holes. Choose the smaller varieties, such as the cabbage lettuce 'Tom Thumb' or the cos variety 'Little Gem'.

Marrow family

Marrows, their mini-version courgettes, pumpkins, squashes and cucumbers are all members of the same family, the cucurbitaceae. They are all half-hardy annuals whose seedlings must be raised indoors and not transplanted to their cropping position until all danger of frost has passed. All are raised by the same method. During mid-April sow two seeds 1 cm deep in a 9 cm pot filled with compost. Allow the seeds to germinate at about 18.5°C (65°F). When the seedlings are 3–5 cm high the weaker of the two should be removed.

If your seeds are F1 hybrids, which are very expensive, you will not want to waste any. The seeds should be started into growth before they are sown. Place a piece of absorbent material such as a paper kitchen towel on a saucer. Thoroughly soak but do not flood. Spread the seeds over the surface, cover to exclude the light and place in a warm position. After 48 to 72 hours (the exact length of time will depend upon the temperature) the creamy white coating of the seeds will burst open and the shoot will begin to emerge. Taking care not to damage the seedling, transfer each seed into individual flower pots and gently cover with 0.5 cm (¼ in) of compost. Place the pots in a warm position and allow germination to continue.

Using either method, by the end of May the seedlings will be ready to transplant into their permanent positions.

Choose a well drained open site which receives maximum sunlight. Where drainage is a problem grow them on a flat-topped mound 30 cm (1 ft) high.

All members of this plant family, except some specially bred cucumbers, produce both male and female flowers. The female flowers can be identified by the tiny immature fruit at its base. Unless the female flowers are pollinated the small embryonic fruit will first turn black and then fall off. Pollination problems are most likely to occur with the first flowers. Later in the season insects usually bring about successful fertilisation. To be sure of pollination you can do it yourself by hand. Pick off a male flower and strip the petals to reveal the yellow pollen-covered stamens. Insert it into the female flower, tapping gently to dislodge the pollen. Make sure the pollen dusts the pistil of the female flower.

The fruits of the marrow family consist mainly of water and it is important to water the plants well during dry spells otherwise the fruit will fall off. All the same, not all the fruits will reach full size, as the plants have an inbuilt mechanism that ensures that they do not carry more than they can raise to maturation. If you want monster fruits like giant pumpkins, limit the number to one per plant.

Courgettes are the same species as vegetable marrows. The varieties sold by seedsmen for courgettes produce a prolific number of fruits from a bushy plant. They are normally picked when 10–15 cm (4–6 in) long. If left on the plant, however, they will grow to full sized vegetable marrows. Small vegetable marrows may be harvested and served as courgettes. When growing courgettes the aim is to produce a succession of small fruits throughout the season. To achieve this the plants must be cropped regularly.

Cucumbers

The short, rough-skinned ridge cucumbers are grown out of doors by the general method (see pp. 38–39). Do not remove the male flowers of these types as you do for indoor cucumbers. Special treatment is necessary to grow the familiar long indoor varieties.

Greenhouse cucumbers

Plant the cucumber seedlings in 25 cm (10 in) flower pots filled with an open loam-based compost. The older varieties have both male and female flowers but, unlike marrows, they will fruit without pollination. In fact if they are pollinated the fruit acquires a bitter taste, so remove the male flowers to stop them pollinating the females. There are now specially bred forms that have only female flowers which save the trouble of removing the male flowers.

Indoor cucumbers need to be able to climb up supports to which they must be tied. They like to have permanently moist roots but they must not be soaked, and they need a humid atmosphere.

Harvest the cucumbers as soon as they are large enough to enable others to develop.

The whole cucumber family is very prone to attack by powdery mildew. Spray with mancozeb as soon as it is noticed. With greenhouse cucumbers the fungus may be persistent and spraying at weekly intervals will be required.

Ornamental vegetables

Even if you have only a small garden and you do not wish to separate part of it off for growing vegetables they may be cultivated together with herbs amongst the flowers. Choose the correct types and they will justify their place by the colour and interest which they provide.

As well as beetroot and members of the spinach family seek out some of the less common vegetables. The recently introduced lettuce 'Lollo Rossa' has attractive fringed and crinkled pale green leaves with a crimson edge. The red chicory 'Palla Rossa', which matures from mid-September onwards, has red hearts with fine white veins.

Globe artichokes situated at the back of a border will add to the layout of a bed as well as providing a tempting fresh vegetable. Sit and study a seed catalogue – you will find a large number of possibilities.

Reasons for growing your own vegetables

- It can save you large sums of money, in spite of the cost of seeds, manures, fertilisers and any other materials.
- Vegetables are fresher and taste better when they are cooked and served immediately after harvesting.
- Different varieties of some vegetables differ considerably in

flavour. You can grow the variety you prefer and also vegetables not usually available in the shops.

- You can enjoy novelty vegetables such as yellow beetroot and striped tomatoes which add interest and colour to your salad bowl.
- Vitamin C, one of the vitamins we are most likely to be short of in our diet, begins to be destroyed the moment vegetables are harvested. Consequently vegetables that can be eaten immediately they are harvested are nutritionally superior.
- You can enjoy vegetables out of season, such as new potatoes with your Christmas dinner.
- If you are fond of mini-vegetables, which are cooked whole, and which may be difficult to find in the shops or are very expensive, then you may grow them as a luxury.
- The sense of achievement is probably far greater in being able to provide your own vegetables than with any other form of gardening.
- You can make a gift to friends that money cannot buy – home-grown vegetables.

18 The Herb Garden

The skilful use of herbs will enhance most meals. Their flavour comes from the essential oils or esters they contain. Yet valuable as herbs are in the kitchen it is not always possible to buy them fresh and they are far more flavoursome and altogether superior when just picked.

Herb is a term used to include all of those plants that have culinary (and in some cases medicinal) uses. Consequently it brings together a variety of plant types, from annuals through to shrubs and trees. For this reason herbs need to be considered separately from a gardening point of view.

Herbs may be grown in a specially set aside area, but the majority of them could share other beds if there is a shortage of space in the garden.

Twelve easy-to-grow herbs

Bay

Bay leaves come from a small tree, the bay laurel. This prefers a well drained, open site and is particularly suited to growing in containers on a patio or forecourt. Bay is particularly resilient to clipping and pruning and makes excellent short hedges for separating parts of the garden.

Buy a container-grown plant during the autumn at which time it can be set straight into its permanent position. Should you wish to produce a bay hedge, raise additional plants by ripewood cuttings taken during late August and early September.

Borage

A hardy annual whose young leaves, used in salads, taste a little like cucumber. The attractive blue starlike flowers can be eaten too. Carried all summer, they have five pointed petals and a pointed centre – the bees love them. Borage is not out of place in a herbaceous border, where once established it will seed itself. Grow it initially from seed.

Chives

A hardy perennial with a mild spring onion flavour. Chive bulbs grow in clumps as a result of continually dividing and are best grown in a series of small batches. Cut the leaves close to the ground as required. Regular cutting maintains a continuous growth of tender young leaves. About every three years, lift and divide the clumps in the autumn, and replant in new ground or freshly manured soil. With their purple flower heads, chive clumps are attractive enough for the front of the border.

Fennel

A hardy perennial herb about 2 m (6 ft) tall whose seeds and feathery leaves have a mild aniseed flavour. The leaves are used to flavour sauces and fish dishes and also make a fine tisane. The variety known as Florence fennel is smaller and an annual. This produces a bulbous stem base which is eaten as a vegetable. Its leaves may be used in the same way as the perennial kind. Fennel will look striking grown at the back of a border. A bronze-leafed form is available.

Grow fennel either from seed or by division of an established plant.

Lavender

This is not strictly a culinary herb although it may be used to flavour wines and liqueurs. It does however have a large number of uses when dried and is an ideal subject for inclusion either in a herb garden or in a herbaceous bed. See pp 148–149 for cultural details.

Marjoram

Marjoram has a sweet spicy flavour and is used mostly in meat dishes, stuffings and omelettes. Pot marjoram (*Origanum onites*) is a perennial and easy to grow. Propagate it by crown division during early March. Sweet marjoram (*O. majorana*) has a more aromatic flavour, but it is only half-hardy and should be grown as an annual. All marjorams like a sunny situation. With their attractive pink, white or mauve flowers they make good plants for the front of a border.

Mint

There are several mints grown for culinary purposes. Probably the most popular is the light green *Mentha spicata* or spearmint. Mints are plants of damp areas, so they should be kept well watered. They are happy in a sunny or partially shaded site. Unfortunately their underground stems, given the chance, will colonise large areas of the garden. In a restricted area such as a herb garden mint can soon take on the role of a weed. Keep it in check by planting the roots in a 25 cm (10 in) pot with holes in the bottom. Propagation is by root division.

Mint can be forced in the greenhouse so that it is available to accompany the first spring lamb. During the summer plant a length of root in a 15 cm (9 in) flower pot. Stand the pot out of doors in a sheltered spot and water regularly. During January, bring the pot into the greenhouse and place it under the staging. Continue to keep it well watered and cover to exclude the light. When the mint has started to produce white stems and pale yellow leaves, bring it out to stand in the light in order that it may become green, at which stage it may be cropped. Carry on harvesting until the outside mint comes into production.

Parsley

A hardy biennial grown as an annual. Germination tends to be slow and erratic. Sow the seeds in a gentle heat during March. Transfer to individual pots before planting out in May. Parsley makes a very attractive border to the vegetable plot.

Rosemary

One of the most fragrant, and pungent, herbs for use in the kitchen. With its attractive greyish-green evergreen leaves, rosemary also makes an excellent hedge or small shrub in a mixed bed.

Give it a site in full sun. Small blue flowers appear about April and continue off and on until September.

Rosemary cuttings root very easily. During May or June take a shoot of the current year's growth about 10 cm (4 in) in length and pull it away from the plant so that it retains a heel. Place it in a flower pot filled with an open compost. Stand the new plant in a sheltered spot during the winter and then plant it out into its permanent position.

Sage

A bushy evergreen shrub with grey-green leaves much used in stuffings, sage is said to bestow wisdom on all who consume it. The seed may be sown in gentle heat during spring or delayed until early summer when it will germinate at ambient temperature. Sage may be placed in its permanent site the same year the seed was sown. Plants can also be raised from cuttings taken in June.

Sage soon becomes very straggly. Take fresh cuttings every second year and use them to replace the original plants. A sunny situation is required.

Tarragon

A perennial about 60 cm (2 ft) in height which prefers a sunny, well drained site. If left unchecked it will spread by its underground roots. About every four years, to regenerate your tarragon, lift it and replant one of the daughter plants which emerge some distance from the declining parent. Tarragon is best propagated by root cuttings taken in summer.

Thyme

There are several forms of thyme, some of which are more suitable for growing on rock gardens. These include prostrate and mat-forming species. The thyme most used as a culinary herb is *Thymus vulgaris* which grows to about 25 cm (10 in) tall. A golden leaved form, 'Aurea', is available. Thyme is used, fresh or dry, for stuffings and flavouring casseroles. Lemon thyme (*T.* x *citriodorus*), which is less pungent, is used in a similar way.

Obtain your plants by sowing seed in warmth during early spring, or by dividing an established plant during March. Grow thyme in a sunny spot.

Pot-grown herbs

The original cottagers' idea was that the herbs should be grown just outside of the kitchen door so that the cook had the minimum distance to walk.

Today this has been taken to its logical conclusion with people actually growing the plants in pots in the kitchen itself. Even if you do not wish to go to these lengths a variety of herbs can be grown in specially designed terracotta pots which can be sited close to the house or, if you are a flat dweller, on a balcony. Only the shorter types of herbs can be grown in this way and usually it will be advisable to plant new specimens each year.

Drying herbs

Herbs dried for use in winter, though lacking the piquancy of fresh material, will retain enough of their essential oils to make them a good substitute.

Gather the herbs when they are in prime condition either just before or at the time of reaching maturity. Once past its peak all plant material rapidly deteriorates. Pick the leaves on a bright day. Lay them out to dry between two sheets of kitchen towel somewhere warm and airy. Aim to dry the leaves as quickly as possible, but never subject them to direct sunlight. That would evaporate their essential oils, which are volatile organic liquids. The loss increases rapidly as the temperature rises, so oven drying is not recommended.

Guide to the growing and cropping of herbs

Herbs for pot culture	Herbs for drying	Herbs for gathering all year round
Bay (as a container-grown tree)	Fennel (seeds only)	Bay
Chives	Marjoram	Rosemary
Marjoram	Mint	Sage
Mint	Tarragon	
Parsley	Thyme	
Thyme		

Grow herbs in terracotta pots conveniently near the kitchen

19 Fruit Growing

There is room for fruit trees in all but the smallest garden providing you choose specimens on dwarfing rootstocks. Virtually all our modern fruit trees are the result of special crosses carried out in scientific breeding programmes, while old favourites, such as the cooking apple 'Bramley Seedling', were the result of good fortune. For years it has been realised that the hybrid varieties are either larger, have a sweeter or better flavour, a more pleasing appearance or greater disease resistance, but they do not grow with the vigour of their wild ancestors. To overcome the problem a tree would be grafted onto the rootstock of a vigorous compatible tree, often the wild form of the hybrid that was being produced. This gave the best of both worlds – a very vigorous root pumping energy into fruit-producing tissue of a different variety. What you had in fact was not one but two fruit trees married together, each doing what it does best.

It was soon realised that the size of the tree was not dependent upon the fruiting variety but the rootstock, and research was carried out to breed types that would produce smaller trees – trees that could be easily trained into special shapes and that yielded a larger amount of fruit for the size of tree.

Rootstocks are now available for growing fruit trees of any desired size, from less than 2 m (6 ft) upwards, so you can grow most varieties of your favourite fruit in a confined space. You can also train a tree to grow in whatever shape you like (see pp. 243–45). However, you must be clear in your mind how you wish to grow your tree and ask the nurseryman to provide the appropriate sapling for the purpose.

Before buying and planting any tree make sure you have the space it needs, and the right situation for it. Most fruit trees require full sunlight but will themselves cast a shadow, rendering the ground underneath them only suitable for growing grass and spring flowers. Large trees often have roots near the surface which can make it impossible to dig the ground. Take all this into account when making your choice of tree.

Pollinators

Pollination in the case of fruit trees is carried out exclusively by insects. During nectar collection they carry pollen on their bodies from tree to tree. The pollen of some trees (e.g. the Victoria plum) will fertilise the female cells of the same tree – these are said to be self-fertile. But in many a mechanism comes into play that stops the egg cells from being fertilised by pollen from the same tree or one of the same variety. Such varieties are said to be self-sterile and they require pollen from a different variety for fertilisation. There are other varieties described as partially self-fertile, which means in the absence of another variety they will yield only limited crops. But all fruit trees, including those described as self-fertile, yield better if a different variety which flowers at the same time – a compatible tree – is planted nearby.

So, before buying a fruit tree check with the nurseryman whether it is self-fertile and, if it is not, what are the compatible varieties for pollination. You will need to buy one of these too. There are even some varieties, known as triploids, where it is necessary to plant *two* compatible varieties. If you have limited space a solution would be to grow a 'family tree', which has several compatible varieties grafted on one dwarfing rootstock.

Remember that it is the flowering period and not the cropping time that is important. For example, if you plant two early (or middle or late) flowering apple varieties, this may easily lead to one early apple and one late.

Among the cherries the acid cooking variety 'Morello' used to be the only self-fertile one. But now there is also a sweet cherry, 'Stella', which does not need a pollinator.

Many people grow apple trees blissfully unaware of the problems of fertilisation and never experience any difficulties. This is because apples, being such popular trees, are also in neighbouring gardens, and the bees, which can travel considerable distances foraging for nectar, visit both in their travels. If you live in an urban area where there are several gardens you may well be able to ignore the question of fertility in apples, but if you try to grow less commonly cultivated fruit you will find it an increasing problem. In an instance where you find you have a fruit tree that flowers well but does not produce a crop then you must purchase a second tree for fertilisation.

Purchasing

Fruit trees grown in the field can be purchased bare-rooted when they have just been lifted from the ground in the dormant season (between autumn and early spring). Alternatively the trees may be purchased as container-grown specimens and planted at any time of the year.

Container-grown fruit trees in spite of being very much more expensive offer few advantages for the gardener. All you are getting extra is a flimsy container and some compost. Garden centres prefer them because they may keep and sell the trees at any time of the year.

A fruit tree can last for many

years and you will probably never need to replace it in your lifetime. While some specimens will afford you a small crop during the first year you will generally need to wait longer to obtain any worthwhile yields. Therefore there is little point in rushing to plant the tree during the late spring or summer. Remember, even if you do plant a container-grown tree in the summer it is unlikely to be any further advanced than a bare-rooted one would be for planting in the following autumn and you will need to keep it continually watered throughout its first summer.

Planting

General instructions for planting bare-rooted trees are given on p. 160.

Pruning fruit trees

Pruning is conducted to control the size and shape of the tree and to direct its energies away from the making of wood and into fruit production. For the purposes of pruning, fruit trees may be divided into two groups. There are the varieties producing fruit on spurs (short branches carrying flower bud clusters). And then there are those known as tip-bearers, whose blossom is produced on the tips of the previous year's shoots.

Apples and pears

The majority of these are spur bearing, i.e. they produce their flowers followed by fruit on short thick stems originating from the sides of the laterals. To maximise spur production pruning must be conducted twice a year. During November, cut the wood of the main laterals back to a bud to keep the size of the tree under control. As well as encouraging fresh wood to develop to take its place, this will stimulate all growth from the laterals. By July you will notice that several long shoots – termed sub-laterals – are growing at right angles to the laterals. Cut back to two pairs of leaves. During August they should be further reduced to two pairs of leaves. Do not attempt to perform the operation in one go as it is necessary to retain enough leaves to generate sufficient food to build up the fruit the tree is carrying.

A small number of apple and pear trees are tip-bearers – these carry their fruit on the tips of the sub-laterals rather than on spurs. If all the branches are reduced during the same year there will be no fruit the following season. Here you should have a rolling programme of pruning, aiming to reduce half the laterals or sub-laterals each year during November. In theory this reduces the size of the crop you will get, but the fruits you obtain will be larger. Tip-bearers are not suitable for growing as either cordons or espaliers. Here the fruit must be carried away from the main regions of growth, which must be restricted.

Occasionally it is noted with old established trees that they carry an enormous crop one year and hardly anything the next when they seem to be recuperating from the previous year's efforts. This problem,

SUMMER PRUNING OF SPUR-BEARING FRUIT TREES

Prune back to the line shown to increase the number of fruiting spurs for the following year

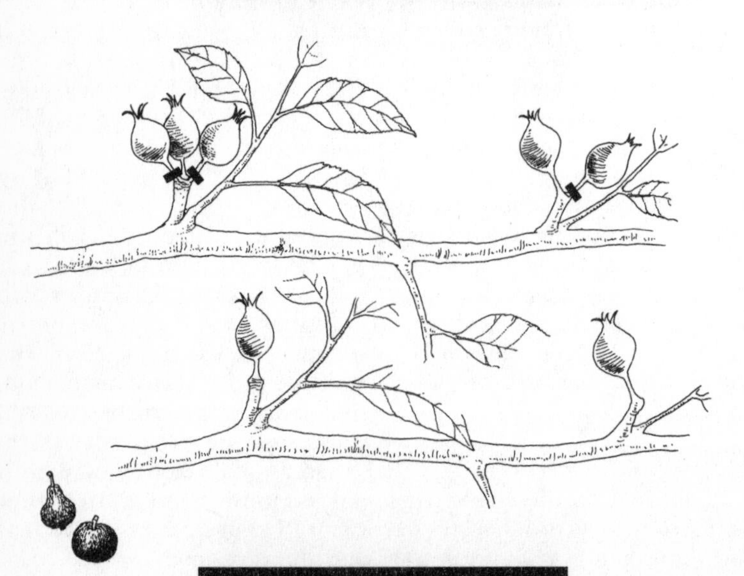

After the June/July fall, reduce groups of young apples or pears growing on a spur to a single fruit

which is only associated with a small number of varieties, is greatly reduced if the trees are regularly pruned.

Plums and cherries

Plums, cherries and other members of the *Prunus* family, which includes almonds and ornamental cherries, all bleed profusely if they are cut during the autumn and winter months, so delay pruning until April. Unlike apples and pears the pruning of plums should not be performed as a routine. Only where there is a complete crop failure or the trees are beginning to reach unmanageable proportions should they be cut back (by up to a third).

Simply because you have had no plum crop for a year or even two years is no reason to rush out with secateurs and saw! The plum family is very sensitive to climatic conditions. Any late frosts while a plum tree is in bloom can result in the loss of virtually all the crop. But a small number of fruits always survive to reach maturation. Not all flowers open at the same time and it is the few that are delayed which produce the reduced crop.

Training fruit trees

When training any tree during the early stages of its development the laterals should be pruned back to a third of their length during November. This will stimulate the shoot. That which comes from the bud lying just below the cut should be trained in position where it will be able to develop the necessary woody growth. Each year the tree should be allowed to become a little bigger until it finally reaches the desired size. It should then be cut back to the same height that it was the previous season.

Fruit tree shapes

Full pyramid. This is the tree you will normally be sold and is suitable for growing all types of fruit.

Half pyramid. A smaller version of the above using a semi-dwarfing rootstock.

Cordon system. Used mainly for the growing of apples and pears (and also gooseberries, see p. 250). Only one main stem is allowed to grow and the fruit-bearing spurs are encouraged to develop from it. Start with a one- or two-year old tree and plant at an angle of about 45 degrees, either against a wall or a wire frame. One of the advantages of this method is that individual trees may be planted as close as 1 m (3 ft) apart, allowing for the cultivation of several varieties in a confined space.

Fan system. Several laterals (secondaries) radiate from the leader (the trunk). The system is ideal for training apples, pears, plums and cherries against walls. Ready trained fans can be purchased to save time.

Espalier. This is a system in which three pairs of laterals are allowed to develop on either side of the leader. It can be used for training trees against a wall or for constructing a screen to separate off part of the garden. During the spring they make a very pleasant feature covered in blossom.

APPLE AND PEAR CORDONS

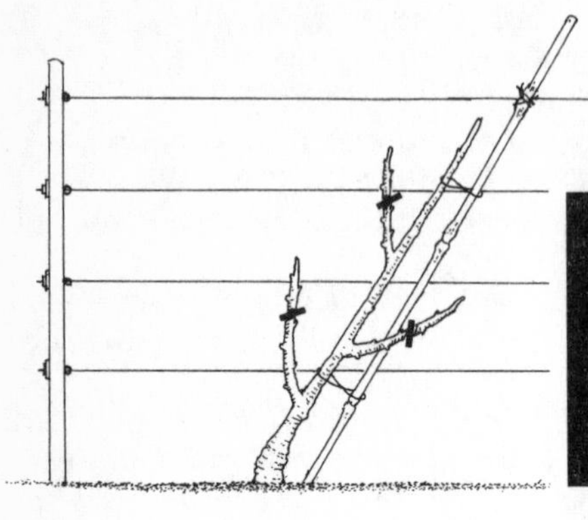

Make a supporting framework of wires set at 60, 90, 120 and 150 cm. In winter, plant a 'maiden' against a cane at an angle of about 45 degrees. Prune off the main stem by about a third of its length, just above a bud. Cut back side shoots to about 7.5 cm (3 in)

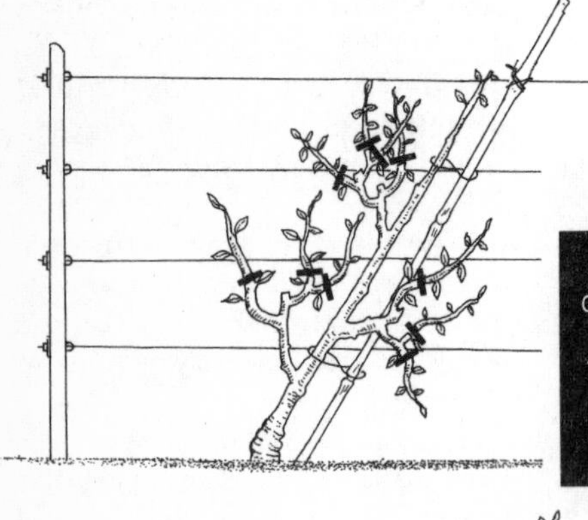

In the following August (mid-July in the case of pears), cut back all the new side shoots arising from the main stem to 7.5 cm (3 in). If any further shoots grow from them, cut them back to 2.5 cm (1 in)

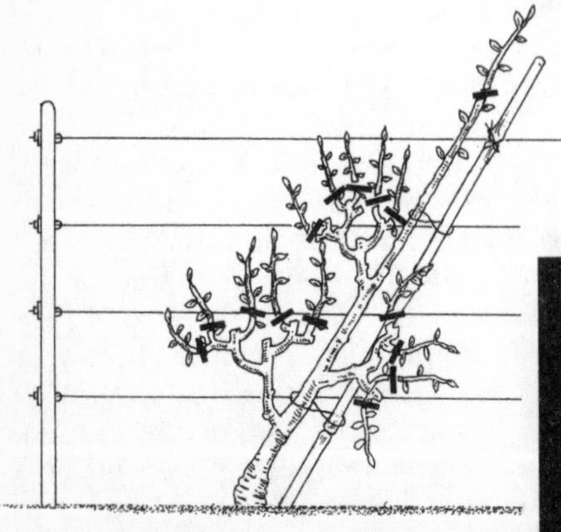

Every subsequent August, cut back new shoots arising from the main laterals to about 2.5 cm (1 in) from their base. If there are any new shoots growing from the main stem, cut them back to 7.5 cm (3 in). Leave the growing tip of the main stem unpruned until it has reached the end of the cane

APPLE AND PEAR ESPALIERS

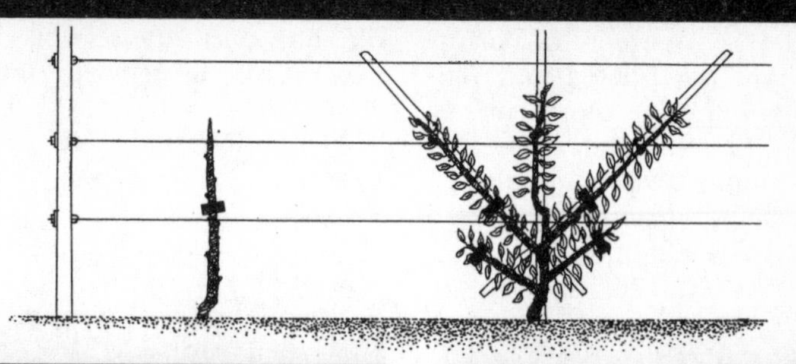

Put up wire supports as for cordons. In winter, immediately after planting, cut back the maiden tree to about 5 cm (2 in) above the first wire

When the espalier is established, cut back the terminal growths of the branches and central leader to the older wood. From then on prune to produce fruiting spurs

During the following summer, several shoots will arise from the leader. The centre branch should be tied to a cane and trained vertically. Train two side branches to 45 degrees and prune back to 7.5 cm (3 in)

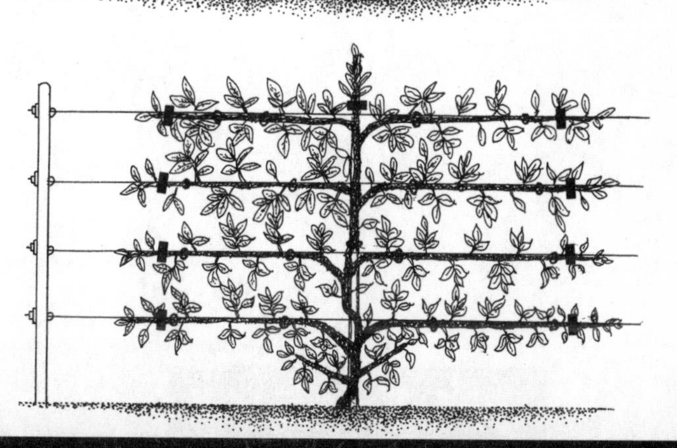

During the second winter, tie the first side shoots along the horizontal wires. Prune the vertical leader to 5 cm (2 in) above the second wire and cut back the horizontal branches by about a third. The process is repeated to form the second tier, with the third tier being made the following year and so on until the required height is reached

Soft fruit

The term soft fruit is used to describe a number of plants which are not related and with varying cultural requirements. But in general they need an open sunny aspect sheltered from the wind and a rich, well drained soil.

Fork over the soil before planting to remove all traces of perennial weeds.

Any weeds such as couch grass that remain will be impossible to dig out once their roots have become intertwined with those of your plant.

Plant the bushes or canes between November and February.

In the spring, after very heavy rain, mulch with compost. Scatter Growmore around the roots each April.

FAN TRAINING OF PLUMS AND CHERRIES

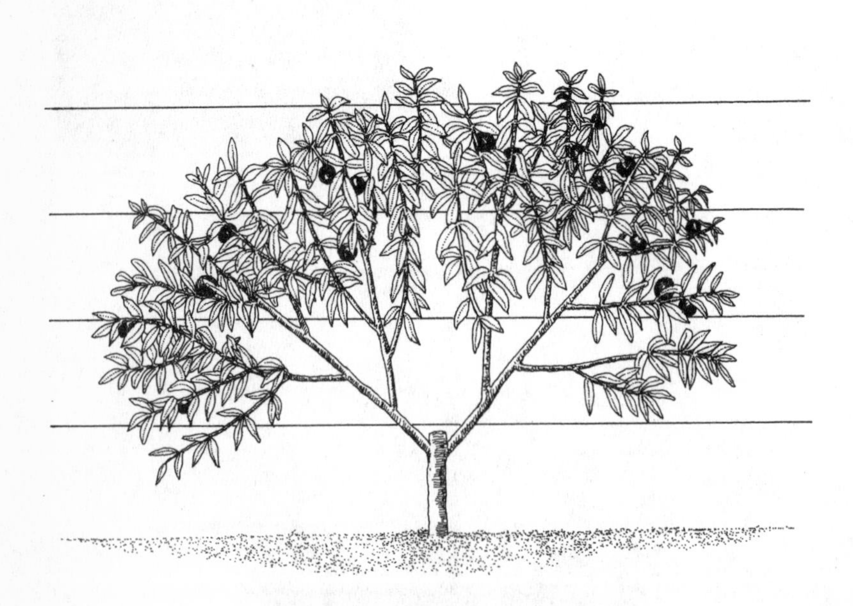

Set up a support system of wires as for cordon apples. After planting stop the leader. When the shoots develop, tie them to canes fixed across the wires in the form of a fan. Continue to tie them in until eventually they reach the ends of the canes after several seasons

Black currants

In the first spring after planting, cut down all the shoots to within 5 cm (2 in) of ground level to encourage strong new growth.

Black currants produce their best crop on wood grown the previous season. In early winter, remove about a third of the fruited branches. Old shoots are dark in colour. Once you have established a pruning system all wood will be regenerated every two years.

Old shrubs may be cut back almost to ground level to encourage the development of new wood, but expect to replace your bushes within ten years. This is done by taking ripe pieces of wood 20 cm (9 in) long and planting them in a nursery bed during September. They will

PRUNING BLACK CURRANTS

Hard prune after planting

On established bushes, remove up to half of the old shoots that have fruited. Cut them either close to the ground or to a vigorous new shoot

be ready for planting out in their permanent positions the following November.

Red and white currants

Both red and white currants form their fruit on short laterals. They could be grown as cordons but are almost universally cultivated as bushes on a short leg.

The pruning is somewhat similar to apples. Once established cut the laterals back by about a third and reduce the fruit-producing sub-laterals to four leaves during the summer. Unlike black currants the same bushes may be grown for several years without replacement.

Gooseberries .

Gooseberries may either be grown as bushes or on the cordon system in which they are grown against wires in a row across the garden. To increase fruiting of bushes, lightly prune them by removing little more that the tips of the laterals.

With a double cordon, once established the two main leaders should be restricted in size each year and the spurs or sub-laterals should be reduced to six leaves during June and then to a double pair of leaves when the fruit has been gathered.

Raspberries

There are two groups of raspberries: summer-fruiting and autumn-fruiting. The former carry their fruit on canes produced the previous season. These crop in July and are the

PRUNING RED AND WHITE CURRANTS

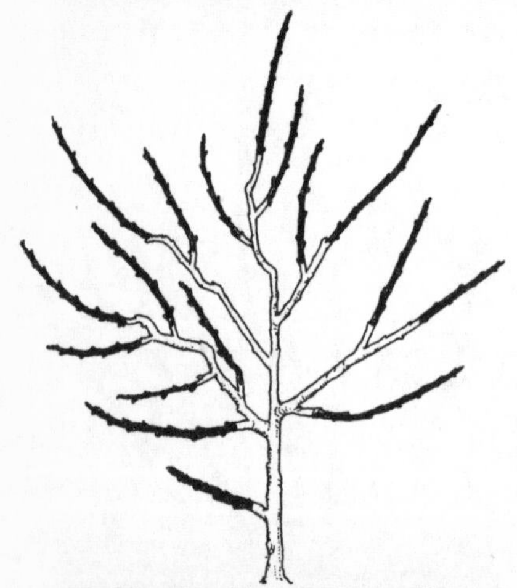

In winter, cut the leaders back by a half to a third and side shoots to 2.5 cm (1 in). Gradually remove old leaders at their origin, allowing new growth to take their place

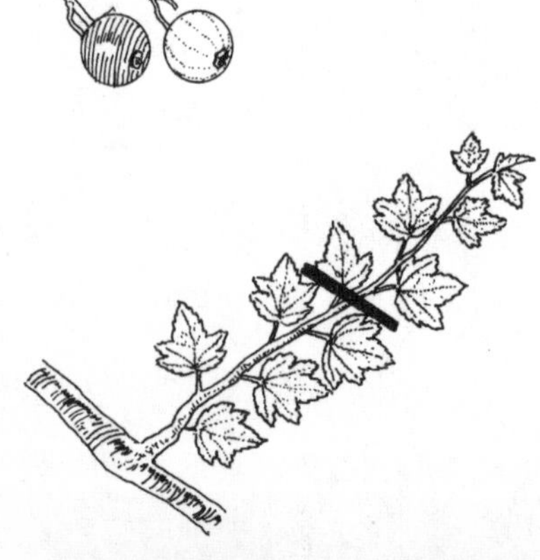

To encourage spur formation, during the summer cut back the laterals to about five leaves

most frequently grown. The others produce their fruit from canes that develop in the current season and crop in September.

Once a raspberry cane has fruited it will die and must be cut back to ground level. As the new cane grows it should be tied into position to the framework. Mature raspberry canes grow to about 2 m (6 ft).

Autumn-fruiting raspberries set fruit on wood produced in the same year. In February, all canes should be pruned to ground level.

Raspberries are very prone to viral infections which appear as mosaic patterns, blotching or a distortion of the leaves. Where this occurs the plants should be dug up. There is no effective treatment for viral infections and since raspberries are propagated vegetatively any offspring will be automatically infected. Purchase canes certified as virus free from a reputable nurseryman.

Blackberries

The cultivated form of the wild plant yields very large crops of succulent fruit. 'Oregon Thornless', as well as being free of thorns, has decorative feathery leaves making it very useful for covering walls and fences. Like raspberries, the canes die after fruiting. Cut out the canes that have borne fruit immediately after cropping and train the emerging new shoots into position.

Loganberries and tayberries

Both are a cross between

PRUNING A GOOSEBERRY BUSH

In summer, on established bushes, shorten laterals to about five leaves

The best fruit is obtained on young wood, therefore the object of pruning should be to maintain a healthy supply of young growth. In winter, shorten main branches by no more than a third of their length. Hard prune in the centre of the bush to keep it open

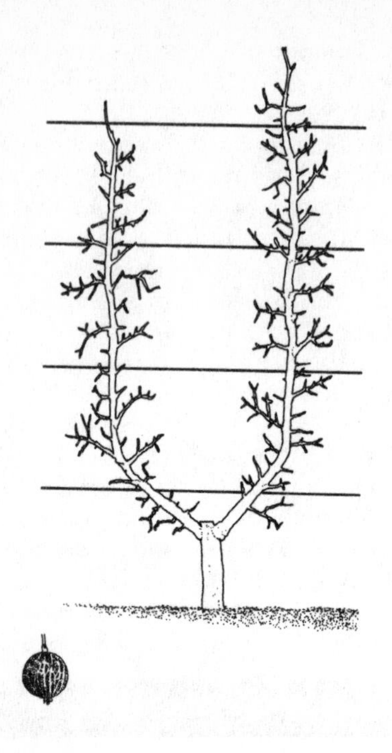

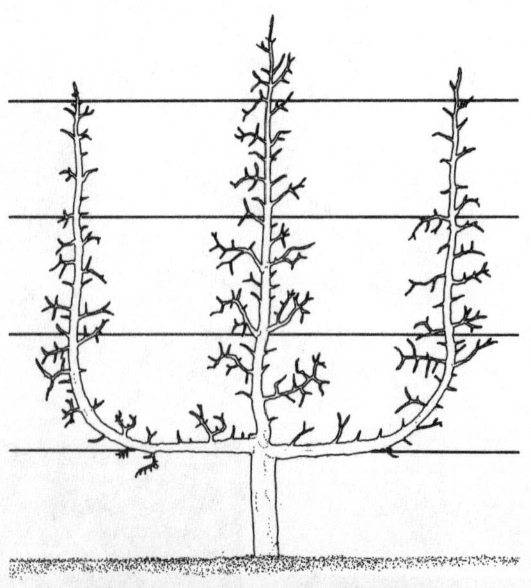

Double and triple gooseberry cordons

TRAINING SUMMER-FRUITING RASPBERRIES

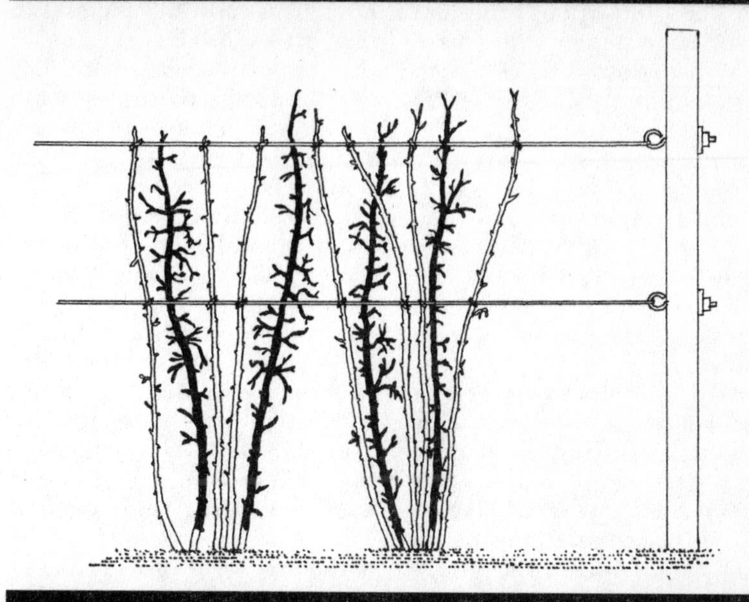

Cut the fruited canes down to ground level when cropping is over. Remove the outer fruiting stems and also the weak ones. Tie in the strongest new shoots (three or four per plant)

During early spring, cut back the tips of the canes

raspberries and blackberries and should be grown in the same way. The fruits of tayberries are much larger than the older established loganberries, from which they look set to take over.

Strawberries

Strawberries are herbaceous perennials unrelated to the other soft fruits. The new varieties now available to the gardener can extend the harvesting season from May to October.

Make your strawberry bed in deep cultivated soil in a sunny position. Late frosts can blacken the flowers, so do not site the bed in a frost pocket. Cloches may be placed over the plants from early April, which can advance the crop by up to three weeks.

New strawberry plants should be set out in their cropping position as early in September as they are available – the sooner they are planted the more time they will have to establish themselves before the winter weather stops growth. Although worthwhile crops can be gathered during the first season, the best and largest crop occurs during the second year. A slightly smaller but nevertheless extremely worthwhile crop will be obtained during the third year, but after that the weight and quality drops off rapidly.

If allowed to lie on the soil, the berries will become spattered with mud during heavy showers. They may be protected in the traditional way by placing a layer of straw under the plants – hence their name. A much

TRAINING BLACKBERRIES AND LOGANBERRIES

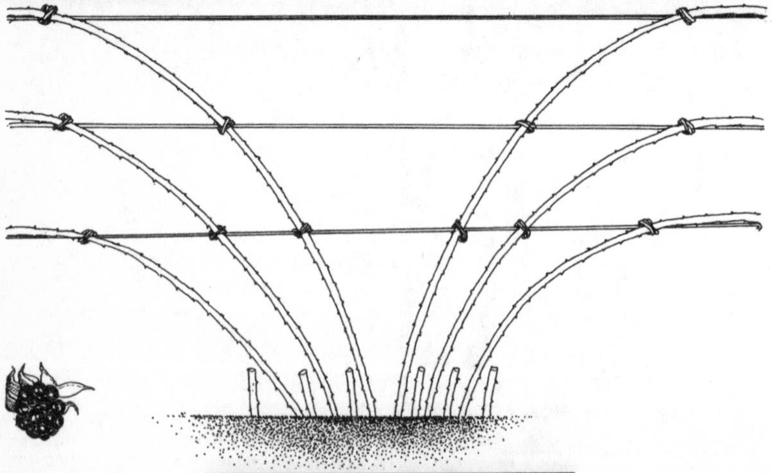

Pruning is similar to summer-fruiting raspberries, but to train the fruiting canes bend them in a fan shape along the wires. Train the new shoots in the centre

better method is to use black horticultural plastic. Apart from keeping the berries clean, it retains moisture, suppresses weeds and warms the ground. To lay it, place the plastic over the plants at the beginning of March following heavy rainfall. Make a hole where each plant is and slip the plastic over the top of it. The edges of the plastic should be weighed down with soil. Once the plants have fruited the plastic can be removed and stored for use in following years.

Strawberries are particularly prone to attack by slugs, both the large surface-dwelling varieties and the small off-white type which lives beneath the soil. Protected from the elements, slug pellets are far more effective under plastic.

Strawberries readily become infected with botrytis, a grey mould which rots the fruit. This is particularly a problem of wet seasons when the humid conditions favour the growth of the fungus. There is no effective treatment other than to inspect the plants regularly following wet weather and ruthlessly discard any berries showing the first signs of the disease – this will help stop the spread of the fungus. The more mature the fruit the more likely it is to suffer from infection, so pick the berries as soon as they are ripe.

The third problem associated with strawberries is that of mosaic leaf virus. If the leaves turn prematurely brown or become distorted for no apparent reason, the plant could be suffering from this disease. Like all viral infections there is no treatment, so when you see leaves displaying colour patterns remove all infected plants and burn them immediately. Because of the susceptibility of strawberry plants to viral infections always buy certified stock from a reliable supplier.

Propagation

Strawberry plants need to be replaced after every third year. To save the expense of buying in new plants, aim at replacing a third of the stock every year by propagation from runners – so long as the plants remain healthy and continue to yield good crops.

Runners are produced in great quantity in July, after the plant has finished fruiting. Each runner can produce several small daughter plants but only the first of these should be allowed to develop, otherwise too much energy will be taken from the parent and the daughter plants will themselves be reduced in size and quality.

As the runner increases its length the plantlet will first show a pair of leaves and then it will begin to develop small roots. As soon as the roots are 1 cm (nearly ½ in) long, place the plantlet in a 9 cm (3½ in) pot filled with compost and pin it in position with a bent paper clip. Leave the runner attached to the parent (this will act as an umbilical cord carrying water and nutrients from the adult plant).

When the plant has clearly reached the stage where it is supporting itself the runner should be severed and the new plant set out in its position in the bed with the minimum of root disturbance.

Grapes

Grapes can be grown successfully out of doors, especially in the south. The main problem is ensuring sufficient warmth for the crop to ripen during the late summer and early autumn. Select the warmest site available – against a south-facing wall is best. Wine grapes grow better out of doors. For desserts, grow a variety such as 'Black Hamburg' in the greenhouse. Grapes require slightly alkaline conditions, but this can be achieved in areas with acid soil by placing a layer of old builders' lime at the bottom of the hole before the vine is planted.

Pruning is critical and should be conducted during the spring prior to the emergence of the first leaves and the flower buds. Allow two laterals to develop either side of the main stem and to grow 2 m (6 ft) in length. The flower buds develop on shoots which emerge during the current year. The spurs carrying the fruits should be cut back to five pairs of leaves during July. Excess lateral growth should also be reduced. Do not over-prune as it is necessary to retain sufficient leaves to produce food for the grapes.

Rhubarb

Rhubarb is not actually a fruit but is used as one. It has a clean fresh taste comparable to apples or gooseberries. The usual method of growing rhubarb is to obtain 'crowns' or roots, which

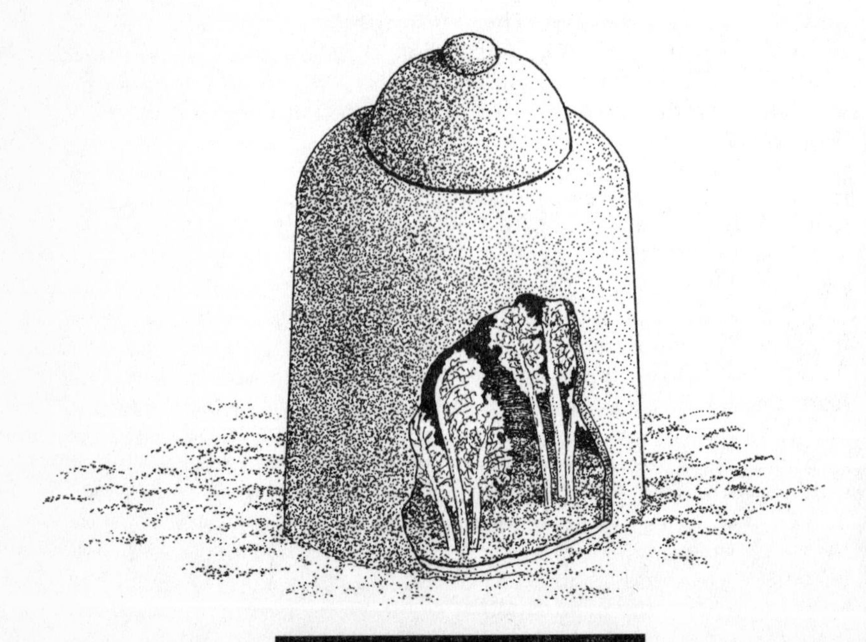

Forced rhubarb

are planted in March about 1 m (3 ft) apart. Rhubarb can also be grown from seed, which may be sown outdoors in March. Alternatively, sow the seed indoors in January, in individual flower pots. As soon as the seedlings have outgrown the pots, plant them out into their permanent positions. It will be another year before you can pull any sticks, unless you can obtain the variety 'Glaskin's Perpetual', which is such a rapid grower that you can pull a few sticks during the year of sowing. Another advantage of this variety is that it has low oxalic acid, so it can be eaten up to October without becoming bitter in flavour. Other varieties should not be harvested after the end of July.

Anyway, after July it is best to allow the leaves to build up food stores in the roots for a good crop next season – just let them die down naturally. Rhubarb is a gross feeder and the plants should be mulched each spring with well rotted farmyard manure.

When harvesting, remove only mature stalks. Grasp the stem low down and twist and pull simultaneously away from the crown. Do not cut as this will leave a site where rot can set in. Pull no more than three or four sticks from an individual plant and allow at least a fortnight to recover.

To divide a mature plant, first lift the root and allow it to stand on the surface. In February divide the root into two by chopping it with a spade. Make sure that each half has three or four of the large buds from which the new growth will originate.

Forcing rhubarb

The earliest rhubarb may be obtained by planting in the greenhouse with the top of the crown level with the surface of the soil. Cover with a terracotta rhubarb pot or, if this is not available, any upturned container providing that it is at least 60 cm (2 ft) high and 45 cm (1½ ft) diameter. Second early rhubarb is obtained by placing a similar container over a crown growing outdoors, in January or February.

Once rhubarb has been forced the crown should be allowed to rest for a year – otherwise discard it.

20 Wildlife in the Garden

There are over a million acres of urban gardens in the United Kingdom, making them one of the most important single resources we possess for conservation. Our garden will be visited by many different forms of animal life seeking to colonise a new area. Whether they remain or not will depend on what the garden contains.

Visiting animals, whether they be birds, mammals, amphibians or insects, give an extra dimension to the garden – they provide movement and sound. Birdsong, the hum of bees, the fluttering of butterflies and the darting of dragonflies add immeasurably to our enjoyment. If wildlife is encouraged by the provision of food plants, breeding places and suitable cover there will always be something interesting to watch.

Not all the animal life in a garden is welcome – there will be slugs, snails and insect pests as well. However, with proper management your garden will contain a vast number of predators to help keep the pests in check. In theory you can ignore pests and rely solely on the predators to control them. Given time, such a balance will occur, though unfortunately there is an interim period in which the pests become established and do significant damage before the predators have had the opportunity to build up their numbers to an effective level.

There is a common misapprehension that a wildlife garden is created simply by allowing it to become overgrown. Nothing is further from the truth. If you ignore a once cultivated piece of land, it will eventually only support the most vigorous species. You will end up with rank weeds such as couch-grass, docks and brambles. These will support a few species, but you will entice a good many more to your garden if you diversify as much as possible.

So controlled planting is essential, and the overall design must be considered carefully too. A bare fence or brick wall will be virtually of no use to wildlife. A thick hedge, on the other hand, will provide cover and nesting places for birds, and there will be food for them there as well. Native species of trees and shrubs along with their close relatives support the greatest variety of insects and their grubs, which are part of the food chain. Where there are insects birds automatically come along.

Consider including a hawthorn, rowan and an elder

tree in your garden. As well as being native plants, their berries are greatly appreciated by birds. And no wildlife garden should be without a pyracantha or cotoneaster whose berries help sustain birds during the winter and seem to be particular favourites with them.

To entice bees and butterflies, plant a *Buddleia davidii* and other flowering shrubs, and grow a clump of *Sedum spectabile* in a mixed border. Most blue flowers attract bees, which gives a very wide choice. Flowers such as honeysuckle, jasmine and petunia will attract hawkmoths at night.

During September, fallen apples will be visited by red admiral and peacock butterflies – and probably wasps as well. Though wasps are regarded as a nuisance, it must be remembered that they play a valuable role in catching the caterpillars of insect pests on which they feed their young.

The gardener's allies

Insects definitely to be encouraged are hoverflies, lacewing flies, ladybirds and ground beetles.

Hoverflies can easily be mistaken for wasps, owing to their imitative markings. They should never be killed because their larvae devour aphids in vast numbers. Lure the female hoverfly to your garden by growing plenty of flowers with a flat, open structure, such as members of the daisy family. She is able to reach the pollen – her food – with her short proboscis. Unlike the hoverflies, both the

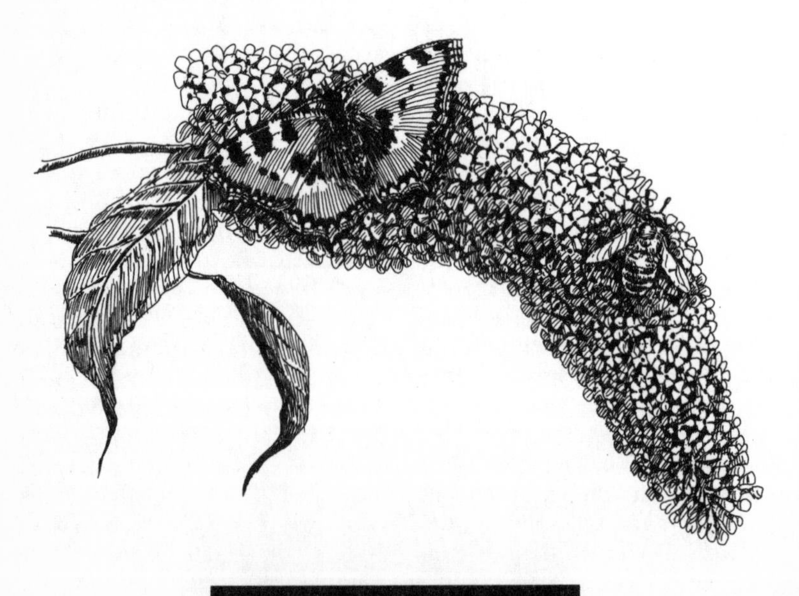

Buddleia flowers produce copious nectar

USEFUL INSECTS

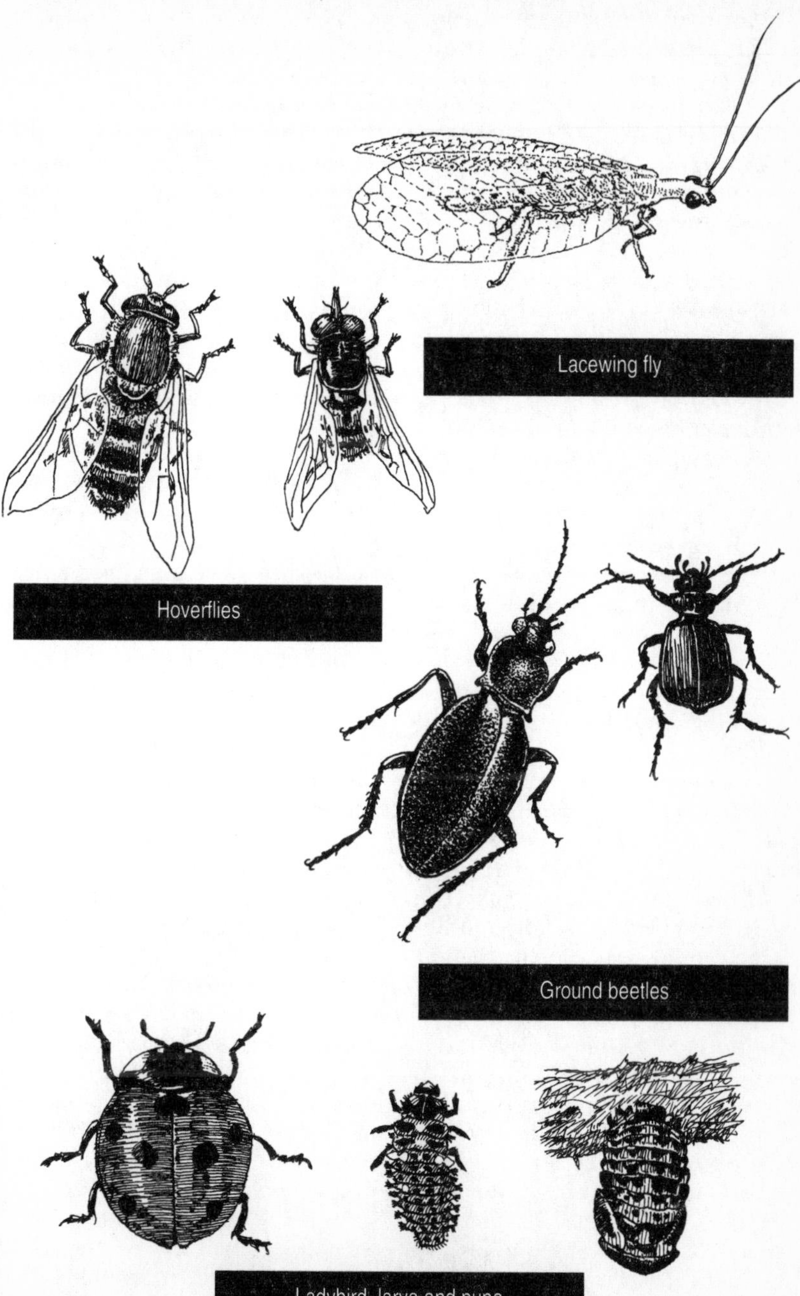

adults and larvae of ladybirds are carnivores – they live solely on aphids.

Ground beetles have shiny black wingcases, sometimes with a violet sheen, and powerful jaws. You may or may not find them attractive to look at, but they certainly do a wonderful job demolishing slugs, snails, wireworms and the grubs of insect pests. They hunt at night and need shelter by day. You can encourage them by providing a few flat stones to crawl under.

Frogs and toads will also help to keep the slug population under control. They need water, of course, and without a pond no wildlife garden would be complete (see Chapter 13 for details on construction).

Hedgehogs are excellent slug-eaters too. They tend to come and go, but one way to encourage them to stay is to provide a small pile of logs they can crawl into for shelter – and perhaps even raise a family. Incidentally, do not try to entice hedgehogs by putting out saucers of milk – although they enjoy milk, it's bad for them.

Insect-eating birds are also the gardeners friends. The robin, which follows fearlessly behind us as we dig, searches the soil and consumes large quantities of leatherjackets and various other grubs and pupae in the ground. Tits collect innumerable caterpillars for their young. Blackbirds, thrushes and starlings constantly scour the garden. Thrushes are particularly valuable allies as snails form a large part of their diet.

Damage by birds

Unfortunately, birds can sometimes be real nuisances. Pigeons can strip unprotected brassica plants in winter, and bullfinches damage the buds of soft fruits. Sparrows tend to tear up yellow-coloured flowers such as crocuses. And when starlings, blackbirds and thrushes turn their attentions to our fruit trees and bushes they cease to be a welcome sight. The only answer is to cover the crops with netting or erect a fruit cage.

When using netting, make sure it is taut to avoid entangling birds.

To prevent birds eating newly sown lawn grass seed, cover the area with a mesh of cotton threads.

Non-chemical control of pests

In addition to encouraging the predators that keep slugs, snails and insect pests under control there are other means of protecting your plants that do not require the use of chemicals. These often involve stopping the pests coming into contact with the plants – you create some form of barrier.

An important rule is to be vigilant – inspect your plants frequently. As soon as a pest appears it is a simple matter to deal with it with finger and thumb, or boot. Insect pests, in particular aphids, multiply at prodigious rates, so if they initially go unnoticed you could soon have a major problem.

Cabbage white butterfly

Both large and small white

species have at least two generations a year. When you see the butterflies on the wing, check the undersides of cabbage leaves for the eggs which look like a collection of tiny yellow torpedoes. As you see them destroy them. Any that you miss will turn into greenish-yellow caterpillars that grow rapidly each day. They leave large ragged holes in the leaves and their evil smelling droppings on what's left of the cabbage can quite put you off wanting to eat it. Hand-picking is as effective as any chemical treatment.

Cabbage root fly

Attack by the cabbage root fly is revealed by bluish leaves and wilting. If you remove the plant from the ground you will see small white grubs writhing around the root. They restrict the growth of the plant by eating away the fine roots – it can seldom be saved. The female fly is on the wing from late spring onwards. She lays her eggs on the plant stem where it meets the soil. Here prevention takes the form of collars which makes it impossible for the fly to reach this spot with her ovipostor – she will go away and try elsewhere.

Cut discs out of felt or some material like carpet underlay about 8 cm (3 in) in diameter. Make a small hole in the centre of each disc no larger than the stem of the young cabbage plants, and then make a slit from the centre to the circumference. The disc should fit quite snuggly.

Carrot fly

The fly first appears in late

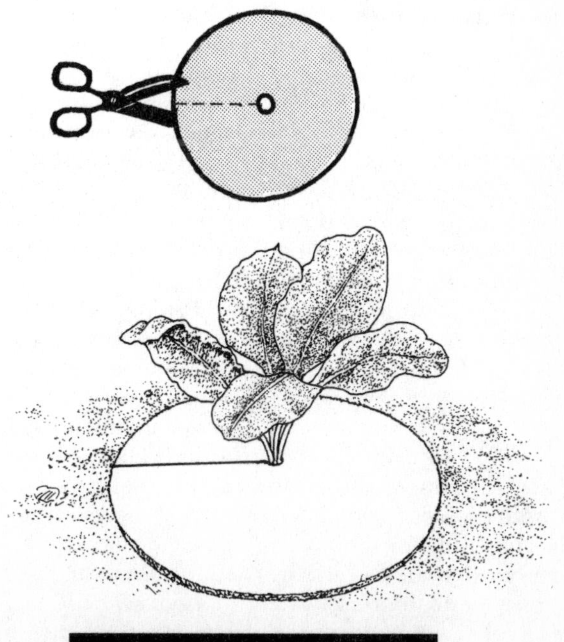

Protection against cabbage root fly

May, searching for carrots and related plants. In its search, the insect flies quite low over the ground. The eggs are laid near the stems and when the grubs hatch out they first eat the fine roots and later tunnel into the taproot itself. A sign of carrot fly attack is a reddish discoloration of the leaves.

You can prevent the carrot fly reaching your crops by making barriers around them out of polythene. The height should be at least 45 cm (18 in) – the pest does not fly any higher.

Another way to beat this pest is to grow a resistant variety of carrot such as 'Sytan', 'Ingot' or 'Fly Away'.

Slugs and snails

Slugs and snails present one of the most difficult problems in the garden. Most active during the hours of darkness, they tend to seek out your seedlings and most precious plants, ignoring weeds which are much less succulent and tender.

Picking them up and squashing them underfoot is one way of dealing with them. Sprinkling a barrier of lime around vulnerable plants is another. The slugs having sensitive skin are reluctant to cross the chemical, which unfortunately soon disappears in the rain.

It is possible to trap slugs by sinking a container into the ground and filling it with beer. Though you will find quite a large number drowned in it they will amount to no more than a fraction of the garden population.

Whitefly

Trap whiteflies in the greenhouse with a piece of yellow card or plastic covered both sides with petroleum jelly. Suspend the card, which should be about 15 cm (6 in) square, 2 m (6 ft) above the ground. Gently tap any infested plants to disturb the whiteflies, which will tend to fly about looking for somewhere to alight. They will be attracted by the bright yellow colour and of course once they have settled on it there is no escape.

Winter moth

One of the most effective barriers used by gardeners is a grease band round apple trees to thwart the winter moth. The green caterpillars, about 2.5 cm (1 in) long, attack the developing leaves in spring. The adult moths emerge in winter or early spring from pupae in the soil. The females have only vestigial wings and therefore must climb the tree to lay their eggs. To prevent them, tie a band of greaseproof paper smothered in grease or petroleum jelly round the trunk. Do this as early as October.

Biological control in the greenhouse

Certain predators which feed almost exclusively on one type of pest can be purchased by mail order. They are totally effective in an enclosed environment such as a greenhouse. Once they have consumed all of their food supply they will die.

Encarsia formosa is a parasitic wasp that attacks whitefly, and is supplied as pupae. *Aphidoletes,* a

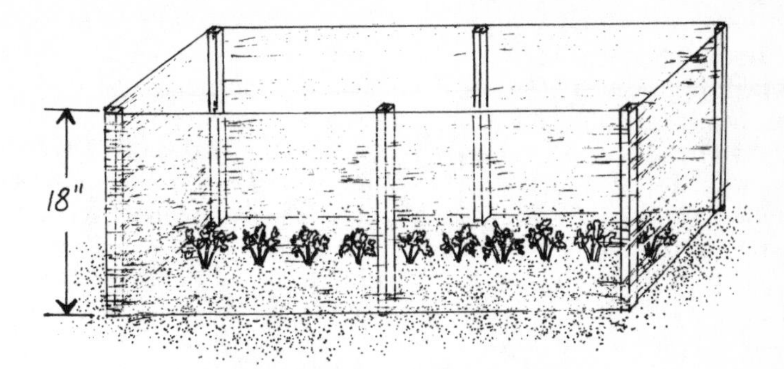

Barrier against the carrot fly

A home-made slug trap (a plastic coffee cup sunk to its brim and filled with beer)

midge that can be bought in the larval stage, controls greenfly.

Red spider mites are frequently a problem in conservatories and greenhouses. Another mite, *Phytoseiulus*, preys on them, though it needs a temperature of over 25°C (80°F) to thrive. When the pack arrives, the contents are sprinkled among the infested plants.

Once you get a mealy bug infestation you will have difficulty getting rid of it. A ladybird, *Cryptolaemus*, and its larvae will reduce the population considerably, but they need a temperature of 20°C (63°F) or more and a high humidity to work best.

A bacterium, *Bacillus thuringiensis*, is a biological control extremely effective against caterpillars yet does not harm other insects. It is sold in sachets of dried spores which are mixed with water and sprayed on the affected plants. When the caterpillars eat the sprayed leaves the bacteria paralyse their gut and so they die.

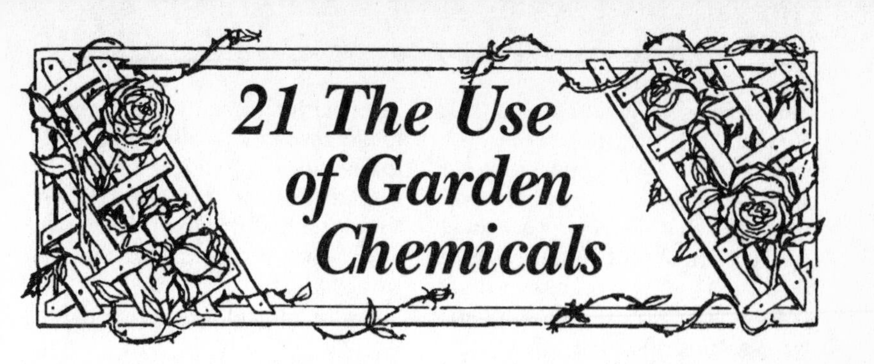

21 The Use of Garden Chemicals

Pests in a well-balanced garden can often be kept down to an acceptable level without resorting to chemicals. Many garden plants are virtually trouble-free, so one could stick to these to minimise the use of sprays. Unfortunately, the more choice and desirable plants are often the ones that pests prefer too, and to grow them you should be prepared to use pesticides. Most plants are capable of withstanding a limited attack, but it is another matter entirely if an onslaught reaches epidemic proportions. At least chemical methods are always there when other means cannot deal with a problem effectively.

Chemical methods of control are often depicted as villains of the piece, leaving residues and being responsible for indiscriminate destruction of wildlife. This may have been true in the past but it is not the case with modern insecticides. Some selectively destroy certain types of insect, leaving others unharmed. For example, pirimicarb kills aphids and has no effect on its natural predators, such as ladybirds.

A common misconception is that any naturally occurring substance is safe whereas anything man-made is dangerous. This is too simplistic a view, because some of the most powerful poisons known occur 'naturally' (e.g. botulin, and snake venom). The real objection to many of the so-called safe methods is that they are less effective than spraying with man-made chemicals. In my opinion, even in a garden designed to encourage wildlife there is also a case for the controlled and responsible use of chemical sprays. Having said that, I must emphasise their use should be kept to a minimum and only for specific problems. The danger is that the natural enemies of pests will be destroyed by the sprays, unless they are used correctly, leaving future generations of pests unchallenged. (Also, over-use of pesticides could lead to some of the pests developing a resistance to the chemical by undergoing genetic change.)

Why, you may be asking, should it be necessary to help nature restore the balance? When a new garden is created we bring in plants whose origins are from the four corners of the earth, with the powers of survival bred out of them. Non-indigenous species, lacking inbuilt defences, will be particularly susceptible to the pests and diseases of the region.

No longer is it a case of the survival of the fittest but the promotion of what man decrees shall be allowed to grow. For our hybrids to survive we must provide them with manures and fertilisers and remove their natural competitors – those plants we call weeds. We must also protect them from various types of animal that would destroy them (are not pests simply the 'weeds' of the animal world?). The question is: when should we introduce chemical methods? The answer is simple: when all other methods have failed.

Types of insecticide

Insecticides can be divided according to whether they are extracted from plants or are man-made.

Plant extracts

These extracts include pyrethrum (from the plant of that name) and derris (from the roots of a range of plants). They are quickly broken down into harmless substances, making them acceptable to many environmental gardeners.

Man-made insecticides

These are of various chemical compositions, but the most important are the organophosphorus and carbamate compounds. There are also some synthetic pyrethroids, such as resmethrin, which being nonpersistent are very safe.

Contact insecticides

All insects have an exoskeleton of chitin, a horny, protein-based armour. But there are some insecticides able to penetrate this armour and kill them. Such insecticides are termed contact insecticides, as they work when they touch the insect. They will also work if the insect eats a sprayed leaf.

To be effective, the insecticide has to be widely distributed, especially reaching the undersides of leaves where pests tend to congregate.

Among the most commonly used contact insecticides are diazinon and malathion, from the organophosphorus group, and pirimicarb and carbaryl, from the carbamate group.

Systemic insecticides

Insecticides described as systemic are absorbed into the plant's sap, and only kill insects that suck the sap. Any creatures that merely alight on the plant remain unharmed.

Dimethoate and heptenophos, from the organophosphorus group, are systemic insecticides available to gardeners under trade names (dimethoate is also a contact insecticide).

The contact insecticides carbaryl, pirimicarb and pirimiphos-methyl can also be considered as partial systemic insecticides because they travel short distances within a plant.

Choice of insecticide

Several insecticides marketed for the home gardener are combinations of systemic and non-systemic substances. These can be used with confidence against all pests.

A few plants are sensitive to certain insecticides – a sort of allergy – and could be damaged by them. Where this is likely to occur there is normally a warning on the packet or container.

Always check the label for the harvest interval – the period of time that must be allowed to elapse between application and gathering edible crops.

Insecticides are sold as powders, sprays and aerosols. Where fairly large areas must be covered sprays are the most practical. For smaller applications that do not warrant making up a large quantity of solution, powders are best. Aerosols are useful for very small applications but are expensive.

Effect on flowers

The part of a plant most vulnerable to chemical burns and stains is the flower. It is the part that attracts bees and other useful insects. If you cannot avoid spraying when the plant is in bloom make sure that none of the chemical comes in contact with the flower. The one exception to this rule is the spraying of fruit trees, especially apples and pears as pests lay their eggs in the blossom.

Weedkillers and fungicides

Herbicides and fungicides act either by contact or systemically (translocation through the tissues). They vary in their persistence, i.e. the time taken for the chemical to degrade and therefore become inactive. Some weedkillers are selective in the kinds of plants they kill. These can be particularly useful for lawns.

Really deep-rooted perennial weeds, like bindweed, can only be effectively eradicated by application of a systemic weedkiller (e.g. glyphosate).

The contact herbicide paraquat is used to kill weed seedlings in the soil. It is very quickly inactivated, so the bed can be sown or planted very soon afterwards.

One of the systemic fungicides most widely used is benomyl. This is effective against a wide range of fungal diseases with the exception of potato blight and rust fungi.

Safe handling of garden poisons

Pesticides are poisonous, designed to kill. Used correctly, neither the environment nor the operator will be harmed. The same goes for fungicides and weedkillers. To ensure absolute safety, always observe the following precautions in addition to those printed on the label.

1 Keep all garden poisons clearly labelled and out of the reach of children.
2 Always dilute to the concentration recommended by the manufacturer. Stronger solutions may burn the plant tissues.
3 Use plastic gloves when mixing up or working with garden poisons.
4 If any chemical comes in contact with the skin, wash it off immediately.
5 Avoid breathing in any fumes.
6 Thoroughly wash out all equipment after using.
7 Never use any poison in the vicinity of a water garden as it will endanger the fish.

Pests and how to deal with them

Aphids

Minute sap-sucking insects which, owing to their rapid rate of reproduction, quickly form colonies. Where there are large numbers, leaves will be found covered with a sticky substance that they excrete, called honeydew, which can lead to sooty mould. In addition to any damage they inflict, aphids are responsible for the spread of viral infections.

Black aphids (blackfly) are particularly troublesome on broad beans. Cabbages are susceptible to mealy coloured aphids that congregate on the undersides of the leaves which they distort. Greenfly is seen on roses and many other plants.

Spray with a systemic pesticide immediately any aphids are seen.

Cabbage root fly

Once a plant is affected there is nothing you can do to save it. Prevent attack by applying chlorophos, a soil insecticide, when sowing and transplanting. Alternatively, use collars (see p. 263).

Cabbage white butterfly

The caterpillars of the large and small white butterflies attack all members of the brassica family. They are best dealt with by non-chemical means (see pp. 262–63).

Carrot fly

The small white larvae eat the fine roots and tunnel through the taproots. Spray the soil with bromophos during May. Alternatively, avoid the problem by physical barriers (see pp. 263–64).

Celery fly

Damage is caused by the grubs which tunnel in the leaf tissue (parsnips are also attacked). Remove badly affected leaves and spray with malathion or a systemic insecticide.

Earwigs

All gardeners will be familiar with this long brown insect which has pincer-like appendages at its tail-end. Earwigs feed on the petals of flowers, particularly dahlias, chrysanthemums and other members of the daisy family.

Pesticides can damage flowers, so use the old-fashioned inverted flower pot method to control them (see p. 207).

Froghoppers (leafhoppers)

These little bugs about 5 mm ($\frac{1}{4}$ in) long attack roses and many other ornamental plants. They leap off when disturbed. The immature insects hide themselves in masses of froth known as 'cuckoo spit'.

Froghoppers are sap suckers, causing mottling of leaves and can also introduce viruses. Spray with malathion or a systemic pesticide.

Leaf miners

The larvae of various species of flies and moths tunnel into different kinds of plants. For example, among others there are chrysanthemum, apple, lilac and holly leaf miners. Vegetables have their miners too (see celery fly on p. 270). Blotches or sinuous lines appear in the leaves. Chemical control is not usually necessary – affected leaves can be removed. But if attacks are severe or persistent spray with a contact insecticide.

Mites

Mites are near relatives of the spiders and so not really insects. Usually they are very tiny, even microscopic.

The big bud mite is a serious pest of black currants, causing some buds to appear swollen and abnormally round in winter. In the spring, the infested buds may not open. Destroy all affected buds or badly affected bushes. The mite can spread the virus that causes reversion disease. Bushes affected decline in vigour and crop poorly. Destroy them, as there is no effective cure.

Fruit tree spider mites attack apples and plums and related trees. They suck the sap and cause leaves to turn brown and fall off. Control by spraying with a systemic pesticide such as dimethoate.

Red spider mite is a problem in greenhouses where they prosper in the conditions afforded. They are destroyed by a wide range of contact and systemic pesticides. (For biological control, see p. 265.)

Moth caterpillars

Ornamental garden plants and fruit trees may be attacked by the caterpillars of a variety of moths. Usually they can be ignored as only a few isolated leaves or branches will be affected.

Winter moth can be prevented from spoiling apple crops by the

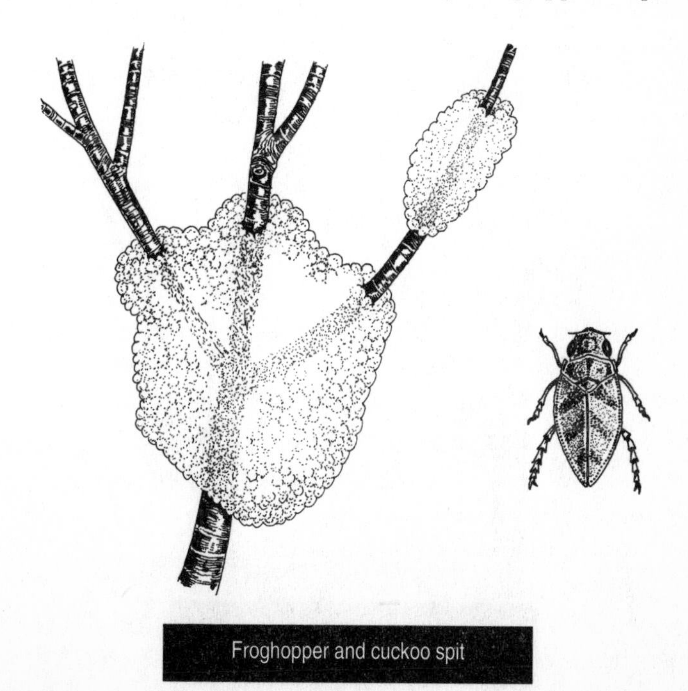

Froghopper and cuckoo spit

use of grease bands (see p. 264). Spray caterpillars, when seen, with contact insecticide, but not during flowering.

Pea moth maggots are a problem with maincrop peas which are at a crucial stage of development when egg-laying occurs. Spray with insecticide as soon as the young pods set (see p. 218).

For tortrix moth, see p. 265.

Narcissus fly

The maggots eat away the bulb from the centre, causing decay. Not only daffodil and other narcissi bulbs are at risk, snowdrop and bluebell can also be attacked. The foliage becomes thin and yellow.

Stop the flies from laying their eggs in the bulbs by covering the gap left when the foliage dies down. Dust the overlying soil with chlorophos in June.

Onion fly

Onions, shallots and other members of the genus *Allium* can be attacked. The first signs are yellowing leaves. If you pull out the bulb you will see the maggots in it. Eventually all that would be left is a rotting bulb. Remove and destroy all affected plants. Prevent the problem by spraying with a soil insecticide such as chlorophos on sowing or transplanting and every fortnight thereafter if necessary.

Raspberry beetle

This is responsible for the small maggots in all cane fruits. Spray with a contact insecticide such as malathion or rotenone a week or two after flowering is

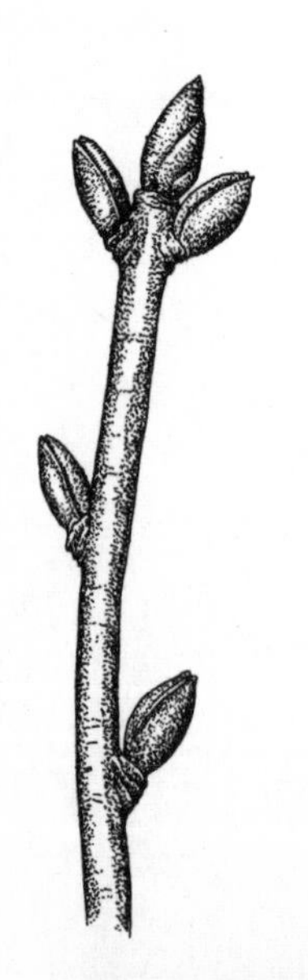

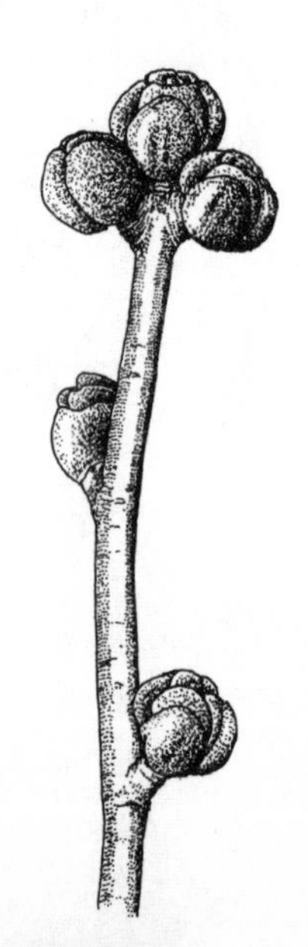

A healthy black currant shoot (left), and one affected by big bud mite (right)

over. Spray raspberries and blackberries again as soon as the fruits start to turn pink.

Sawflies

There are several species of sawfly whose caterpillars attack garden plants. Those of the gooseberry sawfly can completely strip the leaves of a gooseberry bush so that it is unable to produce fruit. Look out for little caterpillars and either hand pick or spray with malathion as soon as they are seen.

Apple sawflies first tunnel under the skin of the developing fruit, making a ribbon-like scar, and then burrow into the flesh. The affected apples often fall in June or July, when the caterpillars will leave to pupate in the soil.

To prevent infestation, spray with a contact insecticide just after the apple blossom has fallen. Gather and destroy any affected apples.

Caterpillars of the leaf-rolling sawfly are to be found in May on various bushes, particularly roses. The leaves curl up while the larvae are feeding on them. Remove affected leaves. Spray with malathion.

Scale insects

These look like small oval limpets and cling to leaves, stems or tree branches. They are found on a wide range of trees and herbaceous plants and can be especially troublesome in a greenhouse or conservatory. Only the young scales move about the plant to spread the infestation. The adults are immobile.

The protective covering of

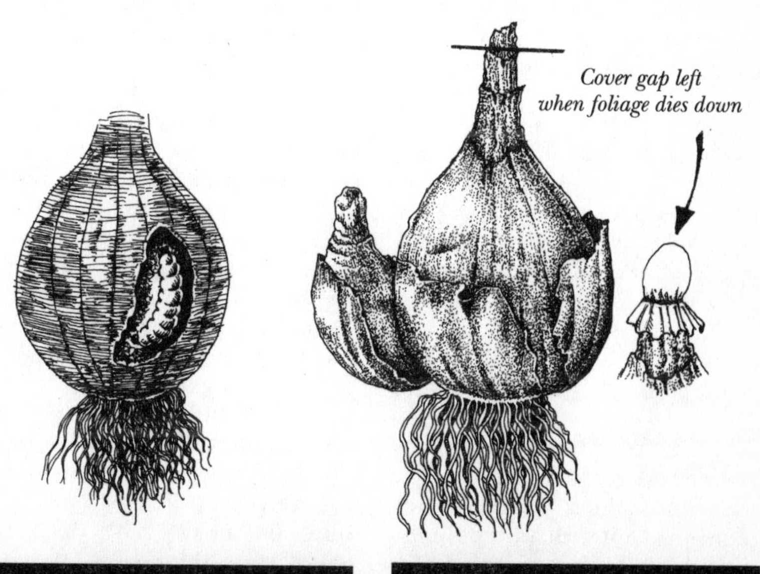

Grub of narcissus fly in a bulb

If the neck of a bulb is exposed, the narcissus fly can gain entrance to lay her eggs

scale insects shield them from insecticide sprays. Malathion is effective when the young insects are hatching. For adult scales, try a systemic insecticide. If the infestation is limited, you can squash the scales by hand.

Slugs and snails

These will attack all seedlings, cuttings and other tender growths. Wherever you see large quantities of vegetation eaten away, suspect these molluscs. Trails of slime will remove any doubt. Most damage tends to occur during the spring and early summer and again during the late summer and early autumn. They are at their most active following rainfall and at night. You are unlikely to be able to eliminate them completely as they will travel large distances in their search for food. During prolonged dry spells their attacks may cease completely, lulling the gardener into a false sense of security.

There are non-chemical methods of combating them (see p. 264), but slug pellets are the most effective protection for vulnerable plants. These should be placed under broken pieces of pot to protect them from the rain.

Wasps

Wasps eat large holes in the sides of ripe fruit, whether remaining on trees or on the ground. When gathering apples, pears and plums, take care not to grasp a fruit with a wasp on it.

Wasp nests are composed of a grey, papier mâché material and can be larger than footballs. They are often found in lofts, outhouses and even below ground. Sprays specifically for destroying them are obtainable. **Caution**:

Do not approach a nest unless you are wearing protective clothing, including a face mask.

Wasps also play a positive part in the garden (see p. 260).

Weevils

These are a group of beetles which have a prolonged snout. The larvae of the blossom weevil feed on developing flower buds of apple and pear trees. Affected buds fail to open. The adult weevils feed on the leaves during the summer and overwinter in bark crevices. The eggs are laid in spring. Grease bands placed round the tree trunk to trap winter moths will also be effective against the blossom weevil. If the problem recurs annually, spray with a contact insecticide just before the buds open.

The pea and bean weevil chews notches round the edges of pea and broad bean leaves, and their grubs feed on the roots in late spring. Damage is not likely to be serious and the yield should be unaffected. Affected plants and the soil could be dusted with derris to control the insects and prevent future attack.

Vine weevils can be particularly difficult to eradicate. The white larvae, up to 8 mm ($^3/_8$ in) long, are sometimes discovered in the compost of ailing pot plants. They feed on roots, while the adults feed on leaves. Any grubs discovered should be removed and destroyed.

Whitefly

These are small sap-sucking insects with white bodies and wings. They can infest a large number of plants, notably cabbages, tomatoes, fuchsias, rhododendrons and viburnum.

The immature whiteflies are to be found in clusters on the underside of the leaves. Whitefly are chiefly a problem in the greenhouse where heavily infested plants may wilt and die. Spray with a systemic insecticide such as dimethoate.

Wasps eat holes in the sides of ripe fruit

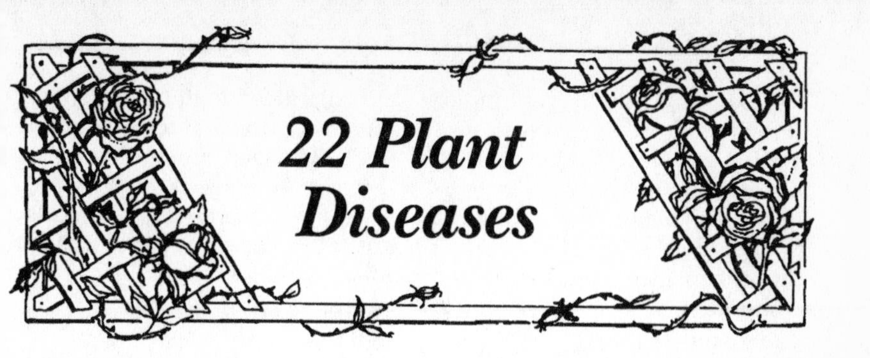

22 Plant Diseases

Organisms causing diseases in plants fall into three groups: fungi, bacteria and viruses. Of these, fungi are the most significant.

Fungi

Fungi were formerly classified as plants but are now usually placed in a separate kingdom. They are a very large group (some 80,000 species have been recognised), which include toadstools, rusts and yeasts.

Although there is great diversity of form and size, fungi have certain features in common. Normally they have threadlike structures called hyphae, which are often grouped in a much branched structure called a mycelium. The reproduction method is based on spores. They all lack chlorophyll and so are unable to synthesise carbohydrates from carbon dioxide and water. Instead, they usually live either as parasites or obtain their nutrients from dead organic matter. Sometimes a parasite kills the host plant and then continues to extract nutrients from the dead tissue. Thus it will be seen why many fungi are disease organisms. On the other side of the coin, fungi help maintain soil fertility by decomposing organic matter.

Fungi that feed on live plants generally enter through wounds or damaged tissue and once inside spread rapidly. Common fungal diseases of plants include blights, moulds, canker, damping-off, leaf spots, mildews, rusts, smut and wilts.

Most fungi are specialist feeders growing on only one particular plant or plant family, though some affect a wide range of plants. Many thrive under the same sort of conditions – warm and humid – so prevention and control tends to be similar for different fungal diseases. Good hygiene and ventilation is essential. And the gathering up and destruction of all diseased tissue as soon as it is spotted will go a long way towards preventing a recurrence of the problem.

It is important to keep a sharp look out for signs of attack so that early action may be taken.

As with insecticides, check on the fungicide label what is the harvest interval that must be allowed to elapse before gathering edible crops.

Botrytis (grey mould)

This common disease can affect virtually all types of plant. It occurs on leaves, stems, flowers and fruits, appearing as grey, furry growths.

Cool, damp conditions, similar to those required to root cuttings, favour this mould – so beware! Always dip your cuttings into a fungicide or a combined fungicide and rooting preparation, and use a sterilised compost.

To control botrytis, as soon as it is seen spray with benomyl.

Soft fruits are particularly prone to botrytis infection, especially in wet summers. Do not spray. Gather all fruit as soon as it is ripe and destroy any on which the mould is seen. With luck the following summer may be a dry one, when the problem should not recur.

Canker

This can affect most woody plants and appears as blister-like irregularities on the stems. The fungal spores enter through small damaged areas where the sapwood is exposed. In the case of apple canker, woolly aphids are often responsible for the small wounds by which the fungus gains entry. Left untreated, the disease will spread, leading to the destruction of tissue including the flowering spurs. With a sharp knife cut out all the infected tissue, exposing healthy bare wood. Once you have established a clean wound, paint it with pruning paint.

Club root

This can affect all brassicas and other members of the Cruciferae family (radishes, turnips, wallflowers, stocks,

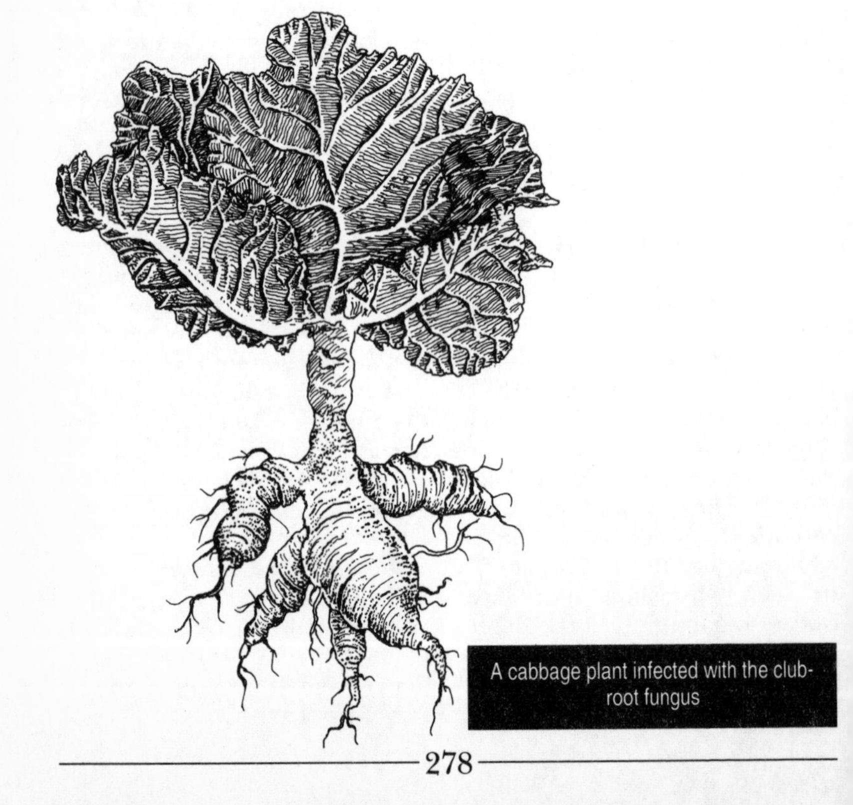

A cabbage plant infected with the club-root fungus

candytuft, etc.). The roots become swollen and distorted, like gnarled fingers and thumbs. They cannot take up water and nutrients adequately, so the plant first develops discoloration of the leaves and becomes stunted. Eventually the roots go rotten and stink.

The fungal spores remain in the soil for as long as 20 years, and are easily spread from place to place when soil is moved (e.g. on boots, garden tools, etc.). For this reason it is advisable to grow your own brassicas from seed rather than buy plants which may be contaminated.

Twenty years is a long time to desist from growing brassicas. This need not be necessary, however. The fungus only thrives in acid or badly drained soils. So improve drainage and lime the plot to keep the pH high. It helps to start young plants in pots of sterile compost. When planted out they will be large enough not to be damaged to any extent on contact with the fungal spores.

Damping-off

The fungus can affect seedlings and sometimes young plants from cuttings – they collapse and die for no apparent reason.

Normally the fungus lives on dead and decaying matter in the soil and will only attack seedlings if they are overcrowded or overwatered. Avoid the problem by using sterile seed compost and clean containers.

If signs of damping off appear, water with a copper fungicide.

Honey fungus

The fungus most commonly affects trees and shrubs, which are killed. Honey-coloured toadstools appear near a dying or dead plant. If you tear off a piece of its bark, white sheath-like fungal growth (the mycelium) may be visible.

Dig out and burn any affected tree or shrub without delay, removing as much root as possible. Replanting with trees or shrubs is possible after two years. Meanwhile, plant herbaceous subjects on the vacant patch (these do not usually succumb to the fungus).

Leaf spots

Most plants are susceptible to spots on their leaves caused by one species of fungus or another. Generally this is not a problem, but roses are an exception. Black spot on rose leaves becomes more pronounced as the season progresses. It leads to yellowing and even complete defoliation with resulting inability to produce new wood and buds.

Some rose cultivars are much more prone than others to this disease. To grow them they must be sprayed throughout the season with a suitable fungicide such as benomyl. One of the qualities sought in modern roses is resistance to fungal infection, though even with these the disease can be a problem in some areas.

Mildews

Powdery mildews produce a white coating of spores on leaves and stems. Different species of these fungi have evolved to live on various garden plants. Among the ornamentals, roses, chrysanthemums, michaelmas daisies and forget-me-nots are particularly prone to infection. Gooseberries, apples and various vegetables are susceptible too. The disease often occurs in hot, dry summers when the plants are lacking in water. It is difficult to control once established. Spray with a systemic fungicide at 14-day intervals as soon as it is noticed. Prevention is better than cure, so you could start spraying before it has had a chance to appear and repeat fortnightly.

Mildew is a particular problem under glass where it can totally destroy the cropping capacity of plants such as cucumbers. Infected leaves must not be put on the compost heap but burnt immediately. When first detected in the greenhouse, stop the build-up of humidity and allow plenty of ventilation.

Downy mildew is unrelated to the powdery mildews, and is a particular problem on young vegetables. Cabbages and lettuces are likely to be affected most but spinach and peas can also suffer. The disease is recognised by yellow or brown patches with white tufts on the foliage. The fungus penetrates deeply into the leaf tissues. Control it with a fungicide such as mancozeb.

Potato blight

This is a serious disease that can affect tomatoes as well as potatoes. The leaves develop yellow or brown patches, and if you turn them over you will see signs of white mould. In dry weather the foliage becomes brittle, in wet weather the haulm may rot. The rot spreads to the potato tubers, producing brown patches in the flesh.

Black spot on rose leaves

Immediately brown patches are noticed on the leaves spray with a fungicide such as mancozeb. Destroy any diseased tubers and haulms and make sure no tubers are left in the ground as they could infect next year's crop.

Rots

A term used to describe a variety of fungal infections that cause breakdown of plant tissue. Rot-causing organisms prosper in damp conditions where the soil is poorly drained. Too much shade and overcrowding are further factors conducive to rot. Once it sets in there is usually no effective treatment. On woody plants, the affected area must be cut out.

Once the problem is recognised, you could plant the crops in a different, more suitable part of the garden the following year. If the problem occurred in an unusually wet season, the chances are it will not reappear again in subsequent drier years.

When storing potatoes and root crops such as carrots and parsnips, make sure they are all sound. Inspect them now and again and destroy any that are rotting. The same goes for apples and pears, and the bulbs and tubers of ornamental plants.

Rust

Different species of rust fungus attack quite a few garden plants. Those most commonly affected include leeks, chives, mints, chrysanthemums, holly-hocks and antirrhinums. Clusters of black, brown, red or yellow powdery spots appear on the leaves and stems and plant vigour is affected. Leeks will survive a rust attack and produce an edible crop. Badly affected leeks can be removed to limit the spread of the disease.

Both indoor and outdoor chrysanthemums may be infected with white rust, in which case use mancozeb fungicide.

Roses can get rust as well as other fungal diseases, but whereas benomyl is effective against black spot and powdery mildew it will not do for treating rust. Use mancozeb or a proprietary combination fungicide and insecticide specially for roses.

Scab

A general term used to describe rough or discoloured patches on the surface of fruit and vegetables.

Apple and pear scab is first seen as small black marks on the foliage which spread to the fruit causing scarring and cracking of the skin. Although the apple will remain edible after peeling, its keeping qualities may be diminished. Prune all affected shoots. During June, spray the tree with benomyl. In the autumn, reduce the number of spores available to reinfect next year's crop by gathering up and burning all fallen leaves.

Potato scab shows as rough brown patches on the tubers. The problem seems to be confined to light, dry, alkaline soils low in humus. Common potato scab does not affect the flavour or the storing qualities of potatoes. If you want scab-free potatoes for exhibition purposes or for jacket baking, dig a trench and place in it a large quantity of compost. plant the potatoes in the compost and cover with soil. Remember never to lime the ground before planting potatoes.

Silver leaf

A serious disease common on plums and other members of the genus *Prunus*, although other trees and shrubs can get it too. The first sign is the foliage acquiring a silvery sheen. Dead branches will be noticed and when these are cut through with a saw the wood will appear stained brown-purple. The disease spreads from the branches to the main trunk and finally the whole tree dies.

The tree might be saved if at the first signs of infection you cut back the dead wood until you find live tissue all the way through the severed stem. Burn all diseased tissue immediately.

Bacteria

Bacteria are present everywhere – in air, water, soil, plants and animals. Just a handful of garden soil would contain thousands of millions of these microscopic, single-celled organisms. Unlike fungi, bacteria are rarely the primary cause of disease in plants – most are harmless. Only five genera are known to infect plants, though they infect a wide range. Perhaps most important to the gardener are the types that spoil stored fruit, vegetables, bulbs and so on. These cause tissues to disintegrate – what is known as a soft rot. To prevent soft rot when storing,

Scab on an apple

check none of the produce is damaged and keep it in a cool, dry, well-ventilated place.

Halo blight

This is a bacterial disease affecting French and runner beans. Small brownish spots surrounded by a yellow halo appear on the leaves. Destroy affected plants (the disease is spread by infected seed).

Viruses

Viruses are so small that they are below the resolving power of an ordinary light microscope. Structurally they are comparatively simple. Outside living cells they are more like chemicals than living organisms and have been isolated in crystal form. When viruses enter living cells they behave like parasites, using the host cell's enzymes for their own metabolism. The cell breaks down and new viruses are released.

Viruses spread throughout a plant very rapidly and are not just confined to where the symptoms appear. For this reason, as soon as a viral disease is suspected, destroy the whole plant (it cannot be cured).

Although viruses cannot be seen, their effects are often all too evident. Common signs of viral infection in plants are discoloration, mottling and puckering of the foliage. This sort of infection is called mosaic disease. The plants tend to be stunted and flowerbuds may fail to open. Potatoes, as well as being susceptible to mosaic virus, are commonly attacked by the leaf roll virus, which causes the leaves to become dry and turn brown at the edges.

Viruses are transferred from one plant to another by sap-sucking organisms such as aphids. It is quite possible-for a plant to survive an attack by sap-sucking insects but then be killed by the viruses they carry.

Nutrient deficiencies

Not all plant diseases are caused by fungi, bacteria or viruses. A deficiency of a particular mineral in the soil can also produce a disorder. The amounts of different elements in a soil largely depends on the type of rock from which the soil was derived and the humus material it contains. But even when a soil has what would appear to be adequate amounts of the necessary elements, plant growth may be poor. The explanation is that when a soil is very alkaline chemical reactions take place rendering some elements, especially iron, less available to most plants. While there are plants well adapted to living on alkaline soils, others will be deficient in nutrients.

Shortage of nitrogen, phosphorus and potassium is unlikely to occur if general fertilisers are regularly applied. The part played by minerals is dealt with on pp. 20–22. The following is a brief summary of deficiency symptoms of the essential elements.

Nitrogen (N)

A deficiency will result in small, pale coloured leaves and the plant will be slow to reach maturation. Remedy: apply plenty of organic matter and a well-balanced fertiliser. Commonly affected plants: leafy vegetables. An excess of nitrogen will produce too much growth which will be soft and unable to withstand the winter.

Phosphorus (P)

A deficiency results in small discoloured leaves, which may drop prematurely, weak growth, and reduced flowering and fruiting. Remedy: apply a phosphate fertiliser or bone meal.

Potassium (K)

Deficiency can result in growth that is destroyed by winds and frosts and with a decreased resistance to disease. Leaves may curl at the apices and margins, and there may be poor flowering and fruiting. Remedy: apply a general fertiliser each season.

Calcium (C)

Leaf tips may blacken. Remedy: apply lime. Commonly affected plants: apples, tomatoes, lettuces, brassicas.

Magnesium (Mg)

A deficiency of magnesium will show as a yellow band between the veins of leaves. Remedy: apply a magnesium-containing fertiliser. Tomatoes are particularly vulnerable because of their rapid rate of growth. Remedy: dissolve a teaspoonful of Epsom salts (magnesium sulphate) in 10 litres (2 gallons) of water and use it to water the plants once every two weeks.

Iron (I)

Insufficient iron may give rise to a condition called chlorosis, in which the leaves are yellow, though with green veins. The condition commonly comes about as a result of an alkaline soil. Remedy: apply sequestered iron.

Commonly affected plants: acid-lovers such as rhododendrons.

Manganese (Mn)

This is only required in minute amounts (a trace element). Deficiency is only likely to occur on heavy, wet, alkaline soils and shows as a yellowing between the veins of leaves. Remedy: apply a fertiliser containing trace elements, for example one based on seaweed.

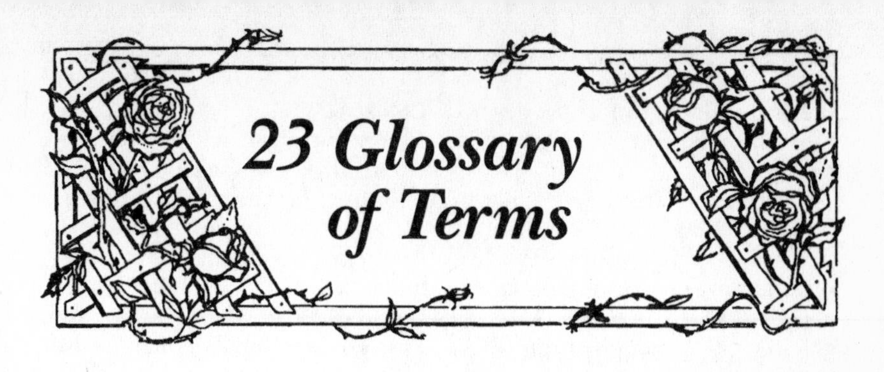

23 Glossary of Terms

Acid
Description of a soil with a pH below 7.0. Acid soils have the advantage of being able to support the widest range of shrubs. To grow certain vegetables successfully, lime must be added to acid soils.

Aeration
The breaking up of the soil by mechanical means such as hoeing to allow air to enter the medium. Also applied to the process of turning over a compost heap.

Alkaline
A description applied to soil with a pH in excess of 7.0.

Alpine
Generally describes plants that require a well drained soil and grow happily in close association with rocks and pebbles.

Annual
A plant that completes its life cycle from germination to setting seeds all in one growing season.

Anther
The terminal portion of the *stamen* which holds the pollen.

Axil
The angle between the upper side of a leaf and the stem on which it is borne. This is the usual position for lateral buds.

Beard
The hairy growth on the outer petals of certain irises.

Berry
A fleshy fruit enclosing seeds, e.g. black currant or grape.

Biennial
A plant that completes its life cycle in two growing seasons. In the first year leaves are produced, and in the following year it flowers, sets seed, then dies.

Blanching
Arresting the development of chlorophyll in any part of a plant by excluding light.

Bolting
The tendency some plants have when placed under stress, such as during a drought, to flower and run to seed prematurely.

Bonsai
A method for creating dwarfed trees. They are grown in small containers and kept to a fraction of their natural height by a combination of severe root and top pruning. By training with wires, twisted gnarled effects are achieved which give the impression of artificial ageing.

Bract
A modified leaf at the based of a flower stalk on a flowering shoot. Usually bracts are scalelike and inconspicuous but sometimes they are large and brightly coloured, e.g. shrimp plant (*Beloperone guttata*). Since such bracts tend to remain long after

the true flowers are dead, an impression is given of longevity.

Break

To grow out from an axillary bud. Pinching out the growing tips of a plant stimulates the production of secondary buds and makes it bushier. In the growing of chrysanthemums this usually results in better quality flowers.

Bud

A compact, undeveloped shoot containing embryonic leaves and flowers.

Bulb

An organ of vegetative reproduction, which may be regarded as a modified shoot consisting of a comparatively short stem enclosed by fleshy scales in which food material is stored. The scales may be either scale-leaves (e.g. tulip) or leaf-bases whose upper parts have withered (e.g. onion). Buds are present in the axils of the scales, and in the spring one or more develop at the expense of the stored food material into a flowering shoot.

Bulbil

A small, immature bulb, sometimes formed around the base of certain full-sized bulbs, such as hyacinth. Bulbils are also found in the leaf axils of certain lilies.

Calyx

The outermost part of a flower usually composed of modified leaves (sepals).

Cambium

The layer of growing tissues, just below the bark of trees and shrubs. Cambium layers are the parts which must marry together to form a union in a graft.

Chlorosis

A condition caused by a fall in chlorophyll levels, giving rise to a yellowing of the leaves. It can come about through a mineral deficiency, poor light or virus infections.

Chlorophyll

The green colouring matter in plants by means of which they build up carbohydrates from carbon dioxide and water, using energy from sunlight, in the process called photosynthesis.

Chromosomes

Minute threadlike structures which occur in the nucleus of every animal and plant cell. They are responsible for hereditary characteristics. A mixture of chromosomes from each parent is present in the nucleus.

Clone

A group of identical plants produced by vegetative propagation and hence of the same genetic constitution.

Compost

1 Material formed by the controlled decay of soft plant tissue by bacteria.

2 A mixture of various substances such as loam, peat, sand, gravel and fertiliser to form a range of materials in which to sow seeds, place cuttings or grow plants in pots.

Conifer

Any tree which produces its seeds in cones. Conifers do not produce true flowers. Their leaves are needlelike or linear and generally evergreen.

Cordon

A method of training and restricting the growth of fruit trees and bushes so that all the fruiting spurs are carried on one or two (double cordon) leaders.

Corm

An organ of vegetative reproduction consisting of a swollen stem base containing food material. It differs from a bulb in that it does not contain an embryonic plant. Growth develops from the buds at the top of the corm. Examples are crocus and gladiolus.

Cultivar

A man-made hybrid, the result of crossing two or more species, varieties or other cultivars.

Corolla

The collective term for the petals of a flower. The part within the *calyx.*

Curd

The dense mass of immature flower buds of broccoli, particularly cauliflowers, which are eaten.

Dead-heading

The removal of flowers once they are past their best, for cosmetic effect or to stimulate the production of fresh heads.

Drill

A small furrow in the ground in which seeds are sown.

Drupe

A succulent fruit consisting of a fleshy outer layer surrounding a hard single seed, e.g. cherry, plum. Blackberries are composed of several drupes fused together.

Espalier

A trained fruit tree with one leader and side branches growing from it at angles of 90 degrees.

Etiolation

A phenomenon exhibited by plants raised in insufficient light. The stems become abnormally

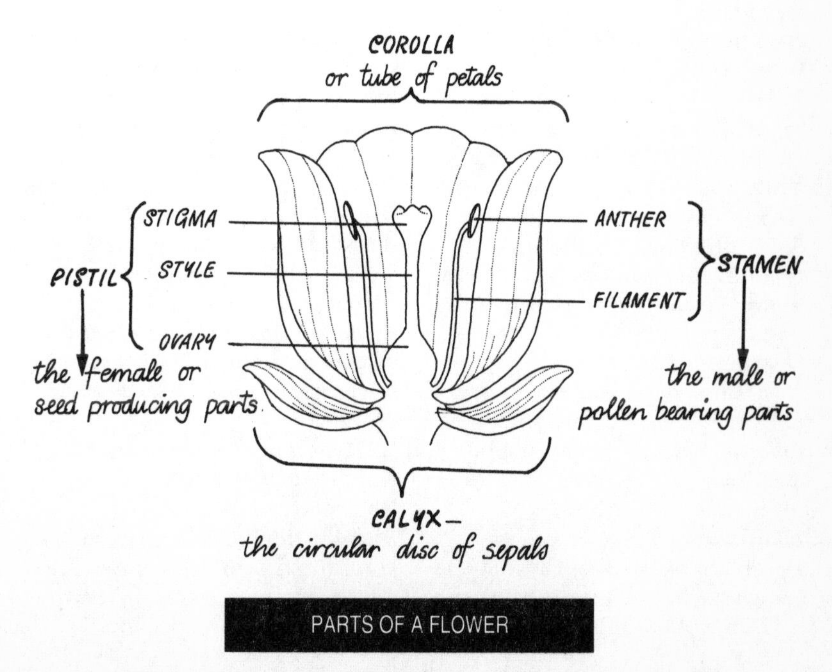

PARTS OF A FLOWER

long, leaves are reduced in size, and the plants become pale and even yellow because of a lack of chlorophyll.

F1 hybrid
Describes seed produced by the careful crossing of two pure-bred, closely related parents. The resulting plants are usually more vigorous and uniform than ordinary hybrids.

Fertilisers
Substances rich in one or more plant nutrients that are added to the soil.

Floret
A small flower that forms part of a large flowerhead, such as is found in members of the daisy family.

Flower parts
See diagram on p. 287.

Friable
Description of a soil that has been worked and readily breaks down to a crumbly mass.

Fungicide
A compound that kills fungi.

Genes
Individual units that control hereditary characteristics. A chromosome contains many genes.

Genus
A group of similar, closely related species. Species of the same genus often hybridise together.

Grafting
A method of propagation where the rootstock of one plant is married with the stem or bud of another to produce a new individual.

Half-hardy
Describes plants that can only be grown out of doors during the frost-free part of the year. Shrubs and perennials that can survive most winters in sheltered situations but are unable to withstand severe conditions may also be termed half-hardy.

Hardening off
The process of gradually acclimatising seedlings and cuttings raised in warmth indoors to outside conditions. This can be achieved by placing them outdoors during the daytime and bringing them inside during the night prior to planting out in their permanent positions.

Hardy
Describes plants which survive the winter out of doors.

Herbaceous perennial
A plant that lives for many years without forming any permanent woody growths. These perennials usually die down to ground level each autumn and shoot again during the spring.

Humus
The dark substance resulting from decomposition of vegetable matter in the soil. It retains moisture and plant nutrients.

Hybrid
The result of a cross between parents that are genetically different – usually different species or distinct varieties.

Incurved
Applied to chrysanthemums whose petals grow upwards and inwards, forming a ball-shaped bloom.

Inflorescence
The flowering shoot.

Inorganic
In horticulture, a chemical compound or fertiliser not derived from a once-living source.

Insecticide
A compound which kills insects and other pests.

Lateral
A side shoot. In fruit trees any branch coming from the main branch, trunk or leader.

Leader
The main stem of a plant or the trunk of a tree.

Lime
Calcium hydroxide, added to the soil to rise the pH and to release the final traces of nitrogen from manure.

Loam
A soil where there is a balance between the humus and mineral content. Good quality loam for potting composts can be made by stacking turves with the grass side down and allowing to stand until it becomes a friable mass.

Maiden
A fruit tree a year after being grafted.

Marginal
A plant which grows in perpetually moist soil or in the shallow part of a pond – in the margin between deep water and dry land.

Microclimate
The climate in a small part of the garden which may differ from the rest, or the climate of the garden in general which may differ from the surrounding locality.

Microscape
The landscaping of a very small area of ground. The visual relationship between plants within a bed.

Mulch
A layer of manure, compost or inert material placed around trees and shrubs to help retain moisture and to stop the growth of weeds. It may, depending upon composition, provide nutrients.

Mutant
A plant that is physically different from other members of its species as a result of a change in its genetic structure.

Naturalising
1 The growing of plants, bulbs for example, under trees or in lawns and allowing them to spread undisturbed.
2 The process by which introduced flora colonise an area and spread like natives, e.g. the common rhododendron (*R. ponticum*).

Offset
A short *stolon* (runner) which forms a daughter plant at its tip, e.g. *sempervivum.*

Organic
In horticulture, describes materials that were once living.

Oxygenator
A plant which grows under water. The oxygen it releases as a result of photosynthesis immediately dissolves in the water.

Perennial
A plant which lives for many years. Gardeners usually apply the term to herbaceous plants which die back in the autumn.

Petal
One of the parts of the *corolla* of a flower, usually brightly coloured and conspicuous – to attract pollinating insects.

pH
The pH scale is a measure of acidity or alkalinity, based on the number of available hydrogen ions (H^+). A soil with a pH of 7.0 is neutral. All values above this,

i.e. 7–14, are alkaline whilst those below, 0–7, are acid.

Picotee
Petals edged with a different shade of colour to the rest of the flower.

Pistil
The female reproductive organs of a flower consisting of stigma, style and ovary.

Pollen
The male reproductive cells of flowering plants.

Reflexed
Describes petals or leaves that are bent sharply backwards, e.g. cyclamen petals. Chrysanthemums classified as reflexed have petals curved outwards and downward, and are overlapping.

Rhizome
A horizontal underground stem, sometimes creeping, serving as a storage organ, e.g. certain kinds of iris, mint and couch-grass.

Runner
See *stolon.*

Scion
A shoot or bud of one plant that is grafted onto the rootstock of another.

Self-coloured
Describes a flower of a single, uniform colour.

Self-fertile
A term applied to any variety of fruit tree that does not require another variety to pollinate its flowers to produce fruit.

Self-sterile
Describes trees that require a pollinating variety nearby to produce fruit.

Sepal
One of the divisions of the *calyx*, which protects the flower bud. Though usually green and leaflike, as in the case of roses, the sepals may be brightly coloured, as, for example, in fuchsias.

Spadix
The fleshy spike containing the true flowers in members of the arum family.

Spathe
A large modified leaf, sometimes brightly coloured, surrounding the spadix of an arum.

Species
A sub-division of a genus. Plant species are genetically similar and originate in the wild. They are the result of natural selection as opposed to artificial breeding, and grow true from seed.

Spit
One spade's depth.

Spore
Reproductive bodies, usually microscopic, occurring in lower plants (such as ferns and mosses) and also fungi and bacteria. Spores in massive numbers become detached from the parent and give rise either directly or indirectly to new individuals. Bacterial spores serve mainly as a resting stage in the life cycle, to preserve the bacterium through periods of unfavourable conditions. Many bacterial spores can germinate after years of dormancy. Distribution of spores is by wind, water or animals. Resting spores are a means of survival through unfavourable conditions.

Spur
Very small lateral branches on trees, notably apples and pears, which produce the flowers and ultimately the fruit.

Stamen
The male reproductive organ of

a flower comprising a tiny stalk (the filament, bearing at its apex an *anther*, which produces the pollen.

Standard
A tree or bush such as a rose or fuchsia in which about two thirds of the height is made up of bare trunk and the top third is the canopy.

Stolon
A prostrate creeping stem that roots at nodes, producing many new plants, e.g. strawberry runner.

Stool
Root crowns of herbaceous plants, which are lifted to produce cutting for next year's plants, e.g. chrysanthemums.

Stopping
The removal of the growing tip of a stem either to restrict height or to develop bushiness of the plant.

Stratification
A means of breaking down the dormancy of certain kinds of seed. Seeds need to be exposed to a low temperature for a few weeks before sowing for good germination. One way of doing this is by placing them in the refrigerator (but not the freezer).

Sucker
A shoot growing from the roots of a plant.

Synonym
Abbreviation: syn. An alternative botanical name for a plant, particularly one resulting from reclassification of species. Even though knowledge improves and particular species are assigned to a new genus, old names persist for many years. Consequently many references quote the new name beside that of the old.

Taproot
The main root which goes straight down.

Tuber
A swollen underground stem (e.g. a potato) or a swollen root (e.g. dahlia) contain stored food material.

Variety
A naturally occurring variation of a species. The term is frequently used for the modern varieties which originated in cultivation, though these are more correctly referred to as cultivars.

Vegetative propagation
Cuttings, division, layering and grafting as a means of multiplying plants instead of by seeds.

Weeping
Describes a tree or shrub whose branches hang down. Often combined with a standard to form a weeping standard in which the branches hang down from a considerable height.

Index

C

R

S

Y

Z